Eduardo E Zamora

D0874221

Elementary Patrology

ELEMENTARY PATROLOGY

+

The Writings of the
Fathers of the Church

BY

ALOYS DIRKSEN, C.PP.S.

B. HERDER BOOK CO.
15 & 17 South Broadway, St. Louis 2, Mo.
AND 33 Queen Square, London, W.C.

Library of Congress Catalog Card Number: 59-13390

IMPRIMI POTEST: S. W. Oberhauser, C.PP.S.
                 Provincial

IMPRIMATUR: ✠ Joseph E. Ritter, S.T.D.
              Archbishop of St. Louis

June 24, 1959

*Printed in the United States of America
by Vail-Ballou Press, Binghamton, New York*

To

THE RIGHT REVEREND OTTO J. KELLER

PASTOR, ST. BAVO CHURCH

MISHAWAKA, INDIANA

Preface

This book is what its title indicates, an elementary patrology. It is meant to introduce the reader or student to the treasure of patristic literature. There is little original in the book and it represents practically no independent research. It is the product of teaching experience, some reading in the fathers and a study of the chief manuals and handbooks of patrology. Above all else these pages are designed to be a tool for the student of patrology and the average reader. The book is meant to be a relatively inexpensive tool, also. For these reasons there are no footnotes, there is no bibliography, and quotations from foreign languages have been reduced to a minimum. The few Greek words that occur have been transliterated. There are also several Latin quotations because these have found their way into standard use in theology. These are freely translated. Those writings of the fathers that are commonly cited by Latin titles in theological literature, are given in Latin in these pages, also. Generally a free translation of the title is added. This is not done when the title would seem to be self-explanatory or when the work is described in such way as to make the nature of the writing clear. In a large number of instances the writings of the fathers have been given an English title that would seem to give the reader an adequate idea of the work.

The whole work is arranged into two parts or books and an appendix. This, too, is in line with its general objective. Book One treats of the main movements and currents in patristic literature and the most important men and writings of the era of the fathers. Book Two lists in alphabetical order for ready reference, names and items of patristic writers that are not discussed in Book One. However, most of these are mentioned there. In this way the pages of Book One are not cluttered with a profusion of names. After all, an ecclesiastic, even though he is most important in church history, should not be given space in an elementary patrology if most of his writings have not come down to us. Finally the appendix lists alphabetically most of the less known and obscure heresies that one meets in the early Church. This should be a handy tool in itself since information about many of these is hard to come by.

The choice of material for Book One and the arrangement of these materials had to be made in somewhat arbitrary fashion at times. In the main the conventional pattern of handbooks of patrology is followed. The variations from this pattern can best be seen in the following outline of Book One.

Part One: The Beginnings
    Section I.   The Earliest Writers
    Section II. The Battle Against Empire, Pagan, Jew and Heretic
    Section III. Scientific Theology and Its Beginnings

Part Two: The Golden Age
    Introduction
    Section I.   Greek Writers of the East
    Section II. Syriac and Armenian Writers
    Section III. Western Writers

Part Three: The Decline
    Section I.   The West
    Section II. The East

Should these pages help the student beginning his theological studies and inspire him, or any other reader for that matter, to a greater love of the fathers and their writings, the author will feel richly rewarded. A word of thanks is due the author's former students in St. Charles Seminary and St. Mary's Novitiate, whose interest in patristic studies prompted the writing of this elementary patrology. Also, a grateful prayer for former teachers of the author, who brought him to a love of patrology: Victor Wagner, C.PP.S., Patrick J. Healy, and Heinrich Schumacher. Finally, the author's gratitude is due Charles J. Davitt, C.PP.S., for reading the proofs.

ALOYS DIRKSEN, C.PP.S.

Contents

BOOK TWO: OTHER PATRISTIC
WRITERS AND WORKS

Introduction

Patrology is the scientific study of the fathers of the Church. As such it is a division of the history of Christian literature and, excluding the canonical writings of the New Testament, covers Christian literature from its beginning to Isidore of Seville (636) in the West and John Damascene (749) in the East. Ordinarily, Christian literature is divided into three periods:

1. The beginnings and emergence of Christian literature from the apostolic age to the emancipation of the Church in 313 by Constantine or to the Council of Nicea (325).

2. The Flowering and Golden Age of Christian literature from 313 or 325 to Leo the Great (461) or to the Council of Chalcedon (451).

3. The Period of Decline, 451 or 461 to 636 in the West and 451 or 461 to 749 in the East. The patristic age is generally concluded with Isidore and John Damascene because neither the West nor the East produced any significant literature for a considerable time after the passing of these great fathers.

Patrology is chiefly a theological science, although the study of the fathers is most valuable also as an auxiliary science to other branches of learning such as linguistics, Latin, Greek, archaeology, history, and others. To the student of theology the study of the fathers is most important because their writings are one of the *loci theologici* or sources of theology. Melchior Cano (1560) who coined the phrase defined the *loci theologici* as storehouses in which the theologian can find the needed theological arguments either to refute or to prove. He distinguished seven such sources in the strict sense of the term, viz., scripture, tradition, *magisterium* of the Church, councils, popes, fathers, and theologians. To these he added three others which he regarded as annexed or nonproper sources, viz., human reason, philosophy, and history.

If we now wish to divide the patristic age with greater emphasis on the fathers as a source of theology we may roughly make these divisions:

1. The earliest writers put Christian truths in concrete formulas for simple instruction. Such were the apostolic fathers.

2. As the Church grew and spread Christian writers came to grips with the religious, political, and philosophical ideas of the Roman Empire. This period produced the great apologists Justin, Athenagoras, Aristides, Irenaeus, Tertullian, and others.

3. Next, at the beginning of the third century we have the start of scientific presentation of the truths of Christianity such as the *Adversus haereses* (Against Heresies) of Irenaeus and the *Peri archon* (On Fundamentals) of Origen. The centers of such activities were Alexandria and Antioch. There emerged other centers of learning and schools but these two were of most far-reaching influence. The Alexandrians were Neoplatonists and characterized by a tendency to mysticism, symbolism, and allegorizing, especially in the interpretation of Sacred Scripture. On the other hand, the Antiochians were Aristotelians and characterized by a concrete realism and literalism. From these schools came the great geniuses, orthodox thinkers, and heretics of the next centuries. Alexandria produced Clement (211), Origen (255), Athanasius (373), Cyril (444) and the Cappadocians, Basil (379), Gregory of Nyssa (394), and Gregory Nazianzen (390). These are the orthodox luminaries of the Alexandrian school, from which emerged also Apollinarianism, Monophysitism, and Monothelitism, to mention the most nettling errors. Antioch spawned Nestorianism, Pelagianism, and the heresiarch Arius, but gave us the towering genius of John Chrysostom (407).

4. The latter half of the fourth century, through the fifth, saw the grappling of great minds with the sublime mysteries of Christianity and their defense against the attacks of heretics. Besides the Easterners already mentioned there appear the great Westerners, Hilary (366), Ambrose (397), Jerome (420) and the greatest of all the fathers, Augustine of Hippo (430).

5. By the second half of the fifth century most of the con-
flagration of controversy had subsided except for Monothelitism,
Iconoclasm, and a few lesser heresies, though in these there was
violent and acrimonious fighting such as in the battle of Origenism. That we speak of the next decades as a period of decline
does not prescind from the emergence of some great men. Besides Isidore and the Damascene there were Gregory the Great
(604) in the West and Maximus Confessor (662) and Sophronius
(638) in the East. But we have come to the end of the patristic
age, the first of the three great epochs into which the history of
dogmatic theology can be commonly divided, the other two of
which are the scholastic and the modern eras.

The name patrology was coined by a Lutheran theologian, Joh.
Gerhard, who in 1653 published a "Patrology." The practice persisted well into the nineteenth century of including in a
"Patrology" all Christian writing up to the Middle Ages or even
to the Reformation. Today, however, it is commonly accepted
that the centuries in which the Church Christianized the Graeco-
Roman world constitute a distinct epoch, the patristic age. The
practice of publishing handbooks of ancient Christian literature,
including therein the canonical books of the New Testament, has
now also largely been discontinued. On the other hand, as the
remains of the first Christian centuries have been unearthed,
patrology must, because it is one of the *loci theologici*, gather in
other things that are not the writings of the fathers. Inscriptions,
acts of the councils, acts of the martyrs, liturgical texts, monastic
rules, lives of the saints, creeds and symbols and fragmentary remains of varied kinds all fall within the province of patrology
to the extent they can be of service to the dogmatic theologian.
Even the writings of heretics, as Jerome pointed out long ago,
are within the province of the science of patrology. They throw
light not merely on the environment of the fathers but also, in
many cases, illuminate their statements.

Patristics is sometimes used to designate the science of
patrology. The term comes from *Theologia Patristica* and has
been in use since the seventeenth century when it was employed
to distinguish the study of the fathers from *Theologia Biblica,*
Theologia Scholastica, Theologia Symbolica, and *Theologia*

Speculativa. The history of dogma has developed out of the *Theologia Patristica.*

"Father of the Church" is a term of strictly ecclesiastical origin but it is most expressive and natural as designation for the bishop and teacher of a community. We find it used frequently. Augustine extended the term in one instance by citing Jerome as a father. Jerome himself did not use the term "father" but coined a new one, "ecclesiastical writer." Thus all theological writings of Christian antiquity could be included. Vincent of Lerins in his *Commonitorium* returned to the earlier meaning of father by emphasizing that the writer must be orthodox. He was the first to propose an adequate theory of a theological proof from the fathers. The oldest list or catalogue of names of the fathers is found in the so-called Gelasian Decretals. This work also emphasizes the need of communion with the "Holy Roman Church" as a mark of a father.

Thus gradually there came to be established the four marks of a father of the Church: *doctrina orthodoxa* (orthodox teaching), *sanctitas vitae* (holiness of life), *approbatio ecclesiastica* (Church approval), and *antiquitas* (antiquity). All four marks, however, are to be interpreted in a flexible and wide sense. Some fathers held erroneous views and the claim to ecclesiastical approbation and a declaration of sanctity must be taken according to the times.

"Doctor of the Church" is a title given to a father or writer who has merited a special sanction of the Church. A Doctor may lack the mark of antiquity, but he must be distinguished for learning. In the liturgy of the Church today, a Doctor of the Church enjoys his own feastday Office and the Credo at Mass. Beyond this he has received a special recommendation as a religious and theological teacher. This was a gradual development. Vincent of Lerins spoke of the fathers as *magistri probabiles* (reliable teachers) and then gradually the number of such was sifted and weighed. Already in the sixth century Hilary, Ambrose, and Augustine are named as the outstanding fathers of the West. Before the ninth century Jerome came to be added to the list. They were likened to the four rivers of Paradise, and Boniface VIII officially conferred on them the title *egregii doctores ecclesiae* (outstanding teachers of the Church). These four remain the "great doctors of the West." As time passed others were added by the Church.

Basil, Gregory of Nazianzus, and Chrysostom are the great doctors of the East. To these Pius V, in 1568, added Athanasius. There is perhaps a reflection of the teaching on the Trinity in the acceptance of three doctors up to Pius V.

The authority of the fathers is based on the teaching of the Church that they are one of the *loci theologici*. As such, then, the teaching of the fathers enjoys infallibility when there is unanimous agreement among them (*unanimis consensus patrum*), and then only. In all other cases each statement of a father must be weighed and taken for what it is worth.

The history of patrology, although the name derives from the seventeenth century, goes back to Eusebius (339). (See the Introduction to his great work.) He lists writers both orthodox and heretical. He also gives quotations and in the case of many writers he tells us all that we know about them. Often what he quotes is all that is left of their writings.

Jerome was next in the field with his *De viris illustribus*, written in 392 in answer to the ridicule of pagans that Christians had no literary men. In 135 sections he lists writers from Peter to himself as of the year 392. He lists heretics, also Philo, Josephus, and Seneca, so that Augustine chides him for not sifting the heretics from the Catholic writers. Worse faults of the work, however, are incorrectness and partiality. But the work is of immense importance because for some writers it gives all the information we have. For the first seventy-eight sections, Jerome is much indebted to Eusebius' *Ecclesiastical History* and *Chronicle*.

Gennadius of Marseilles continued the work of Jerome under the same title (c. 480) by adding ninety-nine titles. He is scholarly and valuable though his work is tinged by his Semi-Pelagianism.

Isidore of Seville continued the work of Gennadius with special emphasis on Spanish writers. His work, entitled *De viris illustribus* and written (615–618) is less scholarly.

Ildephonse of Toledo (667), a disciple of Isidore, next added fourteen biographies of ecclesiastics, only eight of whom are writers and all are Spaniards except Gregory the Great. This narrow nationalism greatly reduces the value of his work.

The dark ages, as enemies of the Church delight to call those years when the fire of letters and learning burned bright only in the monasteries and the turmoil of the times left little chance for intellectual endeavor outside these institutions, found no need or demand to produce histories of patrology. In 1112 Sigebert of Gembloux compiled a *De viris illustribus* in which he followed Jerome and Gennadius and added data about theologians of the early Middle Ages in the West. No Byzantine writers are mentioned. Ten years later, 1122, Honorius of Augustudunum compiled a similar list, *De luminaribus ecclesiae*, and in 1135 there appeared the *De scriptoribus ecclesiasticis* of the Anonymus Mellicensis, so named after Melk in Austria where it was first found. The best work to appear during these years was the *De scriptoribus ecclesiasticis* of the Abbot John Trithemius. This work published in 1494 presents information about 963 writers, some of whom are not theologians. For the fathers he also depends on Jerome and Gennadius.

The reformation so-called revived and revitalized the study of patrology because on the one hand the rebels accused the mother Church of having fallen away from the teaching of the fathers, and on the other the great Council of Trent directed attention to tradition and the fathers. In 1613 Bellarmine produced his *De scriptoribus ecclesiasticis liber unus*. He was followed by a French work in sixteen volumes, published 1693–1712 by Tillemont and a twenty-three volume work by Ceillier that appeared 1729–1763. For further details any standard handbook may be consulted.

Printed editions of the works of the fathers appeared very early. Though uncritical, these early printings are valuable because the manuscripts on which they were based have mostly been lost. In 1618 the French Benedictine congregation of St. Maur was founded in Paris. Some great scholars were attracted to the foundation and the edition of early Christian literature produced by the Congregation is in some cases still unsurpassed. The most complete printed edition of the fathers is found in the massive *Patrologiae cursus completus* edited by the Abbé J. P. Migne (1875). The most modern and critical, though not complete, editions of the fathers are those of the Vienna Academy for the Latin and the Berlin Academy for the Greek. Further details are to be found in any standard handbook.

English editions of the fathers may be found in any of the standard handbooks of patrology. See, especially, the following: Quasten, J., *Patrology*, Vol. I (1950), Vol. II (1953); Cayré, F., *Manual of Patrology and History of Theology*, translated by H. Howitt, Vol. I (1930), Vol. II (1940); Altaner, B., *Patrology*, translated by Hilda Graef.

BOOK ONE

The Main Currents and the Great Writers of Patrology

PART ONE

The Beginnings of Patristic Literature to the Peace of Constantine

The Earliest Writers

I. The Apostolic Fathers

In 1672 J. B. Cotelier published his *Patres aevi apostolici*. The two volumes contained the work of five writers: Pseudo-Barnabas, Clement of Rome, Ignatius of Antioch, Polycarp of Smyrna, and Hermas. Thus came into use the term, "apostolic fathers," as a designation for the authors who had either been taught by the apostles directly or by their disciples. Next Papias of Hieropolis and the author of the *Epistle to Diognetus* were added to the list, making seven. In modern times the *Didache* also has been added. Besides these writings the *Martyrium* of Polycarp and the letters of Ignatius were usually included among the apostolic fathers. Quadratus, though a later apologist, was also sometimes added to the group. Again the so-called II Clement is at times included, as is the Apostles' Creed.

Today it has been suggested that the term apostolic fathers be discontinued because the works mentioned do not make a homogeneous whole. There is considerable difference in their time and place of origin. There also is a great variety in the nature or kind of these writings. However, the term is likely to continue in use because it has become hallowed in years. It is most suggestive in meaning as a designation for the writings that appeared before the end of the first century or in the beginning of the second. It is to such writings that the term should be limited. Then they would number seven: I Clement to the Corinthians, Ignatius of Antioch, Polycarp of Smyrna, Didache, Papias of Hieropolis, the Epistle of Barnabas, and The Shepherd of Hermas.

1. CLEMENT OF ROME (c. 96)

Clement was the second or third successor of Peter as Bishop of Rome. Nothing further is known of his identity but he is accepted as the undisputed author of a letter to the Corinthians. It has been suggested that he was a convert from Judaism by those who are impressed by his familiarity with the Old Testament. There is even stronger evidence of a pagan background. Clement was a name in frequent use and no connection can be established between Pope Clement and the man of Phil. 4:3 or the companion of Barnabas. Legend associated him with Titus Flavius Clemens, a consul, and with the royal household. Legend also exiled him to the Chersonesus and martyrdom. The so-called Clementine *Recognitions* have handed down these and other stories of Clement's association with Peter. Two letters on Virginity, two Epistles to James the brother of the Lord, and a second Epistle to the Corinthians have been attributed to him but we have only the one genuine letter, the authorship of which is undisputed.

Clement wrote his letter to Corinth when that church had flourished for many years after Paul had restored order and when the messengers carrying Clement's letter from Rome had "from youth to old age" (63:3) lived exemplarily among the Christians of Rome. Yet he could call Peter and Paul heroes of "our generation" (5:1) and refer to the persecution of Domitian as going on or only most recently over (1:1). He must then have written about the year 96. The scant evidence he offers on the constitution of the Christian community confirms this (42–44).

An Exordium states the purpose of the letter and contrasts the former happy state of the Corinthian Church with the misery caused by a schism. Part I (4–36) points to envy as the cause of dissension and exhorts to virtue, especially to repentance. Part II (37–59) treats more directly of affairs at Corinth. An Epilogue (59–65) gives us the oldest Christian liturgical prayer outside the New Testament and concludes with a forceful demand that peace be restored. Clement quotes the Scriptures copiously, freely as a rule. The letter shows him to have been otherwise well educated. There is no evidence that his letter is dependent on any other writing.

The most significant importance of Clement's letter is that by it he intervenes in no uncertain way to establish order in Corinth. He does so unsolicited. He writes "through the Holy Spirit" (62:3). Submission to him is submitting to "the will of God" (56:1) and to disobey "what has been said by Him through us" (59:1) is dangerous sin. Furthermore, it was Clement's duty to intervene (59:2) and he demands action (65). All this points to the primacy of the bishop of Rome, especially since John the Apostle was then still living. Clement's authority is evident too in that his demands were carried out. His letter was so highly esteemed and so well received that it was placed on the level with the writings of the apostles and Sacred Scripture.

The letter also witnesses to the existence in the local churches of ecclesiastical authority not dependent on charismatic gifts. Other points to be noted in the letter are: the martyrdom of Peter and Paul in Rome and the latter's journey to Spain (5), the many martyrs of Nero's persecution (6), the apostolic succession (44:1–3), the mystical body (44; 46:7), the resurrection from the dead (24–25), the distinction between clergy and laity (40:5), prayer for civil authorities (61), and the long prayer (59:4–61:3). Clement teaches the inspiration and inerrancy of the Scriptures and witnesses to the Pauline letters to the Corinthians. Above all the letter should be studied as an edifying pastoral letter.

2. IGNATIUS OF ANTIOCH (c. 110)

Ignatius Theophorus was the second or third bishop of Antioch. In his old age he was brought to Rome to suffer martyrdom in the arena. His condemnation to beasts suggests that he was not a Roman, though his name is. His letters show his great prominence in Asia Minor. On his way to Rome delegates from various communities met him en route at various stops. These visits occasioned his letters. There are seven addressed to the following: Ephesians, Magnesians, Trallians, Romans, Philadelphians, Smyrneans, and Polycarp. He died under Trajan, around 110.

Nothing further is known of Ignatius, but a beautiful and heroic soul speaks from the letters.

Legend has Ignatius a disciple of Peter and John. His long life would not make contact with the apostles impossible. His second name, Theophorus, gave rise to a legend that he was the little child whom Jesus took when He blessed the children. His letters, too, suffered in transmission. They were cut in number and size in one recension and interpolated extensively in another. Spurious letters also were circulated at a later date. Today there can no longer be any doubt that the seven letters found in the so-called middle recension are genuine. The long and vicious attempts to discredit them have all ended in failure.

That the letters should have been so vigorously attacked is not surprising because Ignatius is an indisputable witness to the hierarchical constitution of the Church at the beginning of the second century. Where Clement and the *Didache* do not seem to distinguish between bishops and priests, Ignatius mentions bishops, priests, and deacons in all of the churches to which he writes, except Rome. As a rule he names them and, above all, he insists on unity and harmony of action by them. The bishop is head as Christ was. Under him are the priests as in the college of apostles, and serving them are the deacons.

Ignatius writes to the Romans in altogether singular vein. His purpose in his other letters is to exhort to caution against error and to urge unity and obedience to ecclesiastical authorities. His tone is that of a man of eminence who expects to be heard and obeyed. He writes to the Romans, on the other hand, as one addressing one more eminent than himself. The introduction to this letter is long, solemn, and heavy with expressions of respect and esteem. There are six superlatives and Ignatius characterizes the Roman Church as "presiding." His readers well knew his meaning but the entire passage is somewhat unclear to us. It would seem to point to the primacy of Rome. The whole letter expresses some of the most beautiful Christian sentiments of all patristic literature as Ignatius pleads that the Roman Christians should in no way intervene but permit him to achieve martyrdom for his beloved Master.

The letters show Ignatius to have been a strong and beautiful soul, a clear thinker, and a sturdy Christian. He attacks heresy, especially Docetism, clearly expounding both the divinity and humanity of Christ. The Eucharist is for him a sacrifice of Christ's flesh and blood and the place where it is celebrated is called *thusiasterion* (place of sacrifice). He teaches the Virgin Birth and speaks of it as a stratagem to conceal the Incarnation from the Devil. He treats of baptism, matrimony, and virginity, but he is most clear and emphatic in his teaching on the Church. "Where Christ is, there is the Catholic Church." The organization of the Church is hierarchical and monarchial. Authority is in no way connected with or dependent on charismatic gifts. The bishop is high-priest and teacher; not to be in communion with him is heresy. Baptism, Agape, Eucharist and marriage must all be celebrated under his authority. And that the Roman Church, through the bishop of Rome, presides over the churches would seem to be clearly indicated in the letter to the Romans.

3. DIDACHE (c. 80–90)

The *Didache* is probably the oldest patristic document. Its full title originally was, "The Lord's Instruction to the Gentiles Through the Twelve Apostles." The author and place of origin are unknown. In fact the work itself was discovered only at the end of the last century. The place of origin of the little book was probably Syria, though Egypt is not entirely out of question because of its popularity there. It was written some years before the end of the first century. This is indicated by the makeup of the Church when it was written. It is not impossible that some of the materials of the work derive from the apostles and that several older pieces were brought together in its composition.

There are four sections in the little work: a moral catechesis on *The Two Ways*, a liturgical instruction on baptism, fasting, prayer, and the Eucharist, on bishops and deacons (priests are not mentioned), on Sunday worship, and an eschatological treatise.

The catechesis on *The Two Ways* sets forth Christian ideals of life and the evils of paganism. Baptism is by immersion although infusion is valid in case of necessity. The form of baptism is trinitarian. Wednesday and Friday are days to fast and the Lord's prayer is to be said thrice daily. A Eucharistic prayer is reproduced, though the actual celebration of the sacrament is not described because of the "discipline of the secret." Some have referred this prayer to the Agape but without compelling reason. A recently discovered fragment of doubtful authenticity adds a prayer for the consecration of oil used in baptism and confirmation after the Eucharistic prayer. The Eucharist is a sacrifice and is to be preceded by a confession of sins, as is Sunday worship.

The disciplinary section deals with the regulation of charismatic gifts, charity, and charitable works, prophets, teachers, apostles, and other details that give a good insight into the life of the primitive Christian community. The whole work is concluded by a short eschatological discourse. The *Didache* contains the oldest collection of canon law and served as a basis for later disciplinary works such as the *Didascalia* and Book VII of the *Apostolic Constitutions*.

4. POLYCARP TO THE PHILIPPIANS (156)

Polycarp, appointed bishop of Smyrna by the apostles, was a disciple of John the Evangelist and a teacher of Irenaeus. He was martyred in 155 or 156 after being a Christian eighty-six years. He wrote several letters but there have been preserved only his Epistle to the Philippians and a fragment of another that he wrote to accompany a bundle of Ignatian letters he was forwarding to the Philippians as a "covering note." This is ordinarily printed as section thirteen or fourteen of the full letter to the Philippians. Polycarp also made a trip to consult Pope Anicetus for the Quartodecimans and, although nothing was settled, the two parted friends. Nothing further is known of Polycarp except what the *Martyrium Polycarpi* tells, but when he died there passed a man who had known well those who had known the Son of God in the flesh.

The short "covering note" was written before news of Ignatius' martyrdom had reached Smyrna, around 110. It recommends the letters of Ignatius highly and asks for news about him.

The second letter was written some time later, about 135 perhaps. In it Polycarp exhorts the Philippians to unity and harmony, gives pastoral direction to the priests and deacons, warns against errors, especially Docetism and Judaizers, and exhorts to charity, almsgiving, prayer for each other and for civil authorities. He cautions against avarice, citing the case of a priest named Valens.

5. PAPIAS (after 130)

Papias, a disciple of John the Apostle and a friend of Polycarp of Smyrna, was bishop of Hieropolis. About the year 130 he wrote his *Explanation of the Sayings of our Lord*. Only fragments of the work have been preserved but the little that is left is extremely precious, for Papias is the earliest and most important witness to the authorship of the Gospels. The most controversial fragments are those containing reference to an Apostle John and a Presbyter John and what Papias says about Mark. However, Papias is not speaking of two Johns but mentions John twice, once to class him among the apostles and a second time to indicate that John was still living at the time, and heard him lecture, whereas the other apostles had passed away. Papias states that Matthew wrote first in Aramaic, that Mark wrote down Peter's preaching but only in some logical order. Eusebius had a low estimate of Papias because the latter was a Chiliast and reported some other fantastic things. Eusebius also found Papias' double mention of John convenient because he questioned the inspiration of the Apocalypse and denied that John the Apostle had written it.

Many later historians, some of whom were not too critical, cite Papias, e.g., Philip of Side, George Hamartolos, Andrew of Caesarea, Anastasius Sinaita, Maximus Confessor, and Photius. The earliest writers to mention and quote Papias are Irenaeus, Eusebius, and Jerome.

6. PSEUDO-BARNABAS (130–140)

This is not a letter because it has neither an introduction nor a conclusion. It is a theological treatise. Neither was it written by Barnabas since he was dead by the time it appeared. Neither could Barnabas, the companion of Paul who called the Old Testament the Pedagogue to the New Testament, have spoken so disparagingly of the Old Testament or have so wildly interpreted it. Pseudo-Barnabas ascribes the origin of the Old Testament to the devil and he explains much of it in very bizarre fashion. The work was written after the destruction of the Temple in Jerusalem but it is hard to say how late it appeared. It cannot be later than 140. The work may have originated in Alexandria in view of its popularity there.

The first part of Pseudo-Barnabas is dogmatic in content (1–17). Part two (18–21) is moral, describing the two ways, the Way of Light and the Way of Darkness. In the dogmatic part the author wants to give the genuine meaning of the Old Testament that his readers may have perfect knowledge. The Old Testament, although given to Moses, was meant for Christians. The Jews in their observance and interpretation of the Old Law were misled by an evil angel. Some of the author's interpretations are fantastic. The second part then describes the Way of Light and the Way of Darkness, giving various moral precepts and a catalogue of various vices and virtues.

Although there is little dogmatic content in the work, it teaches the pre-existence of Christ, who became man to suffer for us and to let the persecutors of the prophets fill up their measure of iniquity by putting Him to death. Baptism confers sonship of God and makes us temples of God. Abortion is condemned, Sunday is the Lord's day, and from the Hexaemeron the author concludes to Chiliasm.

7. THE SHEPHERD OF HERMAS (c. 140)

Hermas, according to the trustworthy Muratorian Fragment was the brother of Pope Pius I and a contemporary of Pope Clement. He cannot therefore be the Hermas of Romans 16:4. His work is commonly included among the apostolic fathers. In reality, it is an apocryphal Apocalypse. In some circles it was for a time regarded as canonical Scripture.

The book derives its title from the angel who appears to Hermas in the guise of a shepherd. The work is arranged into five Visions, twelve Commandments or Mandates, and ten Similitudes or Parables. In the beginning the Church, as an elderly matron that grows younger, appears charging Hermas to preach repentance (Vis. 1–4), and Vision three seems to indicate a penitential discipline in existence. Vision five makes a transition to the next part in which the Angel of Repentance, appearing as a shepherd, instructs Hermas in Christian living and morality. The last part treats of repentance again. Similitude nine seems to be a later addition. It repeats and develops the vision of the Tower. The addition probably was made necessary by the delay of the Parousia which Hermas thought imminent.

The twelve Mandates treat in order: faith, simplicity, truthfulness, chastity, meekness and patience, discrimination of angels, fear of the Lord, continence, trust in God, avoiding sadness, false prophets, and warfare against cupidity and evil desires. The Similitudes treat of love of earthly things, kindness and benevolence, good and evil in the world, fasting, penance, value of affliction, building the tower, and a final admonition by the angel that Hermas clean up his domestic affairs.

Hermas was a simple soul but devout and firm in his Christian faith. There would seem to be no reason to question the several autobiographical notes in his writing, that he was a manumitted slave who later lost all that he had gained by honest endeavor as a free man. Hermas is not a theologian, but what he has to say on repentance (Mand. 4,3,1 ff.; 5,7,1 ff.), on the Church (Vis. 2,4,1 ff.; 3,3,31; Sim. 8,13,1), baptism (Vis. 3,3,5; Sim. 9,16,1), and marriage (Mand. 4,1,8; 4,4,1 ff.), are of great importance. His Christology is a bit muddled (Sim. 5,6,5; 9,1,1; 9,16,5). He teaches the value of works of supererogation (5,3,3) and gives a catalogue of seven virtues (Vis. 3,8,1 ff.). He is a good homely psychologist (Mand. 5,2,5 ff.; 6,2,1 ff.) He is a definite witness to the necessity of baptism, the indissolubility of marriage, and he refutes the error of those who held that the early Church was rigorous in dealing with sinners. Hermas is surprised at having heard that there were some who preached a single repentance. He himself is convinced that the imminent Parousia will leave time for only one repentance but otherwise repentance is always open and available, even for the adulterous woman who has been put away.

The whole Shepherd, even if somewhat tiresome reading, is filled with excellent moral reflections. These account for its popularity and make the lengthy book well worth reading.

Hermas is the first writer to speak of stations of fasting (Sim. 5,1,1 ff.) and the first to mention the two cities so well discussed later by Augustine in his "City of God" (Sim. 1,1 ff.).

8. II CLEMENT (c. 150)

This little work is neither a letter nor the work of Pope Clement as a comparison with I Clement easily shows. It is the oldest Christian sermon or homily that has come down to us. That it is a sermon is evident from the composition of the little work and from the two statements in it (17,3:19,1). How it came to be associated with Clement and the Corinthians is not known. It may have originated in Corinth. The Syrian Church for a time regarded it as Scripture.

The sermon is rather general in scope but its homiletic and hortatory tones are evident in every line. However, a few points of dogmatic interest stand out. The Incarnation of the "Prince of Incorruptibility" and His suffering for us are clearly stated. Baptism is the seal. The sinner has ready access to repentance. There is no rigorism in the sermon, and the necessity of good works is stressed. Though the term "Mother Church" is precisely not used, the Church is depicted as a mother. Throughout the preacher is influenced by Paul.

9. THE PRESBYTERS

Some ecclesiastical writers speak of various traditions handed down from the ancients. See Papias, Irenaeus, and Clement of Alexandria. These ancients or presbyters (elders) appear to include the generation of Christian leaders that still had direct contact with the apostles. Whether they committed anything to writing is not known. An example of these traditions is the story of the robber whom John the Apostle converted. Clement of Alexandria has preserved it for us.

10. THE APOSTLES' CREED

Our Apostles' Creed, a profession of faith in twelve articles, so well known and loved today, has been in use in the West since the sixth century. We find it in use in Gaul, Spain, and a little later in Ireland and Germany. In the East it was not known until the fifteenth century. The tale that each of the apostles contributed an article to its form can also be traced back to the sixth century. The name Apostles' Creed goes back to the fourth century (in Ambrose and Rufinus) when, however, it did not yet have its present form. This is a matter of slow development. A formula of twelve articles is found, at the earliest, in Caesarius of Arles and in the liturgical books of Rome and Gaul. The nucleus of the Creed, however, may go back to the apostles, thus justifying the title and forming the basis for the legend of its composition by the Twelve.

Rudimentary Creeds are found in the New Testament and in the apostolic fathers (Acts 8:37; I Cor. 15:3 ff.; 1 Pet. 3:18–22; I Cor. 8:6; II Tim. 4:1; Ignatius: *Eph.* 18:2; *Smyrn.* 1:1 ff.; Irenaeus, *Adv. haer.* 3,1,2; 3,4,1 ff.; *Epistola Apostolorum* c. 5, and the oldest, the trinitarian formula of baptism, Matt. 28:19). The acrostic Ichthus also contains a credal formula. The papyrus *Dêr-Balizeh* and Irenaeus, *Adv. haer.*, 1,10: 4,33,2–3 have similar formulas.

The credal formularies of the second century are characterized by an elaboration of the formulary for professing Christ so that the Eucharistic Euchology (Preface of the Mass in the liturgy) became a confession of faith in Christ. By the beginning of the third century there were eight or nine articles. The Apostolic Tradition of Hippolytus has preserved for us the Roman Creed which must be regarded as the nucleus of all the Western Creeds. The Oriental Creeds seem to have developed independently in Jerusalem and Caesarea. However, great as the development may be, "all the doctrinal elements to be found in the Apostles' Creed appear already about the end of the first century in the numerous and varied formulas of faith which are contained in early Christian literature" (Quasten, J., *Patrology*, I, p. 27).

II. The Apocrypha and Folk Tales

The New Testament tells all too little about our Lord and those associated with Him. Too little is known also of the heroes of primitive Christianity. What wonder then that pious imagination should get busy to satisfy the curiosity of early Christians. The result was all manner of tales about the apostles, about Mary, the Infancy, and the early life of the Holy Family. Christian imagination literally seethed with stories about these things and, even though the auditor knew them to be tales of the imagination, he delighted and revelled in their repeating. Many accepted these narratives as historical fact but many others recognized them for what they were, endeavors to please, to entertain, to edify, and to satisfy curiosity by telling what might have happened. How soon these things were put to writing or attained the form in which we know them today is, for the most part, rather unimportant. So is the fact that some circles placed some of these writings on the level of Scripture. The most important fact about them is that, as a whole, they were accepted for what they were.

However, not all these writings were meant to entertain and edify. Some were written by heretics to spread their errors. The name of an apostle or some highly revered name was attached to a writing to gain it entrance to the reading public. However, in these the error is so patent that little harm was done and the word Apocrypha, attached to them, came to change its meaning. Originally, apocryphal did not mean spurious but something hidden. The writer of an apocryphal book pretended to reveal something that was hidden or unknown, something that was so sacred it could be committed only to the select initiates. But soon, because of the bizarre and extravagant contents of these writings, the word apocryphal came to mean spurious or false.

Of what use are the Apocrypha? They supply most valuable information about early Christian customs and throw light on the common man's way of life. They reflect common beliefs of the people. If the facts they allege are untrue or suspect, they still tell us what the early Christians would like to believe about our Lord, His Mother and His apostles. They represent the earliest beginnings of Christian folklore, legends, and romantic writing. We have these writings in the form of a later day, but the contents and basis of this literature are older. Finally, they are a most important source to illumine Christian art which would be in great part unintelligible without them.

The production of books in imitation of parts of the Bible is older than Christianity. Judaism produced a considerable body of Apocrypha which are called Pseudepigrapha in non-Catholic circles. These are of great importance in the study of the New Testament. However, some of them are very difficult to use because so popular were they that Christians interpolated them. Chief of these are:

1. The Ascension of Isaias;
2. The four Books of Esdras;
3. The Book of Enoch and Secrets of Enoch;
4. The Testament of the Twelve Patriarchs;
5. The Apocalypse of Baruch.

Turning now to Christian productions, mention may first be made of the Clementine *Romances, Recognitions,* and *Homilies.* They spin the most varied and interesting legends and tales about Peter and Clement of Rome and his family. All the rest of the romantic fiction of this early period may be classified as New Testament Apocrypha and, like the New Testament literature, fall into four classes—Gospels, Acts, Epistles, and Apocalypses. They imitate their New Testament models and purport to have New Testament writers as authors. Some are heretical, some are such heretical writings corrected and edited by Catholics, and a large part is the work of orthodox authors who wrote for edification. A comparison with the canonical New Testament, even a quite cursory one, betrays the spurious nature of the Apocrypha, and the Church made short shrift of their claims to inspiration. Irenaeus speaks of their great numbers.

1. APOCRYPHAL GOSPELS

1. The Gospel according to the Hebrews
2. The Gospel of the Egyptians
3. The Ebionite Gospel
4. The Gospel according to Peter
5. The Gospel of Nicodemus
6. The Protoevangelium of James
7. The Gospel of Thomas
8. Arabic Gospel of the Childhood of Jesus

9. Arabic History of Joseph the Carpenter
10. The Gospel of Philip
11. The Gospel of Matthias
12. The Gospel according to Barnabas
13. The Gospel of Bartholomew
14. Heretical apocryphal gospels known only by name are those of Andrew, Judas Iscariot, Thaddeus, Eve, Basilides, Cerinthus, Valentinus, and Apelles. Because of their apocalyptic nature these works are sometimes called Gospel-Apocalypses

2. APOCRYPHAL ACTS OF THE APOSTLES

The Apocryphal Acts can truly be called the earliest Christian historical novels and adventure stories. Though many display heretical tendencies, they are generally not interested so much in theological matters as in historical and geographical things such as tales of the adventures of the apostles in foreign, far-off lands. They are not entirely fanciful for at times the basis in historic fact of some of the tales can be established. They often throw much light on early Christian life and worship. However, their inferiority to their model is again at once apparent. A certain Leukios is often mentioned as author of some of them since the fifth century.

1. The Acts of Paul
2. The Acts of Peter
3. The Acts of Peter and Paul
4. The Acts of John
5. The Acts of Andrew
6. The Acts of Thomas
7. The Acts of Thaddeus

3. APOCRYPHAL EPISTLES OF THE APOSTLES

There are not many apocryphal Epistles of the Apostles. Yet one or the other found canonical recognition in some limited circles.

1. The *Epistola Apostolorum*
2. Apocryphal Epistles of Paul to the Laodiceans, to the

Alexandrians, the so-called third Epistle to the Corinthians, and the Correspondence between Paul and Seneca

3. Apocryphal Letters of Disciples of Paul. Of these Pseudo-Barnabas has already been discussed. There is also an *Epistola Titi discipuli Pauli, De dispositione sanctimonii*

4. APOCRYPHAL APOCALYPSES

The Apocalypses are characterized by fantastic flights of the imagination for the most part and sometimes, as the Shepherd of Hermas, are far removed from their model, the Apocalypse of John. Some approach the letter form, e.g., the *Epistola Apostolorum.*

1. The Apocalypse of Peter
2. The Apocalypse of Paul
3. The Apocalypse of Stephen
4. The Apocalypse of Thomas
5. The Apocalypse of St. John
6. The Apocalypses of the Virgin

III. Acts of the Martyrs

Even as our Lord walked the bitter way to Calvary, His followers have in great numbers given their lives for His Name's sake. How many will never be known. Without going into further detail the following statements should be consulted: Eusebius (*H.E.* 6,42,1 ff.; 7,11,20; 8,6,6; 8,9,3–4; 8,11,1 ff.); Lactantius (*Div. inst.* 5,11), and the Passions of Sts. James and Marian (12). Origen's statement (*C. Cels.* 3,8) is often cited to show that the number of early martyrs has been exaggerated. However, Origen was writing before the bloody persecutions of Decius, Valerian, and Diocletian. Furthermore, Origen is saying in the context that God would not let all the Christians perish. Elsewhere he speaks of many victims and Pope Clement tells of many who suffered as early as Nero. The persecutions were a matter of ebb and flow.

The accounts of the martyrdom of Christians are among the earliest remains of Christian literature. The earliest students of these writings used to divide them into six groups:

1. Official court reports;
2. Accounts of eyewitnesses;
3. Accounts based upon court records or the written report of eyewitnesses;
4. Accounts, based on no written document, but made up of some facts embellished by the imagination;
5. Romances that are totally imaginative;
6. Forgeries meant to deceive the people.

Besides these Acts of the Martyrs, there are the works of such fathers as Eusebius, Prudentius, Chrysostom, Basil, Augustine, Socrates, and others who wrote accounts of martyrs. Eusebius, to mention only his works, wrote *On the Ancient Martyrs* and *On the Martyrs of Palestine*. Ordinarily, the official court records or accounts patterned on them are called *Acta*. All others are referred to as *Passiones* or *Martyria*.

A simpler classification is in use today. The official court proceedings are grouped together to form the *Acta* or *Gesta Martyrum*. In a second group are put all eyewitness accounts. These are called *Passiones* or *Martyria*. Then all the legends and stories of the martyrs, composed for edification, sometimes even long after, are classified in a third category. These last are unreliable and even fantastic. They were meant to amuse and to edify.

How can the authenticity of these acts be determined? The best evidence is external, such as the fact that they are quoted by early and reliable writers. Internal evidence, too, such as accuracy of date, terms used and description of procedures, will help recognize the mark of authenticity. No one could question the Acts of Polycarp, Justin, and Cyprian, for example. Absence of extravagant miracles or even of many elements of the miraculous would weigh in favor of authenticity because of the natural human tendency to enlarge, e.g., Martyrdom of Polycarp (16), where the phrase "a dove and" is a later addition. But it would be a great error to reject the substantial truth of any account because of miraculous content. Though the miraculous story be fiction it might have a solid basis in fact. A good case in point is the three versions of the martyrdom of Procopius, each of which builds on the other. Better yet is the later story of Elizabeth of Hungary who placed a leper in her bed to nurse him. Her angry husband was illumined by grace to appreciate her charity so that he saw Christ in the leper. This entirely trust-worthy detail was later embellished so that the Duke found, not a leper, but the crucifix in the bed.

Many authentic Acts of the Martyrs have been lost to us be-cause many of the persecutors, especially Diocletian, destroyed all the Christian books they could. Furthermore, the average reader usually preferred the more elaborate and adorned accounts. As a result we find many manuscripts of the later and embellished copies but frequently only one of the authentic original. How-ever, many of these tales have found their way into the second Nocturns of the Breviary.

The modern sophisticated reader will now ask why the Acts of the Martyrs, especially those of the third or even of the second group, should be studied at all. The answer is simply that we can learn much and derive great edification from the account of the witness and example of the holy martyrs. For this the Acts of the Martyrs are of even greater importance. Nowhere proportionately can we throw so much light on Christian belief and practice of the early Church as in the comparatively small bulk of this kind of literature.

In the first place, the Acts of the Martyrs quote the canonical New Testament profusely but hardly ever cite any of the books that were regarded as inspired only in certain limited circles. Be-sides this, they attest to the following Catholic practices and be-lief: infant baptism; martyrdom, a baptism of blood; celebration of the anniversaries of martyrs as their birthdays; celebration of Holy Mass on their tombs, and the veneration of the Blessed Mother.

Classifying the Acts of the Martyrs into the three groups we have:

1. The Acts of St. Justin and His Companions, The Acts of the Scillitan Martyrs in Africa, and The Proconsular Acts of St. Cyprian.

2. The *Martyrium Polycarpi*, The Letter of the Churches of Vienne and Lyon to the Churches of Asia and Phrygia, The Passion of Perpetua and Felicitas, The Acts of Carpus, Papylus and Agathonice, and The Acts of Apollonius. The Acts of Ptolemy and Lucius, The Acts of Potamian and

Basilides, The Martyrdom of Pionius, The Acts of Maximillian, The Acts of Marcellus, The Acts of St. Felix, The Acts of St. Dasius.

3. The Acts and Testament of the Forty Martyrs. To these are to be added the Acts of the Persian Martyrs and the Acts of the Martyrs of Edessa. Other writings, such as the Acts of the Roman Martyrs, belong rather to the sphere of Hagiography. Though they are of much later date than their subjects, this does not preclude the historic existence of their heroes such as Agnes, Cecilia, Felicitas and her seven sons, Hippolytus, Lawrence, Sixtus, Sebastian, John and Paul, Cosmas and Damian, the "Four Crowned," Clement, Ignatius, Irenaeus, and others.

In this connection should be mentioned the ancient catalogues of martyrs or martyrologies. They are chiefly: The *Depositio episcoporum* and the *Depositio martyrum* found in the *Roman Chronographer of 354;* the *Martyrologium Carthaginiense;* the *Martyrologium Syriacum;* the *Martyrologium Hieronymianum,* and the *Synaxarium ecclesiae Constantinopolitanae.* In the Greek Church the Synaxaria or Menaea are the counterpart of the Western Martyrologium or martyrology.

IV. Early Documents on Liturgy and Canon Law

The *Didache* is the oldest work on canon law, Church organization, and the liturgy that has been preserved for us. A number of writings of later date have been influenced by it or even based on it. Though of a later date, they reflect earlier conditions and ecclesiastical discipline. Some of them even trace their lineage back to the apostolic age. They are so important because they detail the progress of the Church.

1. THE APOSTOLIC TRADITION OF HIPPOLYTUS
(c. 215)

On the chair of the third century statue of Hippolytus is inscribed the title of a work of his, long thought lost. It is called

Apostolic Tradition. A work entitled *The Egyptian Church Order* has long been known to students of early Christian literature. It is now certain that the two works are one and the same. The latter title came to the work because it first became known in Ethiopic and Coptic translations and because this work of Hippolytus seems to have wielded great influence in the East, especially in Egypt. It was of little importance in the West. However, its discovery has given us the oldest, after the *Didache*, and most important source of information on the organization and life of the early Church. The *Apostolic Tradition* has again served as a basis for later works, chiefly for Book VIII of the *Apostolic Constitutions.* There is an *Epitome* of this Book VIII that is, however, misnamed because it draws independently on the *Apostolic Tradition* and gives only excerpts of Book VIII. This *Epitome* has also circulated under the title *Constitutions by (per) Hippolytus* and must have been published shortly after the *Apostolic Constitutions.*

The *Apostolic Tradition* is arranged into three parts treating respectively of the clergy and hierarchy, of the laity and, in the last part, of the liturgy and church observances. Part I treats of bishops, priests, deacons, confessors, widows, readers, virgins, subdeacons, and the gift of healing. The Eucharistic liturgy is also covered and the prayers found in the work indicate that the earlier practice of free composition was being abandoned. Part II treats of converts and catechumens, of baptism, confirmation, and Holy Communion, and discusses the trades and professions proscribed for Christians. The description of baptism gives us the first Roman Creed. Part III treats of the Sunday, fasting, prayer, daily Communion and care of the Eucharist, as well as some other early practices.

2. THE DIDASCALIA (early third century)

The full title of this work is "Catholic Teaching of the Twelve Apostles and Holy Disciples of Our Savior." It is a Church Order published early in the third century by a bishop in Syria for converts from paganism there. The work is based on the *Didache* though the author also draws from Hermas, Irenaeus, the Gospel of Peter, and the Acts of Paul. He is not much of a theologian and the *Didascalia* contains little dogma. It is chiefly canon law and moral instruction. The *Didascalia* in turn served as the chief source for the first six books of the *Apostolic Constitutions*. A reading of the *Didache* and the study of the *Apostolic Tradition* of Hippolytus, will suggest the ground covered in the *Didascalia*. Whatever doctrinal discussion is to be found in the work is directed against Gnostics and Judaizers. There is detailed discussion of penance but no rigorism in the matter. In general the work covers all details of Christian life and practice.

3. THE APOSTOLIC CHURCH ORDER
(early fourth century)

This is a most important source of early canon law. The author and place of origin are not known. The first sections (1–4) are a mere revision of the *Didache*. The rest is moral instruction (5–14) and disciplinary regulations (15–29). The moral instructions follow the pattern of *The Two Ways*. The last part treats of bishops, priests, lectors, deacons, and widows. The work may have originated in Egypt since it was held in high esteem there.

4. THE APOSTOLIC CONSTITUTIONS (c. 380)

The author of this work seems to have been the Arian author of the Pseudo-Clementines. The full title is *Canones ecclesiastici Apostolorum* and the work was condemned by the Trullan Synod (692), except for chapter forty-seven or the Apostolic Canons, as having been falsified by heretics. The first six books (of the eight) cover the same ground as the *Didascalia* and are valuable for showing the progress and development of the Church since the *Didascalia* was written. Book seven is an enlargement of the *Didache* and contains, besides the matter of that work, prayer formularies, among them a morning prayer that is close to the Gloria of the Roman Mass, and instructions on the catechumenate and baptism. Book eight is the most important part of the book. It is based on the *Apostolic Tradition* of Hippolytus and has preserved for us the oldest complete liturgy of the Mass, the so-called Clementine Liturgy (6–15). This book treats of the charismatic gifts (1–2), the liturgy of the several orders (3–22), regulations on confessors, virgins, widows, exorcists (23–26), and converts, holydays and other matters (27–46). The last chapter (47) contains eighty-five Canons, which were circulated independently also as the 85 Apostolic Canons.

5. THE 85 APOSTOLIC CANONS (c. 380)

As mentioned in discussing the *Apostolic Constitutions* above, these 85 Canons are from the pen of the author of that work and make up chapter forty-seven of its eighth book. The Canons are adaptations of the legislation of Antioch (341) and Laodicea (343–381). Canon 85 gives a list of the canonical books of Sacred Scripture.

6. THE TESTAMENT OF OUR LORD JESUS CHRIST (after 450)

This work is a revision and an elaboration of the *Apostolic Tradition* of Hippolytus in two books. Book I has, as an introduction, an otherwise unknown apocalypse (perhaps the *Epistola Apostolorum*) and purports to give the instructions of Jesus to His disciples before His ascension, including instructions on the signs of the end of the world and on how affairs are to be ordered in Christian assemblies. Book II covers regulations governing the Christian's life from baptism to burial. The Eucharist, Agape, and Christian burial are described in detail.

7. THE CANONS OF HIPPOLYTUS (c. 500)

This work is a clumsy redaction of the *Apostolic Tradition* of Hippolytus. It probably was published in Syria shortly after 500.

8. THE PAPYRUS DÊR-BALIZEH (third century)

This fragmentary papyrus found in a Coptic monastery contains elements of a third century Mass Liturgy.

9. THE EUCHOLOGIUM OF SERAPION OF THMUIS (middle of the fourth century)

This is a collection of thirty prayers collected and published by Serapion. The *Euchologium* or prayerbook is especially valuable for a study of the Canon of the Mass.

V. Early Christian Hymns and Poetry

The oldest Christian hymns and poetry are found in the New Testament; the Magnificat, the Benedictus, the Nunc Dimittis and the Song of the Angels at Bethlehem. Some passages in Paul have hymn-like qualities and John speaks of a "new song" in the Apocalypse. Ignatius of Antioch to the Ephesians 7:2 seems to be part of a hymn to Christ, the divine Physician. Melito of Sardis (13–14) may be quoting a hymn. The Acts of Thomas reproduce several beautiful liturgical hymns which appear to be older than the narrative. The Acts of John purport to give the hymn which Jesus sang with His apostles on His way to Gethsemane. Hippolytus has preserved a Hymn of the Naasenes (Gnostics) in *Philosophumena* 5,10,2. Clement of Alexandria concludes his work, the *Pedagogue*, with a Hymn to Christ the Savior. There has been preserved for us a beautiful Hymn at Eventide (A.N.F. 2,298) and *Oxyrhincus Papyri* #1786 reveals another ancient Christian song. The *Epitaphs of Abercius and Pectorius* are poetry, as are the *Sayings of Sextus*. The bulkiest poetical works of primitive Christianity are the *Sibylline Oracles* and the *Odes of Solomon*.

The Battle Against Empire
Pagan - Jew - Heretic

I. The Greek Apologists

The earliest Christian writings were designed for guidance, edification, and information. Their number is not great because instruction was oral and converts learned Christian teaching by heart. There was no literary tradition of any proportion, but this was not because early Christians were illiterate and made up of the lower classes only. Paul in his captivity could already send greetings from "those of the household of Caesar" (Phil. 4:22). According to Tacitus (*Ann.* XIII, 32), Pomponia Graecina, wife of Aulus Plautius, conqueror of Britain, was accused of a "foreign superstition" as early as the year 58. She seems to have been a Christian. Domitilla, granddaughter of Vespasian, was banished as a Christian, and her husband, the ex-consul Flavius Clemens, executed (Dion. Cass. LXVII, 14). The family of the Acilii numbered a martyr, Acilius Glabrio, at the end of the first century (Suet. *Dom.* X). Small wonder that Pliny should report in his letter (*Ep.* X, 96) of about 112 A.D. on the phenomenal growth of Christianity in Bithynia. (Read Tertullian, *Apol.* 37.) It was the Discipline of the Secret that explains the lack of an early Christian literature.

As the Church grew, Christians began to be more noticed and their teachings and practices attacked. A new body of literature resulted. The earlier writers had produced chiefly letters and works of a moralizing nature, filled with biblical allusions and references. A group of writers called the Apologists came to defend the Church and even attack her enemies in writing. Their objective was threefold:

1. To refute and repudiate the calumnies leveled at Christians.
2. To plead for and even demand repeal of intolerant and hostile legislation.
3. To prove the truth of Christianity's claims.

To achieve their purpose they had not only to disprove the false accusations brought against the Christians but in their positive demonstration of the truth of Christian belief they had to attack and discredit the absurdities and evil of pagan belief and practices. The truth of monotheism and the resurrection had to be proved.

The chief charges against Christians are reducible to three: immorality, atheism, and "laziness," i.e., *odium humani generis* or *inertia*.

1. Immorality—These charges, though widely circulated, found acceptance chiefly among the lower classes and the ignorant. Christians were accused of all manner of sexual license, of cannibalism (Thyestian banquets) and the like.

2. Atheism—This charge had a twofold aspect. The Christians refused divine honors to the emperor. Yet this emperor-worship was the bond that knit the empire together. They were, therefore, enemies of the state. Again they were regarded as atheists because they offered no visible sacrifice at all. Then, when laws had been passed against the introduction of new religions, the Christians were charged guilty of *religio illicita*. Jews escaped these accusations because they were recognized as a race that had brought its own religion with it.

3. Laziness—Christians were accused much as Catholics often are today, of being enemies of progress and of the best interests of society. The intimate union of pagan religion and the Roman state made it altogether impossible for a Christian to be active in most political and civic affairs because of the danger of becoming involved in idolatry. So they were regarded as bad citizens, not at all interested in the welfare of the state and even hostile to its best interests.

The Apologists wrote much but only a small part of their literary output has come down to us. Our greatest loss is that the many books they wrote against heretics have been lost. These would have been of inestimable value in the study of theology.

Works that have been preserved are directed to the pagans for the most part, though some, e.g., Justin, wrote for Jews. They were addressed to three groups, to the emperor and the senate, to individuals and, finally, to the public in general. Whether those directed to the emperor or the senate ever reached the attention of their addressees may be questioned. In writing for Jews the Apologist endeavored to explain and demonstrate Christian belief, particularly the Messiahship of Christ. Works directed to pagan readers took another turn.

The chief arguments of the Apologists may be grouped under these heads:

1. Christian teaching has transformed the lives of converts, especially in their love of neighbor.

2. The coming of Christ was foretold by inspired writers more ancient and more reliable than the literature of any of the ancient peoples.

3. Christianity is ancient. The New Testament is but a fulfillment of the Old, and whatever of truth is found in paganism is Christian also. Christianity is not young, but can go back beyond Moses who was older than any writers of the pagan world.

4. The miracles of Christ were little used because of the many tales of miracle-working itinerant teachers in pagan literature.

5. Another thought frequently expressed by the Apologists is that God would not restrain the powers of demons but would let the world be destroyed except for the good living and good works of Christians.

These writings of the Apologists are generally superior to the works of their predecessors. A number of them were professional and trained philosophers. Their work is the first attempt at scientific theology and the reconciliation of reason and revelation. It marks the beginning of the absorption of Greek philosophy by Christian theology. Frequently the works take the dialogue form so popular in Greek literature.

The chief pagan rhetoricians and philosophers to attack Christians were Fronto, Lucian of Samosata, and Celsus. Later enemies were Porphyry, Hierokles, and Julian the Apostate.

The chief Apologists known to us are Apollinaris of Hieropolis, Aristides of Athens, Aristo of Pella, Athenagoras of Athens, the author of the Epistle to Diognetus, Hermias, Justin Martyr, Melito of Sardis, Miltiades, Tatian the Syrian, Theophilus of Antioch, and Quadratus.

1. ARISTIDES OF ATHENS (c. 120)

The oldest Apology that has come down to us is the work of the philosopher Aristides of Athens addressed to Hadrian (117–138). The work was long lost until found embedded in the legend of Barlaam and Josaphat. Roughly, the work falls into two parts. Part I (1–14) is a polemic against the Barbarians, the Greeks, and the Jews. Part II, the remainder of the book, describes the Christian way of life. Aristides points out how, of the four "races of men," the Barbarians have gone astray in worshiping the elements, the works of God's creating hand. Next he convicts the Greeks, more subtle than the Barbarians, of inventing their own objects of worship and going even farther astray by attributing human sins and passions to their gods. The Jews, though monotheists and on the way of truth, yet went astray in their vain observances. Finally (15–17) Aristides shows that only the Christians have the true conception of the deity and only they are notable for their purity and high standard of moral living. There is only one God whom all the peoples, Barbarians, Greeks, Jews and Christians must worship and serve. He is the creator of all, conserves all and is Himself immobile, perfect, incomprehensible, and unnamable. It is the prayers of Christians that keeps God from destroying the earth.

2. ATHENAGORAS OF ATHENS (c. 190)

Called a "Christian philosopher of Athens" in the title of his *Supplication for the Christians,* nothing further is known of Athenagoras of Athens except that he also wrote a treatise *On the Resurrection of the Dead.* The only ancient writer to mention him is Methodius. Athenagoras shows himself a far more polished and orderly writer than Justin and far more sympathetic toward Greek philosophy and culture than Justin's student, Tatian.

His Apology or Supplication was written about 177 and addressed to Emperor Marcus Aurelius Antoninus and his son Lucius Aurelius Commodus. In calm and ordered manner he ap-

peals for a hearing (1–3) and then refutes calumnious charges of
atheism (4–30) and cannibalism and Oedipean immorality (31–
36). He concludes with an appeal for justice (37).

His *On the Resurrection of the Dead* is the best ancient
treatise on the subject. He proves the possibility of the resurrection on the part of God's omnipotence (1–10) and the necessity
of the resurrection on three counts. Man, a rational creature, is
immortal and the body must rise to rejoin the soul (11–17). The
body must share in the sentence meted out in the hereafter
(18–23). Finally, man is destined for happiness that cannot be
achieved on this earth (24–25).

Athenagoras gives the best and clearest exposition of the oneness of God and the Trinity and of the place of the angels under
God (*Apol.* 8–10). He has a clear statement of the instrumental
causality of biblical inspiration (*Apol.* 7) and he sets forth the
sublime Christian ideal of marriage and virginity (*Apol.* 33,35).
His description of Christian living (*Apol.* 31–33) should be read
with that of Aristides and the Epistle to Diognetus.

3. THE EPISTLE TO DIOGNETUS (second century)

The author, addressee, and origin of this apology are unknown
as was the writing itself until the sixteenth century. Quadratus
has been proposed as the author and what Eusebius (*H.E.* 4,3,2)
quotes from that author's Apology would fill the lacuna in
chapter 7, 6–7. It might throw light on the last two chapters
(11–12) in which the author claims discipleship of the apostles
and represents himself as a teacher of pagans. This would date
the work under Hadrian. The authenticity of these last chapters
is also called into question because of their difference in style. It
has been suggested that the work draws on Irenaeus and that 7,
1–5 are related to the *Philosophumena* 10,33 of Hippolytus. Such
a conclusion would date the work near the end of the second
century. The serene tone and exquisite simplicity of its presentation, however, speak for an early date at the time of Aristides,
of whose Apology it is reminiscent. Clement of Rome, Theophilus
of Antioch, Apollos, Justin, Apelles, and Marcion have also been
suggested as authors.

The author answers three questions: 1. What God do the

Christians worship and why do they condemn the pagans and Jews; 2. What is their vaunted love of fellow, and 3. Why did Christianity come into the world at so late a date. In answer, the author criticizes paganism and Judaism (2–4) and with lyrical beauty describes the Christian way of life. Christians are the soul of the world (5–6). Christianity is of divine origin (7–8) and came late into the world that man might first realize his own helplessness without God (9). The conclusion points out that if Diognetus embraced Christianity, true love of God and man would soon blossom in him (10).

This chapter (10) ends abruptly. If the last two chapters (11–12) are accepted, as is commonly done, we have a conclusion to the work. But the break between chapters ten and eleven remains unexplained, and there is still a difference in style and tone that is startling.

4. JUSTIN MARTYR (165)

Head and shoulders above the Greek Apologists of the second century stands Justin, the philosopher. Born of pagan Greek parents in Sichem, Palestine, he worked his tortuous way to the truths of Christianity through the maze of current philosophies and the Scriptures. After this he devoted himself exclusively to lay missionary activity for the only trustworthy and useful philosophy. He taught in Ephesus and elsewhere in Asia Minor, founded a school in Rome and died there, a martyr. The authentic Acts of his martyrdom have come down to us. In Rome his chief antagonist was the rhetorician Crescens (Tatian, *Or.* 19,4). Tatian the Syrian was one of his students there. Tertullian (*Val.* 5) calls him "Philosopher and Martyr" and Eusebius (*H.E.* 4,18,1 ff.) lists his many and varied writings. Of these only the *Apologies* and the *Dialogue with Trypho* can be accepted as of unquestionable authenticity. Leo XIII placed his feast on April 14.

The nobility of Justin's character and his honest sincerity speak from every line of the account of his trial and martyrdom, as well as from his own writings, especially the Dialogue. However, he is often tiresome reading because what he has to say is often not well organized and he rarely develops warmth or enthusiasm, discussing his matter in the quiet way of the philosopher. Yet his love for Christian teaching and the truth, even as found in pagan philosophy, glows in every line he has written.

Among the lost writings of Justin and others attributed to him are: *On the Resurrection, Against Heresies* (*Apol.* I, 26), *Against Marcion* (Eus. *H.E.* 4,11,8), *Cohortatio ad Gentiles* (Exhortation to the Gentiles), *Oratio ad Graecos* (Petition to the Greeks), and *De monarchia* (On the Monarchy). It is certain that he was a prolific writer, a fact that may explain the unorganized state of his materials and his rambling style. His penchant for long drawn-out sentences and his preoccupation with the thought of the moment may seem to indicate a lack or total absence of rewriting or revision.

His two Apologies are generally regarded as a unit, though cited separately. Indeed, *Apology II* fits well as a conclusion to the first Apology. It has also been suggested that *Apology II* is a reply to an attack of Fronto of Cirta. Both works are addressed to Emperor Antoninus Pius (138–161) and written in Rome.

Apology I falls into two parts. The first (1–12) refutes the charges against the Christians. The second (13–67) is a positive exposition and demonstration of the truth of Christianity. In it Justin devotes chapters thirty to fifty-three to a proof of the divinity of Christ from the Old Testament. The conclusion (68) is a serious exhortation to the Emperor and there is added a letter of the Emperor Hadrian to Minucius Fundanus, proconsul of Asia, on the correct court procedure against Christians. It is of extreme importance and Eusebius says that Justin himself added it to his Apology (*H.E.* 4,8,8 ff.).

The much shorter *Apology II* goes over some of the ground of *Apology I* but is directed to the Senate and appeals to the innate justice of Roman public opinion.

Justin's Apologies were published about 155 and some time later there appeared his work to the Jews, the *Dialogue with Trypho*. It has been suggested that Trypho may have been Rabbi Tarphon who had fled Palestine during the disorders attending Bar Kochba's revolt (132–135). The disputation may have taken place in Ephesus, though it may also be that Justin is employing a literary device in the Dialogue. The work lacks some of the introduction, and part of chapter seventy-four is missing. The introduction (2–8) is autobiographical. Part I expounds the Christian view of the Old Testament (9–47). Part II demonstrates that worship of Christ is not opposed to monotheism (48–108) and the last section (109–142) points out that Christians are the new people of God and that heathens are called to the New Israel.

Justin brought revelation to reason and proved that revelation does not need the endorsement of reason, but that the truths of philosophy need the light of revelation. In his thinking it was not that Christianity became Greek but that Christianity began to absorb, to transform, and to complement Greek philosophy.

In his search for God, Justin discovered the faltering inadequacy of reason and came to experience the joy of seeing the light thrown on reason by revelation. If an analysis of his theology reveals defects and shortcomings, as in his Christology (*Apology* II, 6), it must be remembered that only a small part of what he wrote has been preserved for us.

For Justin, God is transcendent and cannot be named (*Apol.* II, 6, *Dial.* 127, *Dial.* 60). The Logos is the bridge between God and man (*Dial.* 61) because God is not substantially present in His creation. By his theory of the *Logos Spermatikos*, Justin unites ancient Greek philosophy and Christian teaching. The divine Logos is in Christ in His fullness but in human reason every man possesses a germ of the Logos (*Logos Spermatikos*), though in unequal degree. The prophets of the Old Testament and some Greek philosophers possessed the germ to greater degree and thus arrived at a greater knowledge than others. Greek philosophy drew many truths from Moses, the oldest of writers, and attained others by reason but only Christians have the full and unadulterated truth (*Apol.* I, 46; *Apol.* II, 13). Justin's thinking on the relationship of the Logos to the Father is tainted with subordinationism.

Angels and demons have some kind of corporeity, according to Justin. They are creatures of God. The good angels look after men and the demons seduce men. Satan fell when he seduced Eve; his followers, when they seduced human women. Now they inhabit the lower air and work evil until they are sent into hell (*Apol.* I, 6,26,28,54,57,62; *Apol.* II, 5; *Dial.* 30,57,100,124).

Man's soul also has a certain corporeity and has immortality only by participation in God's life because original sin destroyed its capacity for immortality and deification. This has, however, been regained through the Logos. Justin is a Chiliast though not stubbornly so (*Dial.* 6,45,72,80,99,124).

Of great importance is Justin's testimony to the Gospels (*Dial.* 100; *Apol.* I, 66). He is the first to introduce the idea of Mary as the second Eve into Christian literature. Finally, he has left us a liturgical description of baptism, the celebration of the Eucharist and Sunday worship. There has been keen dispute whether he considered the Eucharist a sacrifice, but his identification of the Eucharist with the sacrifice foretold by Malachy would seem to settle the question. It must further be remembered that we have only a little of his literary output (*Apol.* I, 61–67; *Dial.* 41,117; *Apol.* I, 13).

5. MELITO OF SARDIS (c. 190)

Melito, revered bishop of Sardis in Lydia engaged in prodigious literary activity but little of it is left. His apology, directed to Marcus Aurelius (c. 172) contains the thesis that peace between Church and state is normal and beneficial to both. His *Homily on the Passion* is the earliest Christian homily that has come down to us. We know he wrote treatises *On the Pasch* in which he defended the Quartodeciman position, and an anti-Montanist work on the correct way of life of "Prophets," *On Body and Soul, On the Church, On the Corporeity of God*, six books *On the Law and Prophets* that give us the oldest list of Old Testament books, *On Faith and the Birth of Christ* and three books *On the Incarnation* against Marcion.

The Christology of the *Homily on the Passion* might be misconstrued as Monarchian Modalism but it is very clear on the Incarnation and the Virgin Birth. Christ became man to rescue us from original sin and its effects, from death and the devil. Melito describes the pre-existent Son and His *Descensus ad Inferos* (Descent into Hell) in lines that suggest a liturgical hymn. The Church is the "reservoir of truth."

6. TATIAN, THE SYRIAN (c. 180)

Born of pagan parents in the East, Tatian came to Rome in the course of his extensive travels in pursuit of the study of philosophy. Here he entered the school of Justin and became a Christian. Returning to the East about 172, he fell away from the Church and founded the Encratites who repudiated all marriage and the use of meat and wine, even using water to celebrate their "eucharist." He was active in Syria, Cilicia, and Pisidia, dying around 180 without returning to the Church. He has left us only two works, the *Discourse to the Greeks* and the *Diatessaron*. The former contains a few references to other works.

A reading of Tatian's Oration or *Discourse to the Greeks* will readily show why he could have founded the unreasonable Encratites, and both how much and how little he learned from his master Justin. It reflects many of Justin's philosophical and theological ideas but it also reveals a character far different from the sainted philosopher-martyr of Rome. Tatian is an angry, scolding old man who rants and raves at everything Greek as valueless and productive only of evil and immorality. The introduction challenges the Greeks to prove that they have themselves produced anything worthwhile, and Tatian concludes with another challenge that he be proved wrong. The body of the Discourse falls into four sections: Section I, a Christian cosmology, treats of God, the Logos, creation, eschatology, and man and the angels (4–7). Section II is a Christian demonology and a discussion of what man must do to achieve immortality (8–20). Section III excoriates the Greek way of life in the light of Christianity (21–30), and the last section, IV, treats of the age and the moral worth of Christian teaching (31–41).

The *Diatessaron* is a Gospel harmony presenting one continuous chronological story of Christ "out of four" Gospels. Composed probably in Syriac and put into Greek form, it very early made its way to the West. The Syriac *Diatessaron* was in use by the Syriac Church well into the fifth century and the Greek version influenced the pre-Hieronymian Gospel text.

7. THEOPHILUS OF ANTIOCH (c. 185)

Born in Mesopotamia, Theophilus embraced Christianity in his manhood after a good Hellenistic education (*Ad Autol.* 1,14) and, according to Eusebius (*H.E.* 4,20,1 ff.) became the sixth bishop of Antioch in Syria. His three books *Ad Autolicum* were written shortly after the death of Marcus Aurelius on March 17,

180 (*Ad Autol.* 3,27 ff.) and he died some time later. All his works except the *Ad Autolicum* have been lost. Theophilus writes well, displays a comprehensive knowledge of contemporary thinking and literature, and uses the New Testament far more than the other Apologists. For him the New Testament is equally inspired as the Old Testament and he is witness to John's Gospel (*Ad Autol.* 2,22; 3,12–14).

Book I, in refuting the attacks of Autolicus, treats of God, providence, the Christian name, the resurrection, and idolatry. Book II develops these thoughts and contrasts pagan mythology and the contradictions of Greek poets and philosophers with the Sacred Scriptures. In the third book Theophilus contrasts pagan and Christian living and demonstrates the antiquity of Christianity and its writings.

As a theologian Theophilus has given us several "firsts." He is the first to speak of a "Trinity," to distinguish between the immanent Logos and the Logos sent or uttered, and to give clear expression to the inspiration of the New Testament. In general, his ideas are otherwise those of the other Apologists. He, too, holds that the soul is not by nature immortal but can achieve immortality.

8. RETROSPECT

The Apologists were the men who contributed much to the impact of Christianity on the Graeco-Roman world. They accomplished what the average Christian could not do. The Christian living his life in Christ, living in the world but with eyes fixed on his true home, disregarding all that paganism valued and esteemed, only mystified the average pagan and aroused the anger of the higher strata of paganism. The Apologists explained the "why" of Christian conduct.

Varying judgments are made of the individual Apologists. Here it must be remembered that we have but a small fraction of their literary output. Furthermore, each had his purpose in view. It is, therefore, a mistake to expect anything like an organized and systematic exposition of Christian teaching in their writings. Such was not their intent. On the contrary, they sometimes concealed the "mysteries" of Christianity. Their silence on some points by no means indicates lack of interest. They fought for the fundamental rights of Christians; they defended the honor of the Name and refuted calumnies. Only incidentally did they now and then come near to a disclosure of what the full vision is that makes a Christian, and then only in a vague way.

II. Heretical Literature

Besides Paganism and Judaism three internal enemies plagued the early Church, the errors of Modalism, Gnosticism, and Montanism. Paganism took the lives and property of Christians but the blood of martyrs turned into the seed of ever more Christians. Judaizing tendencies disturbed the discipline of the infant Church by insistence on the Mosaic law and some of its practices. These enemies disparaged especially the divinity of the Messias. The Judaizing movement was geographically contained for the most part. Offshoots of this movement were the Ebionites, Essenes, and Elkasites. Most of the writings of these sects have been lost. There remain only a few Apocrypha and some strains of their thought in the Clementine literature. Modalism, Montanism, and Gnosticism on the other hand for a time threatened the very life of the Church. Modalism struck at the very basic truth of Christianity. Montanism threatened the growth and spread of the Church. Gnosticism attempted to conform Christianity to the world. Any one of these movements, but for the abiding presence of Christ, might have destroyed the Church. A prodigious amount of heretical and anti-heretical literature was produced by the struggle but most of it has been lost.

Of the three errors, Modalism lived longest in various forms. Where the Docetae and similar errors had questioned the complete humanity of the Son of God, Modalism attacked the Trinity and the individuality of the Son as the second Person of the Trinity. It emphasized monotheism to a point where it conceived of the three divine Persons of the Trinity as a threefold mode of being or self-manifestation of the one God. Therefore it denied a real distinction of divine Persons in the one God. According to this error, there is only one principle that created all things, that became incarnate. In other words, Father and Son are merely names for different roles of the deity. With the emphasis placed on the one principle of uncreated being the error came to be known as Monarchianism. It came also to be called Patripassianism after the slogan, "the Father suffered." Noetus originated the error and was condemned for it by the presbytery of Smyrna. His disciples, Epigones and Cleomenes, came to Rome where they spread the heresy. Hippolytus wrote against it there. A certain Praxeas, who was an anti-Montanist, fell into Modalism and spread the error in Italy and Africa. Tertullian wrote against him, as well as against Gnosticism, though he fell victim to Montanism later. A later development of the error was Sabellianism, named after another man from the East who came to Rome to teach his heresy. He reduced the divine persons to mere transitory modalities. Pope Callixtus excommunicated him, but the error persisted in developed and modified form.

Montanism was more a rigorously ascetic way of life than a doctrine. The Montanist idea of the Church was that leadership depended on direct personal inspiration. Montanus, a native of Phrygia in Asia Minor, a region so noted for freakish heresies that some of the fathers used the adjective *Kataphrygian* (according to the Phrygians) for any error to which they could not attach an exact label. About 170 he claimed to have ecstasies, even to be inspired. He was joined by two women, Priscilla and Maximilla, who made similar claims. The heresy spread wide and threatened the progress of the whole Church. Montanus claimed that the Paraclete had descended upon him. He taught that the end of the world was imminent. Therefore Christians should retire from the world and have nothing to do with it. Christians should embrace a most rigid way of life, engage in long fastings and austere mortifications. Second marriages, too, were to be condemned. Montanism was finally condemned by Pope Zephyrinus after a number of individual bishops had taken action against it. The chief orthodox writers against the error are Miltiades, Melito of Sardis, Praxeas the Patripassianist, the anonymous anti-Montanist, Apollonius, and Gaius, a Roman priest under Pope Zephyrinus (198–217).

Gnosticism presented an even more serious threat to the in-

fant Church, but from another angle. Where Montanus claimed
that the Paraclete spoke through him, urging Christians to have
nothing to do with the world, Christian Gnosticism disparaged
faith and emphasized gnosis, i.e., scientific knowledge. It strove
to secularize Christian thinking and to bring Christian living to
conform to the age. Gnosticism as a world outlook sought to
displace Christianity. It is correct to speak of a Jewish and a
pagan gnosis. The Christian gnosis tried to absorb the thinking
of Judaism and the mystery religions. It occupied itself with
the entire gamut of human thinking, the origin of the universe,
the problem of evil, the redemption, God, and the spirit world.
It was a very complex and confusing system of doctrines and
practices. Basic to it was the idea of "gnosis," i.e., the higher insights that come to the favored few while the average believer
has only the common outlook or knowledge. The Gnostic resorted to all manner of allegorizing to come to his gnosis.

Gnosticism spread far and wide in the East and the West and
produced an incalculable volume of literature, gospels, acts,
apocalypses. It also produced the first, though erroneous, attempt
at scientific exposition of Christianity. Gnostic writings far out-
numbered the literary output of the Orthodox. It is only because
truth survives and that Christianity is true, that the young Church
was able to survive. Irenaeus has preserved much of Gnostic
teaching in his *Adversus haereses.*

The last representatives of pre-Christian Gnosticism that we
meet in early Christian literature are Simon Magus, his teacher
Dositheus, and Menander, who was a disciple of Simon Magus.
The chief Christian Gnostics whose names have come down to
us are Apelles, Bardesanes, Carpocrates, Epiphanes, Florinus,
Harmonius, Heracleon, Isidorus, Julius Cassianus (an Encratite),
Marcion, Mark Ptolemy, Theodotus, and Valentinus. To this list
of names should be added the following Gnostic writings, *Pistis
Sophia,* Two Books of Jeû or the *Mystery of the Great Logos,*
the *Gospel of Mary,* the *Apocryphon of John,* and the *Sophia
Jesu Christi.* In 1946 a large collection of Gnostic writings,
thirty-seven complete works and five fragmentary ones, were
discovered in Egypt. These have not yet been fully evaluated
and still await definitive editing and study.

Marcion, the heretic, needs a little more mention. He was called the Pontic mouse in contempt by some of the fathers, but he caused the early Church much trouble. Born in Sinope on the Black Sea in Pontus of a wealthy and prominent family, he was excommunicated by his father, a bishop. Thereafter he turned up in Rome around 140. It seems he had attained episcopal consecration and after he was excommunicated in Rome in July, 144, founded his own church with an hierarchy. In this he differed from the Gnostics of his time who had merely established schools. He was in a way anti-Gnostic in his emphasis on asceticism and disparagement of Gnosis. Basically he condemned the Old Testament and taught that only Paul had correctly understood the teachings of Christ. Only Paul understood that God is the merciful and loving God of the New Testament and that the Old Testament God of stern justice is a distorted concept of the deity. Accordingly he discarded all of the New Testament except Luke and the Paulines. He attracted many followers because of the austerity of his own personal life, and his errors were for a time a serious threat to the young Church. The vitality of the Church is again evident in this conflict with Marcion and his followers.

III. Anti-Heretical Literature

The great mass of Gnostic literature has been lost and with it also, for the most part, the orthodox writings refuting the vagaries of these early heretics. This should not be surprising because once the error had been vanquished the early Christians found little interest in such writings. There have been preserved for us, however, a number of papal and episcopal writings. There are the works of Dionysius of Corinth, Pope Eleutherius, Pinytus of Gnossus, Serapion of Antioch, Pope Soter, Pope Victor I, and Pope Zephyrinus. Besides these names Eusebius mentions the following men whose treatises against the Gnostics have perished completely: Apion, Agrippa Castor, Candidus, Heraclitus, Maximus, Modestus, Musanus, Philip of Gortyna, Rhodon, Sextus, and Theophilus of Antioch. To this list must be added Hegesippus and Irenaeus of Lyons. Both engaged in systematic attempts at a refutation of these heresies and laid the foundations of the beginnings of dogmatic theology. Only a few fragments are left of the works of Hegesippus but there remain two full works by Irenaeus.

Hegesippus laid the foundation of the argument from tradition. Irenaeus built on it, developed, and elaborated it. Hegesippus stated the principle of the argument. "Go," he said, "and visit the churches as I did. You will find that in the churches each one can go back to contact with the apostles through the line of bishops. Thus each church has directly from Christ's apostles what He taught. All the churches," thus Hegesippus continued the argument, "teach the same doctrine and have no knowledge of the new Gnosis spread by heretics. Therefore, though it may be new and attractive, it is not the teaching of Christ." Irenaeus later developed this argument in his *Adversus haereses* (Against Heresies).

1. HEGESIPPUS (end of second century)

Hegesippus, a convert Jew, came from the Orient to Rome by way of Corinth to investigate the goings-on of the Gnostic sects. When he got back home he wrote (c. 180) his five books of Memoirs or *Memorabilia*, containing much ecclesiastical information, though they are primarily anti-Gnostic writings. What is left of his writings is mostly found in Eusebius. Though a good observer and a sincere reporter who was highly esteemed by Eusebius, he appears to lack critical acumen. His list of the popes is still a matter of controversy. But Hegesippus is witness that to find true doctrine one must visit the various centers of Christianity to learn the teaching of tradition.

2. IRENAEUS OF LYONS (c. 202)

Too little is known of the life of this great man. He was born, it seems, in Smyrna and since he could remember vividly the lectures and sermons of Polycarp, there is established a personal contact with the apostolic age through Polycarp. When and under what circumstances he made his way to Gaul is not known. In 177 (or 178) the church of Lyons sent him with a highly commendatory letter to Pope Eleutherius to mediate as presbyter of Lyons in the Montanist trouble. On his return he became bishop of Lyons after the death of Bishop Photinus. When Pope Victor I had excommunicated some Asiatic bishops in the Paschal controversy, Irenaeus wrote to them and to Victor to urge peace. Nothing further is known of Irenaeus. The story of his martyrdom told by Gregory of Tours is too late to be trusted. He died about 202.

Irenaeus is the most important theologian of the second century and may, in a sense, be called the father of dogmatic theology. As a witness to Catholic belief in the second century he is even more important. He can speak for the East and the West, for Rome and Gaul, by reason of his travels and his residence. Despite his preoccupation with ecclesiastical affairs in his own diocese and with general affairs of the Church, e.g., Montanism and the Paschal controversy, he found time to engage in varied literary activity also. However, only two of his larger writings have come down to us: the *Adversus haereses* (Against Heresies) and the *Epideixis* or *Demonstration of the Apostolic Teaching*. All his other writings have been lost except for a few fragments.

The full title of the *Adversus haereses*, so called since it has come down to us only in a Latin translation from the original Greek, is *Detection and Overthrow of the Pretended but False Gnosis*. As the title indicates, this work is in two parts of which the first (Book I) explains and the second (Books II–V) refutes the errors of Gnostics. The first part is valuable because it tells us what the many different Gnostic teachers, from Simon Magus on, taught. He then compares their teaching to Catholic doctrine. Part two undertakes the refutation of Gnosticism from reason (Book II), from tradition and the teachings of the apostles (Book III), and from the teachings of our Lord and the Old Testament prophets (Book IV). The last book is eschatological, treating chiefly of the resurrection of the body. Here Irenaeus expounds his chiliastic views. The thinking in the work is clear and precise but the expression of his thought is that of a busy and distracted executive. This makes the work hard to read because of frequent repetitions and the absence of lucid arrangement. Remarks by Irenaeus throughout the work show that it was written piecemeal and that he added enlargements. He tells us that he did not wish to produce a literary master-piece. He desired only to fill the request of a friend for an ex-position and refutation of the errors of the Gnostics. In that he succeeded and he has left us one of the masterpieces of early patristics.

The Demonstration of the Apostolic Teaching is a simple, apologetic treatment of Christian teaching and differs entirely from the *Adversus haereses*. After telling why he writes (1–3), Irenaeus explains the essential elements of Christian belief (4–42), the Trinity, Creation, the Fall, and the Incarnation. Next he proves the truth of Christianity (42–97) and finishes with an edifying exhortation to Christian living. There is nothing polemic about the book but it is a calm positive exposition of Christian belief. However, it is not a catechesis because of its apologetic tone.

Of all that Irenaeus has written, Book III of the *Adversus haereses* is of the greatest importance. In it he refutes the Gnostics from the teaching of the apostles and from tradition. Its theological content goes far beyond this, but the third book develops the principle of tradition enunciated by Hegesippus, that the truth can be found in any church where the tradition can be traced back to the apostles through a succession of bishops. The Gnostics alleged a new and additional revelation. Irenaeus argues that anything not handed down by the apostles, whom Christ instructed, cannot be revelation. He asserts that one may select any single church or all of them in such an inquiry into the true teaching of Christ. Instead he chooses to take the Roman Church and, in a most controversial passage, witnesses to the primacy of the bishop of Rome. We have the passage only in its Latin form by a translator whom we cannot check as to accuracy. Irenaeus demands apostolicity as proof of correct doctrine, and cites the Church of Rome, founded and developed by the Princes of the Apostles, Peter and Paul. How Irenaeus is to be interpreted can be learned from his contemporaries Tertullian (*De praescr.* 32) and the anonymous writer mentioned by Eusebius, 5,28,3, who name Peter alone as the founder of the Roman Church and the chief source of its authority. In spite of all efforts to interpret

Irenaeus' statement in a different way, he states the pre-eminence of the Roman Church and adds that this Roman Church is conclusive proof of Christian teaching. The only validity of Irenaeus' argument, and it must have had validity or he would not have used it, is that the Christian churches of his day recognized the primacy of the bishop of Rome (Cf. *Adv. haer.* 3,3,2–3).

Irenaeus makes no pretensions to being a speculative theologian. What he has to say about the Trinity is mainly directed against the Gnostics. He clearly states the doctrine of the Trinity but he emphasizes the place of the three divine Persons in the divine economy. In developing his Christology, he clearly teaches the *Perichoresis* or *Circumincessio* of the three Persons and elaborates his teaching of the Recapitulation or *Anakephalaiosis*. He takes his doctrine of the Recapitulation from Paul but develops it. God's plan for mankind, frustrated for a time by Adam's fall, is taken up again in the Second Adam, the Incarnate Son. So the human race is to be restored and everything is to be renewed in this recapitulation.

Man, created in the image of God, lost this gift by original sin. In this restoration Mary plays her part. Developing Justin's theology, Irenaeus points out Mary as Eve's advocate. The whole restoration or recapitulation is through the Church of which Christ is the head. Christ's teaching and His grace are handed down through churches that can be traced back to the apostles and to no others. Hence heretics, especially the Gnostics, have nothing to offer (*Adv. haer.* 3,3,1).

Irenaeus is a witness to the existence of a canon of the New Testament that is complete, except that he seems to have accepted Hermas and rejected Hebrews. For him the New Testament is inspired Scripture and the Gospels are tetramorphous because presented in different form by the four evangelists whom he lists by name in the traditional order. The inspired character of the canonical books is determined by apostolicity and by tradition.

In his sacramental theology Irenaeus teaches transubstantiation, the sacrificial character of the Eucharist, and the existence of a penitential discipline. He is the earliest of the fathers to mention the practice of infant baptism.

In his eschatology Irenaeus is a Chiliast and influenced by his theory of the Recapitulation. All evil will be recapitulated in Anti-Christ, as all good in Christ. Irenaeus must be set down as the greatest theologian and opponent of error in the Church of the first two centuries.

3. THE MURATORIAN FRAGMENT AND THE ANCIENT PROLOGUES TO THE GOSPELS AND PAULINE EPISTLES

By way of an appendix to the study of the earliest anti-heretical Christian writings, the Muratorian Fragment and the Prologues to the New Testament books that have come down to us cannot be passed by. The former is of greatest value while the latter can no longer be as highly esteemed as they once were. The Muratorian Fragment is of greatest importance for the study of the history of the New Testament canon. It is an important witness to the orthodox list of New Testament books in a time when the controversy on the inspiration of the New Testament writings was acute.

Of the Prologues, three groups are important. These were attached to copies of the New Testament writings and served as introductions purporting to tell about the authors and the time and occasion of their writings. A large number of these Prologues are of a late date. The important three groups are: the Anti-Marcionite Prologues to the Gospels, the Monarchian Prologues to the Gospels, and the Prologues to the Epistles of Paul.

- SECTION III -

Scientific Theology and
Its Beginnings

Introduction

About the year 200, Christian literature took a new turn and
made a spurt of tremendous growth. The writings of the second
century were almost entirely apologetic and anti-heretical. Their
main objective was to defend the Church and attack her enemies.
Irenaeus came closest to a systematic presentation of Catholic
truths but he did not even attempt any such work. However,
the Church was spreading not only geographically and numeri-
cally, but through all strata of society. Lawyers, rhetoricians,
philosophers, and intellectuals of all sorts were coming into the
Church and interesting others in Her teaching. For such converts
a simple exposition or catechism did not suffice. Handbooks that
scientifically explained and explored Christian truths became a
need. Even schools or universities came to be needed. No longer
could the individual lay missionary or philosopher satisfy demand
by instructing the few that might come as did Justin "in the
house of Martin, near the baths of Timothy." Thus there sprang
into being the great theological schools of Alexandria, Antioch,
Caesarea, and at a later date those farther East in Nisibis and
Edessa. The schools of Alexandria and Antioch, by all odds, exercised the greatest and widest influence. It comes as somewhat of a
surprise, or even shock, to learn that Rome, the center of Christianity, the pre-eminent church, did not produce any theological
schools and, compared to the East, contributed but little to Christian theological literature. Even the daughter church in Africa
surpassed the Romans. Rome gave us the one Apology of
Minucius Felix. Her greatest contribution to theological litera-

54

ture was made by two rebellious antipopes, Hippolytus and Novatian.

A closer study of the history of the Church in the West and East illumines the picture. All roads led to Rome, even in those days. Rome was kept busy (and this applies also to the African Church) with enemies without and within—real enemies of Christianity, not mere protagonists of a detailed point of theological speculation as the troublemakers in the East so often were. Rome was driven to defend the Christian way of life against paganism without and extremism within. This becomes apparent in the works of third century Christian writers. The writers of the West are preoccupied with the practical values of Christianity as expressed in daily living and with the subjective contribution each Christian must make in a world bedeviled by pagan immorality and heretical extremism. The Easterners, on the contrary, could go on to exploit the truths of Christianity and show their superiority to Greek philosophy and Hellenistic religious thinking. This explains why the great heresies of this age were bred in the East and why the West had comparatively little theological impact on the East. The West, however, had to absorb the reverberations of theological strife in the East in the next century.

1. THE SCHOOL OF ALEXANDRIA

Alexandria, the crossroads of ideas in the ancient world, naturally became the oldest Christian center of theological learning. The Christian school built on the past, pagan and Jewish. Philo was the outstanding spokesman of the latter. The characteristic of the schools is metaphysical speculation and the "allegorical" interpretation of Scripture.

This so-called allegorical interpretation of Sacred Scripture was new only in that the method was applied to Scripture by Christian theologians. Pagan thinkers had long before this tried to find deeper, hidden meanings in the sometimes repulsive tales of mythology. Philo had searched for a deeper significance in those sections of the Old Testament that seemed to have no relevancy for his day. Other Alexandrian Jews had gone before Philo in this task. Reduced logically to its conclusions, this system of interpreting Scripture led to a subjectivity that could produce only chaotic thinking. Though in principle it was based on the idea that a literal interpretation of the Scriptures was often unworthy of God, the allegorical method came near to the ridiculous at times. On the other hand the Antiochian school by its extreme literalism often did harsh injustice to the sense of Scripture.

The chief names associated with the school of Alexandria were Ammonius, Athanasius, Clement of Alexandria, Didymus the Blind, Dionysius of Alexandria, Pierius, and Theognostus. The most illustrious of these and the most influential by far was Origen who even today remains a controversial figure in the history of theology.

2. THE SCHOOL OF CAESAREA

Origen brought the school of Alexandria to its greatest heights but was compelled to flee the city of Alexandria in 332. He settled in Caesarea in Palestine and founded there a school and a library with a scriptorium. His successor, Pamphilus, enlarged the school and library so that Caesarea became the greatest center of Christian learning and scholarship of antiquity. Origen's influence was diffused throughout Asia Minor, Syria, and Palestine. Later these areas became the battleground between Origen's followers and his friends. The school at Caesarea trained such theologians and writers as Eusebius of Caesarea, Gregory Thaumaturgus and the Cappadocians, Basil the Great, Gregory of Nazianzus, and Gregory of Nyssa. In fact, it was indirectly the influence of Origen that led to the establishment of the school of Antioch to fight the so-called allegorical interpretation of Scripture made so popular by the influence of Origen.

3. THE SCHOOL OF ANTIOCH

Lucian, a priest of Samosota who is not to be confused with a pagan writer of the same name and place, is said to have founded the school of Antioch in the latter half of the third century. Antioch had been for years a great center of pagan scholarship and its Christian school was started to counteract the influence of Origen and the Alexandrian school. All these early Christian schools, although theological, were chiefly exegetical. The Antiochian school concentrated on the literal, historical, and grammatical study and exposition of Scripture. Whatever the followers of the Antiochian and Alexandrian schools themselves thought of their approach to the explanation of the Scriptures, subsequent studies in their hermeneutics have shown them less far apart than was at one time held. The Antiochians looked for the obvious and literal meaning of Scripture, whereas the Alexandrians ever sought deeper and hidden meanings. The opposition in the approach to the interpretation of the Word of God by the two schools has often been exaggerated. Fundamentally the two were not too far from agreement in their principles of exegesis. The Alexandrians found the typical sense everywhere, while the Antiochians, going to the opposite extreme, often did not find it where it existed. The former, influenced by Philo, were inclined to speculation and mysticism. The latter, more influenced by Aristotle, were realists and empiricists. The Antiochian school reached its maturity under Diodorus of Tarsus. Two of its most distinguished alumni were the great John Chrysostom and the equally great, but erratic exegete, Theodore of Mopsuestia. The rationalistic approach to the Scriptures was bound to produce error, and the Antiochian school numbers among its products the heresiarch Arius.

4. THE SCHOOL OF EDESSA

The school of Edessa in Mesopotamia was an offshoot of the Antiochian school and reached its maturity under the direction of Ephraem, the Syrian.

5. THE SCHOOL OF NISIBIS

This school was founded by the Nestorian Narsai in 457 when he was driven from the school of Edessa because of his errors.

All these schools, as time passed, departed to some extent from the original principles of their great founders and became embroiled in the theological controversies of succeeding years. Despite the many heresies and the many bitter theological wars in which they had a part, it was these schools that in the end crystallized the great Christological truths of Catholic theology.

But, it should be added here, it was the West that coined the terminology that gives best expression to these truths.

I. Latin Writers

Latin did not become the language of Western Christianity until the second half of the second century, as literary remains and inscriptions attest. Clement, Justin, Hermas, and the other writers treated so far wrote in Greek. Even Tertullian, though he wrote mostly in Latin, wrote some of his works in Greek. Whether he or Minucius Felix is the first Latin Christian writer need not be settled here. The Muratorian Fragment indicates its origin in the period of transition by its bad writing.

Christianity was first preached in Greek to the West, but Latin was the native language not only in Italy but farther afield also. Just as the language of Latium had smothered the older dialects in Italy, so the Celtic, Iberian, and Punic languages were crowded out by the Latin of the conqueror in Gaul, Spain, and in Africa. The political might of Rome used this unification of language for unification of empire and the infant Church used it to spread the Gospel. The earliest remains of Christian Latinity such as biblical texts, *The Acts of the Scillitan Martyrs*, and the translation of I Clement already show some development in the language. From this we may conclude that it was not too long after the first preaching of the Gospel in Rome that the Church began the use of Latin in the spread of Christ's teaching.

The earliest Christian use of Latin was confronted with the problem of expressing the many entirely new concepts of Christ's teaching in Latin. For this the new language was entirely inadequate. The common language of the people lacked the vocabulary. Even Latin words that came close to expressing the ideas of Christ's teaching labored under another shortcoming. They fell short of conserving the necessary reverence for the unique and exalted concepts of the new religion and for the biblical text. Out of this reverence for the sacred text and from the endeavor to reproduce the sense of Scripture as exactly as possible, there sprang up Christian Latinity.

The earliest translators of the Bible into Latin used the every-day language of the time. They were, however, thrown on their own resources in many cases to enrich its vocabulary, syntax, and sentence structure. The product was what may be, for want of a more descriptive name, called an hieratic style or form. These Bible translations, then, definitely threw their impact on the common Latin speech of the Christians and made it clearly distinguishable in many ways from the colloquial Latin of the pagan. In this way, what may be called Christian Latinity came into being around 200.

At the beginning of the third century the Christian writer was faced with the problem of how he should write. He might express himself in the colloquial speech of his fellow Christians. He might press the Latinity of the Bible translations into his service to express his thought. Both these courses were rather impractical. Two other paths lay open. He could adhere strictly to the classical tradition of Latin and express his thoughts in it as well as possible. Finally, he might take a bold new course and create a new Latinity. Minucius Felix chose the former while Tertullian struck out on the new way. However, it should be added here that it is overrating him when he is called the father of Christian Latinity.

The African Church has left us our oldest Latin Christian writings, *The Acts of the Scillitan Martyrs,* proof that the New Testament had been translated into Latin long before the year 180 in Africa. Besides this the early African Church gave us the works of Tertullian, Cyprian, Arnobius of Sicca, and Lactantius. A writing of little importance, *De rebaptismate,* also originated in Africa in Cyprian's time. The traditional view is that Commodianus also was a contemporary of Cyprian. But, we cannot assign him any date or place with certainty. Some few anony-mous Christian writings of no importance also appeared in Africa at this time. The Roman Church has left us, besides a number of papal documents, the works of Minucius Felix, Hippolytus, and Novatian. The Church of Gaul, still represented in Greek Christian literature by Irenaeus, gave us the Latin writings of Victorinus of Pettau and Reticius of Autun.

A. THE ROMANS

The Roman Church was probably the first to shift from Greek to Latin. The quotations from Scripture in the Latin translation of I Clement made about 150 shows that the Bible was already used in Latin then. By the year 250 the change to Latin as the official language of the Church was complete, though Hippolytus still wrote Greek. The shift to Latin in the Liturgy was accomplished in the next century under Pope Damasus (366–384). Other popes who have left us letters, etc., are Callistus, Pontianus, Fabian, Cornelius, Lucius I, Stephen I, Sixtus II, Dionysius, and Felix I.

1. MINUCIUS FELIX (end of second century)

Nothing is known of the charming and widely-read author of *Octavius* except what can be deduced from the work itself and that he was a Roman lawyer. That he was well read is evident from the many allusions and even borrowings from both pagan and Christian writers. That Minucius Felix does not quote or use the Scriptures is to be expected since his Apology is directed to pagans. When he wrote his *Octavius* cannot be determined until the question of his relationship to Tertullian's *Apologeticum* and *Ad nationes* is settled. These were written about 197 and *Octavius* was written before or after, since there is definitely some influence of one writer on the other. Jerome had already presented the view that Minucius Felix is dependent on Tertullian, but there are good reasons for the opposite view.

Octavius is a dialogue in classical form and its nobility of thought and elegance of expression stamp it as the finest of Christian apologies. Three friends, Caecilius, a pagan lawyer, and Octavius, a Christian, engage in a debate along the seashore, with Marcus (Minucius Felix) as referee. In the end the pagan is converted and all are happy. At the time of writing, Octavius had died and the book has some most consoling reflections on death and the after-life. Perhaps the work was partly written as a consolatory effort at the loss of Octavius to his friends. Very often what Octavius says is not debate but meditation.

Caecilius presents the typically pagan viewpoint of skepticism and materialism. Often what he says may be found in the utterances of modern pagans. We can know no more of what is above and what comes after this world and life than the thinkers of old who came to the conclusion of Socrates that what is above us is no concern of ours. Therefore, it is best to keep the gods and the beliefs that have made Rome great. On the other hand Christians are a rude, uncultured, and immoral lot. Their God is a figment of their credulous minds. Their beliefs have nothing to offer but rather threaten to destroy the good life that is, and which Caecilius wants to keep that way (5–13).

Octavius calmly refutes what Caecilius says about Christians and shows that Rome has become what she is by murder and pillage, not through her religion and her gods who were mere men later divinized. He points out that though man cannot see God here below, he can and must find God in His works. It is the knowledge that God is everywhere and that He can be easily found that gives the Christian his serene and happy outlook on life (14–38). Whether Minucius Felix wrote a treatise *On Fate* remains doubtful.

2. HIPPOLYTUS OF ROME (235)

Hippolytus, though not a profound thinker, was a man of varied interests and tremendous literary activity. Probably born in the East, he came to Rome where he functioned as a presbyter. Here Origen on a trip to the Eternal City heard him preach in 212. Shortly thereafter Hippolytus was elected antipope during the reign of Callistus and continued in schism under Popes Urban and Pontianus. During the persecution of Maximinus both Pontianus and Hippolytus were banished to Sardinia where the latter made his peace with the Church before his death in 235. Pope and antipope are venerated as martyrs. Though in life Hippolytus seems to have been a proud and stubborn extremist, Pope Damasus in an epitaph records that before his death Hippolytus urged his rebellious followers to be reconciled to the Church.

The Vatican Museum has a seated statue of Hippolytus. On the chair is engraved a complete list of his numerous writings and his Paschal table. For other lists see Eusebius (*H.E.* 6,22) and Jerome (*Vir. ill.* 61). His works cover so wide a range that he has often been compared to his eastern contemporary, Origen, though he lacks the latter's penetrating thought. Most of them have been lost, not so much because of his heretical tendencies but because he wrote in Greek, and Latin came to supplant Greek in the West not long after his death. His most precious work for us today is the *Apostolic Tradition* or *Paradosis Apostolike*, treated in an earlier chapter, though the value and importance of the *Philosophumena* can hardly be overestimated.

1. The *Philosophumena* or *Refutation of All Heresies*, written after 222 in ten books, was long lost. Books two and three are still missing. Part I (books one to four) can alone be called *Philosophumena*. Hippolytus discussed pagan philosophies in uncritical and inadequate fashion in book one, and seems to have treated the mystery religions in the lost books two and three, while book four treats of magic and astrology. Part II (books five to nine) discusses thirty-three Gnostic systems and concludes with a summary and a Jewish chronology in book ten. The last six books are critical and valuable for the study of Gnostic errors.

2. *Syntagma* or *Against All Heresies* was written before the *Philosophumena*. Though lost it can be fairly well recovered from later writers who used it. He treats thirty-two heretical systems. His extensive use of Irenaeus suggests that he may have been a disciple of Irenaeus.

3. Dogmatic works have all been lost except for *De Antichristo* (c. 200). As the title suggests, this treats of the last days.

4. Exegetical writings cover a great variety of scriptural questions. The *Commentary on Daniel* (c. 204) is his oldest exegetical writing that has come down to us. He explains the Deutero-Canonical parts also. There are a *Commentary on the Canticle*, treatises *On the Blessing of Jacob* and *On the Blessing of Moses* that were very popular.

5. Chronological works include a chronology of the world from the beginning to 234. It attacks Chiliasm. All that is left of *On the Computation of Easter* is the Easter table chiseled into the chair of Hippolytus' statue.

6. Homilies include the following: *On the Passover, On the Praise of the Lord Our Savior, On the Heresy of Noetus* and

Demonstration Against Jews. Most of Hippolytus' exegetical works are of an homiletical nature.

Other works that have been lost or of which there remain only small fragments need not be mentioned. Hippolytus is important in theology as a witness to the inspiration of Scripture, to the resurrection, to the eternity of hell and to the reality of the Eucharistic sacrifice. A vigorous antagonist of Modalism in all its forms, he was, like some other fathers before him, a Subordinationist. He held that God could have made a man God, for which Pope Callistus called him a Ditheist. Hippolytus' greatest error was his extreme rigorism because of which he stubbornly left the communion of the Church, until his death.

3. NOVATIAN (c. 260)

The second antipope was of different mold than the first. Though Novatian is said to have died a martyr under Valerian, his error and the movement he started were given such impetus by him that they persisted several centuries. Baptized clinically but not confirmed, he rose through ordination to a powerful position in Rome by 250. A man of exceptional training in rhetoric, philosophy, and theology, he was the first theologian to write in Latin. His work on the Trinity best illustrates his intellectual gifts. But when Cornelius was consecrated pope in March, 251, Novatian rebelled against the merciful policy toward the Lapsi proclaimed by Cornelius. He had himself elected and consecrated antipope. He and his followers called themselves the Cathari, i.e., the clean, and refused to have anything to do with the Catholic Church, even denying the validity of Catholic baptism. Nothing is known of his last years.

Novatian's most important work is his *De Trinitate.* He sums up the trinitarian doctrines of Theophilus of Antioch, Irenaeus, Hippolytus, and Tertullian but in it he discloses subordinationist tendencies. The Logos is subordinated to the Father as is the Holy Ghost to the Logos. Besides two letters to Cyprian there have been preserved among the writings of Tertullian and Cyprian three treatises by Novatian: *De cibis judaicis, De spectaculis* and *De bono pudicitiae.* The first of these, On Jewish Foods, is a pastoral letter to his followers explaining that the Jewish food laws are no longer binding. Christians need avoid only pagan sacrificial foods. *De spectaculis* (On the Theaters) forbids his followers any part in or attendance at public entertainments of any kind. The last treatise, *De bono pudicitiae* (On the Good of Modesty) is an excellent and edifying discussion of virginity, continence and marital fidelity.

B. THE AFRICANS

The African Church was started from Rome and history shows her ever in close contact with the mother Church. The Gospel was originally preached in Greek to the people of Africa. Even at the end of the second century Tertullian was writing in Greek. However, it is not easy to measure the contribution of the Africans to Christian Latinity. It seems they were the first to bend the Latin language to express the ideas and concepts of the New Testament. Tertullian seems to have contributed most to ancient Christian theological terminology.

1. TERTULLIAN (after 220)

Quintus Septimius Florens Tertullianus was born a pagan about 160 in Carthage and received the finest education. After a career as a lawyer in Rome he returned to Africa. Here he broke with his dissolute past and devoted his pen to the Church. It is doubtful that he became a priest. Around the year 207 he left the Church to associate himself with the Montanists. His intransigent nature would not let him return to the fold and he ended by becoming the head of the sect named after him, the Tertullianists. He died at an advanced age in Carthage after 220. Jerome dates his death as late as 240.

Tertullian can be understood and appreciated only against the background of his time, and his character can be analyzed only by a complete and thorough reading of his works. He contributed as much or more to Christian Latinity as the ancient Latin Bible. His writing is like the music of an organist using all the stops of his organ in bewildering variety. As a Christian he levels his invective at paganism and later, as a Montanist, he is equally unsparing of the Catholic Church.

Tertullian has been called the founder of Western theology and the father of Christology. Both are seriously mistaken evaluations. Keen and versatile though he was, he did not have the balanced mind or the objectivity of thinking to become anything like a leader in those fields. He disparaged human speculation though he had to admit that pagan thinking came near the truth at times and that philosophy still can come close to the truth even now. But faith completes reason.

Tertullian's writings are hard to date and to classify. But we can make three rough categories: apologetic, dogmatic, and ascetic writings. All of them are for the most part polemic but there frequently occur in all of them beautiful sentiments and passages of exalted positive thinking.

The apologetic works of Tertullian are: *Apologeticum, Ad nationes, De testimonio animae, Ad Scapulam,* and *Adv. Judaeos.* The *Apologeticum* (Apology) is the most important of these and it is unique in that it is preoccupied mainly with political charges leveled against Christians. *Ad nationes* (To the Nations), in two books defends Christianity and attacks decadent paganism. *De testimonio animae* (On the Testimony of the Soul) develops the thought of the Apology (17), "O testimony of the soul, which is by natural instinct Christian." *Ad Scapulam* is an open letter to a proconsul of that name in Africa who was especially hostile to the Christians. Tertullian uses an eclipse of the sun as an occasion to remind Scapula of impending divine judgment. *Adv. Judaeos* (Against Jews) points out that pagans, too, have a claim on God's mercy. Part II (9–14) is not genuine but added here from Tertullian's book, *Adv. Marcionem.*

The dogmatic writings of Tertullian are chiefly polemical. There are ten:

1. *De praescriptione haereticorum* (On Prescription against Heretics), written around 200, develops the thought that Catholics alone can claim the truth by legal prescription. They alone have been in possession of the truth from the time of the apostles who bequeathed revealed truth to the churches founded by them. Catholic truth is old, and innovations in teaching are heresy. The Church alone received the Scriptures from the apostles, and heretics have no competency or right to interpret them. Any-

one not in line with the belief and teaching of the churches has no claim to the truth. The last chapters (46–53) list thirty-two heresies and are a Greek appendix written perhaps by Pope Zephyrinus and translated by Victorinus of Pettau.

2. *Against Marcion* in five books began to appear in 207. It refutes the errors of Marcion and proves that God is the creator of the universe (1–2), that Christ was foretold in the Old Testament (3), and that Marcion has adulterated the biblical text. There is no contradiction between the Old and the New Testaments (4–5).

3. *Against Hermogenes*, on the creation of the world.

4. *Against the Valentinians*.

5. *Scorpiace* (About Scorpions), written in 213, is directed against the Gnostics who are the scorpions.

6. *On the Flesh of Christ* was written around 210–212 against the Docetism of the Gnostics. Tertullian says Christ was not handsome (9).

7. *On the Resurrection of the Body*.

8. *Against Praxeas* is the clearest exposition of the Trinity against Modalism before Nicea.

9. *On Baptism* denies the validity of heretical baptism but is otherwise a good exposition of Catholic teaching.

10. *On the Soul* is the first Christian handbook of psychology. It was written around 210–211.

Tertullian has left sixteen books on asceticism and Christian living. Of these, seven were written by him as a Catholic, the rest as a Montanist. A comparison of the former with the latter reveals the progressive deterioration in Tertullian's thinking. However, the Catholic works already show the germs of his later rigorism. The Montanist works contain considerable venom. All these works are of great value for the light they throw on the times. *To the Martyrs*, written in 197 or 202–203, is a short but moving tribute to the heroism of martyrs. *The Shows* (197–200) condemns the pagan theater for its immorality and idolatry. *On Prayer* (198–200) tells how to pray and explains the Lord's Prayer. *On Patience* (200–203) extols the virtue most difficult for Tertullian and points to the spirit of revenge as the greatest obstacle to patience. *On Repentance* (c. 203) outlines penitential practice and the disposition needed before baptism (1–6), and treats of the one repentance after baptism. In this work we have the first distinction between mortal and venial sins, though the terms are not used. *On the Dress of Women* in two books (197–201) excoriates feminine dress and beautification. *To His Wife* in two books (c. 203) discusses mixed marriages and asks his wife to remain in widowhood in the event of his prior death.

After his defection to the Montanists, Tertullian published the following books: *Exhortation to Chastity* (c. 207) advising a widower friend against remarriage as a kind of adultery; *On Monogamy* (c. 217) a violent denunciation of remarriage; *On Veiling Virgins* (c. 207) demanding the wearing of a veil by virgins not only in the Christian assemblies but outside as well. *The Chaplet* (211) is the earliest patristic pacifist tract condemning military service. The chaplet worn by soldiers is for Tertullian essentially pagan. *On Idolatry* denounces certain professions and avocations as essentially pagan. *On Flight in Persecution* (c. 212) denounces flight in time of persecution as opposed to God's will. *On Fasting* is important for the history of fasting in the Church. It is a violent attack on Catholics for what Montanists called laxity in the practice. *On Modesty* denies the Church the right to forgive sins and defends the Montanist position that only those who possess the "spiritual" gift can forgive sins. In it occurs the famous statement on the "peremptory decree" which has come to be called the Edict of Callistus. This work should be read with *On Repentance* to see what the Montanist heresy had done to Tertullian's thinking. *On the Pallium* (c. 210) is a short witty book in which Tertullian satirizes the dress of men and women in general and defends himself against criticism that he had exchanged the toga of the Roman for the pallium of the philosopher.

Tertullian in his own works and other ecclesiastical writers tell of other books. We also read of works falsely ascribed to him. These facts indicate his great and varied literary activity; even the forgeries are tribute to his influence. It is told that Cyprian used to direct his valet in these words when he wanted one of Tertullian's books: "Give me the Master." Tertullian, Cyprian, and Augustine of Hippo are three representatives of the now devastated African Church who symbolize what that ancient and venerable church contributed to early Christianity.

Tertullian could not create a system of theology, yet contributed much to Catholic theology. His greatest contribution is his clear exposition of the doctrine of the Trinity and his Christology, though the latter seems at times to be tainted with Subordinationism. His statements on the Trinity sometimes suggest that he was conversant also with some kind of binitarian formula. Tertullian's next great contribution to theology is in the matter of theological phrases and terms, whose meanings and content he fixed exactly. Many of these are still in use. Thus Tertullian molded the Latin language to the use of Catholic theology. In all his writings his disparagement of philosophy and human reason, his lawyer's mind and his preoccupation with theology are evident.

Tertullian denied virginity in and after Mary's motherhood because he was bent on refuting Docetism in Christology, and he taught clearly and precisely that there are two complete natures in the one Person. He is a Traducianist in his psychology. He deprecated infant baptism because a baby is not yet developed to perform rational acts, but advocates it in case of necessity because of original sin. His concept of the Church is Montanist, which implies a denial of the primacy, not of Peter, but of his successors. The germ of these ecclesiological ideas is found even in his pre-Montanist writings. His is a church of the Spirit in opposition to an hierarchical church. In his teaching on penance he is a rigorist even before his Montanism, but he is an important witness to the penitential discipline and practice of that day. His Eucharistic teaching is Catholic and most important because he fixed and clarified some theological terms. Tertullian was a Chiliast and, though he did not use the term, taught the existence of purgatory. He thought that the end of time was not far distant.

2. CYPRIAN (258)

Born at the beginning of the third century Thascius Caecilius Cyprianus was converted about 246 and consecrated bishop of Carthage around 248. He fled his see in 250 during the Decian persecution. When he returned in 251 the problem of what disciplinary measures were to be taken on those who had denied the faith or betrayed sacred secrets and now wished to be restored to communion with the Church was acute. Cyprian's enemies used a division of opinion to attack him because he adopted severe measures of penance. A schism resulted, headed by Felicissimus and Novatus. Cyprian called a synod, excommunicated his opponents, and set a stern policy in dealing with the *Lapsi* and *Thurificati*, though in the event of another persecution these were to be reconciled. The schism did not do too great damage, even though Novatus went to Rome to support the antipope, Novatian.

Cyprian's last years were saddened by the terrible plague of 252–254 in which he won universal recognition because of his great works of mercy; and also by the bitter controversy on heretical baptism. The African Church denied the validity of heretical baptism in three synods held at Carthage (255–256) under the presidency of Cyprian in opposition to Pope Stephen. Cyprian was martyred in the Valerian persecution at Carthage, Sept. 14, 258. The best source of facts about his life are his letters and the *Acts* of his martyrdom. His *Vita* by the deacon Pontius is not too reliable, being mostly a panegyric or a "Martyrium." Cyprian tells of his conversion in his *Ad Donatum* (To Donatus).

Cyprian was mostly a man of action and his writings are for the most part somewhat occasional and betray his lack of solid, thorough theological training. It was his greatest achievement to steer a middle course between rigorism and laxism in those turbulent times when the Church was sorely beset by persecution and internal strife. He remained the outstanding figure in the West until Augustine and Gregory the Great. His clear exposition of the unity of the Church is his best contribution to Catholic theology. He has left us a number of treatises and a considerable number of letters. All his writings were popular even in the Middle Ages, as the number of forgeries associated with his name attest. We have three lists of his writings, one by Pontius, another by Augustine in his *On the Birthday of Cyprian*, and a third list by an unknown author of 359.

On the Unity of the Church is Cyprian's most important treatise. It was written about 251, and attacks the Roman schism of Novatian and the local African schism of Felicissimus. His own words, "He cannot have God as his Father who does not have the Church as mother" (6), sum up the treatise. The important fourth chapter has come down to us in double form, the one far more favorable to the primacy of the pope than the other. Today both must be accepted as the work of Cyprian, though the so-called "interpolated" and more favorable text appears to have been the earlier.

Cyprian's other treatises cover a variety of subjects. *To Donatus* is an intimate account of Cyprian's conversion that reminds one of Augustine's *Confessions*. *That the Idols are not Gods* and *To Demetrianus* are two works refuting the charge that Christians have occasioned the plagues, the famine, and the wars that afflicted the age. Two treatises are very valuable for the study of the ancient Latin text of the Bible. They are: *To Quirinus*, three Books of Testimonies, a collection of biblical texts against Jews on Christology and on Christian virtues; and *To Fortunatus* (An Exhortation to Martyrdom), a list of biblical texts that might give strength to Christians come to face martyrdom. *On the Lapsed* is a work sent to Rome together with Cyprian's *Unity of the Church*. It explains the reason for the problem of the great number of the Lapsi and the procedure in dealing with them that Cyprian advocated. Several of his treatises seem to echo writings of Tertullian by the same title. Such are: *The Dress of Virgins*, *The Lord's Prayer*, *The Advantage of Patience*, and *On Jealousy and Envy*. The first of these exhibits Cyprian's high esteem for virginity. *On Mortality* is designed to encourage and comfort Christians during the plague. *On Works and Almsgiving* is an exhortation to works of mercy. Both appear to have been meant as pastoral letters.

The letters of Cyprian are his most precious literary legacy. They tell us about a most interesting period of Church history; from their lines speak, besides Cyprian himself, some of the most notable figures of that day. There are eighty-one in all, dealing with a great variety of matters, e.g., that a cleric should not act as a legal guardian or executor (*Ep.* 1); whether a retired convert actor may give lessons in his art (*Ep.* 2); on the abuse of using water instead of wine in the Eucharist (*Ep.* 63), and the abuses connected with the institution called *syneisaktai* (dedicated virgins living with an older ascetic). There is also a letter about a deacon who offended his bishop (*Ep.* 3). Some of these letters are in reality treatises and have sometimes been so titled by later publishers, e.g., Epistle 63, *On the Sacrament of the Cup of the Lord*. There are twenty-seven letters of Cyprian to his people from his place of hiding. They well explain his conduct. There are twelve letters dealing with the Novatian schism. The correspondence with Rome comprises another twelve letters. The controversy over heretical baptism comprises nine letters. Cyprian wrote more letters but this is all that is left. However, these are most valuable to the historian, to the canonist, and to the linguist.

Cyprian was very emphatic and clear in his doctrine on the oneness of the Church, but he did not pursue this teaching to its logical conclusion. That is why he could take his stand in the matter of heretical baptism despite the position of Rome. He called the Church the indivisible garment of Christ and spoke of the law of charity and harmony that bound together the bishops who traced their sees to the apostles. He formulated the principle, "No salvation outside the Church," but he did not see clearly the full implications of the divine commission to Peter and his successors. The African Church and Cyprian were not alone in this attitude and it was not yet possible to distinguish plainly between matters of discipline and matters of faith.

For the rest Cyprian explained the validity of tradition and insisted on infant baptism against his master, Tertullian. His teachings on the Eucharist and penance are important in the history of dogma. Martyrdom, he teaches, admits immediately to the vision of God.

3. ARNOBIUS THE ELDER AND LACTANTIUS
(both after 317)

The African Church of the early fourth century also produced Arnobius of Sicca the Elder and Lactantius. The former rhetorician published a treatise, *Against the Nations* (seven books), of no great profundity or importance. Lucius Caecilius Firmianus Lactantius, a student of Arnobius, is the first Latin Christian poet of importance. He was later called the Christian Cicero.

Upon his conversion he lost his position as a teacher of rhetoric and was reduced to poor circumstances until the Emperor Constantine engaged him as tutor for his son Crispus in 317. Nothing further is known of his life.

A master of expression but totally deficient in theology and unacquainted with Christian literature, Lactantius wrote his *Divine Institutes* as an apology for Christianity. It is an incompetent attempt to explain and prove Christianity. He tries to expose the absurdity of pagan religion (Books I and II) and of pagan philosophy (Book III). Book IV demonstrates that Christ brought true wisdom to man. Books V and VI are the best writing of the work and treat of the true worship of God. Book VII is eschatological.

Besides the *Divine Institutes*, Lactantius has left us an excerpt of that work, the *Epitome*. His *On God's Workmanship* (c. 303) tries to show God's design in the creation of man. *On the Anger of God* is an answer to the Stoics and Epicureans. If God is mercy He must also be justice. *On the Death of Persecutors* describes the evil end of enemies of God's Church. The poem, *The Bird Phoenix*, tells the legend of the bird that arises from its own ashes. There are some spurious works attributed to Lactantius also.

Neither Arnobius nor Lactantius contributed anything to theology. Neither of them was very well instructed. Their only assistance to Christianity was their attractive literary writing. Perhaps Lactantius' best contribution to psychology was his exposition of creationism.

C. THE WRITERS OF GAUL

In Gaul there was no one to succeed Irenaeus of Lyons. Reticius of Autun published a *Commentary on the Canticle of Canticles* and a treatise *Against Novatian*. He was an important ecclesiastic since he was sent by the emperor to synods in Rome in 313–314. Another writer, Victorinus of Pettau (304) in Styria, farther East and not a part of Gaul, is the first Christian Latin exegete. He wrote extensive commentaries but little of his work has come down to us. He was a Chiliast and his style is poor. He may have been the translator and editor of the *Against All*

Heresies which has come down to us as an appendix to Tertullian's *De praescriptione*.

II. The Greek Writers of the East

In the East the earliest and most productive Greek writers are Clement of Alexandria and Origen. After Origen the Eastern fathers, almost at once, are split into two groups: the friends and followers of Origen and his antagonists.

1. CLEMENT OF ALEXANDRIA (c. 215)

Born a pagan about 150, probably in Athens, Titus Flavius Clemens became a Christian and after extensive travels settled down in Alexandria where he succeeded Pantaenus as president of the school of Alexandria around 200. A few years later the persecution of Septimus Severus forced him to flee and he died in Asia Minor sometime before 215. He is the first Christian father who may be classified as a scholar, inasmuch as he devoted all his energies to writing and teaching. The best evidence of his general scholarship is the range of literature that he quotes or refers to: the Old Testament about 1,500 times, the New Testament about 2,000 times, with about 360 passages of the classics. He is the first Christian to attempt a synthesis of pagan learning and Christian revelation. He assembled all that he could find of truth in paganism and demonstrated how these truths found their completion in the revelation of Christ. It is true that in so doing Clement erred at times, but he presents his thinking with genuine enthusiasm and he is a good reporter on Christian living of his time.

Clement was a prolific writer but we have only a homily and what seems to be a trilogy left. The homily, "Who is the Rich Man that is saved?" is an exposition of Mark 10:17–31 and explains the right use of riches. The work concludes with the well-known tale of the robber whom the aged John converted. The other three works are the *Protrepticus* or *Exhortation to the Greeks*, the *Pedagogue*, and the *Stromata* or Tapestry. We find references to other works of Clement but all these have been lost except for small fragments. There are also some spurious fragments ascribed to Clement.

The *Protrepticus* or *Exhortation to the Greeks* is negative in the first part in that it describes the immorality of paganism and the stupidities of the mystery religions. The second part is a positive exposition of Christian thinking. The *Pedagogue*, in three books, is a continuation of the theme of the *Protrepticus*. It tells in detail what is expected of the Christian in his everyday living and concludes with an inspiring hymn to Christ that may have been part of the Alexandrian liturgy. The third work, the *Stromata* or Tapestry, follows a literary device of the time and contains assorted essays on varied topics. In reality this work is not a part of the trilogy projected by Clement in *Paed.* 1,1. He seems not to have completed that plan. The other fragments of his writings preserved for us seem to be notes that he had collected. The most extensive of these are the *Hypotyposes*. They are notes or sketches, as the name implies, on Scripture. Only small fragments remain.

It would be no great exaggeration to call Clement of Alexandria the founder of speculative theology. Following Paul he saw in the Old Testament the tutor to the New. Similarly, Greek philosophy which derived its main basic truths from the Old Testament, according to Clement, was a tutor to Christianity for pagans. Clement came so far even as to think that philosophy could give the pagan the same or equivalent means of grace that the Old Testament institutions gave the Jew. Clement's greatest contribution to Christian thinking was his refutation of the Gnostic position that faith and knowledge are irreconcilable opposites. For Clement the starting point of his inquiry after truth is faith. Reason and philosophy assist in the inquiry, not by establishing or proving the truths of faith, but by clarifying them. This is the true Christian *gnosis* or knowledge which leads immediately to God. Those who do not attain it must bide a time for cleansing before entering heaven. Adam's sin was that he would not let God teach him true knowledge. Original sin is then transmitted, not by generation, but by the bad example of Adam through succeeding ages.

Clement's theology can be gathered only from a reading of

his complete works. Statements of his taken from context will be misconstrued. Thus, because of his opposition to the Gnostic error condemning marriage, he extols the married state over that of virginity. He himself remained unmarried. Again, while he teaches that all sins can be forgiven, he seems to speak of an unforgivable sin committed voluntarily by the Gnostic. There are statements of Clement that may seem to deny the sacrificial character of the Eucharist because he is attacking certain heretical practices. The greatest defect in Clement's theology is that he centers it in the Logos, not in the triune God, though he certainly did not deny the Trinity. Nothing finer has been written than the "Hymn to the Logos" with which Clement concludes his *Pedagogue*.

2. ORIGEN (253)

Origen was beyond question the greatest scholar of Christian antiquity and we know more about his life than we do about any other of the early fathers. Eusebius, Pamphilus of Caesarea, Gregory Thaumaturgus, Jerome, and Photius have preserved for us the details of Origen's life. It had three phases: his early years, his term as president of the school of Alexandria (c. 202–232), and his last years at Caesarea (232–253). Born of Christian parents (c. 186) he received the best of education from Leonidas, his martyr father. His youth was characterized by his passionate devotion to and defense of Christianity, for which he wanted to die. At the young age of eighteen, he began teaching, and when Clement had to flee Alexandria, Origen was appointed president of the school. In this second phase of his life he laid the foundations of his scholarship. He studied philosophy under the Neoplatonist Ammonius Saccas and even tackled Hebrew, but with indifferent success. He visited Rome about 212 and during the persecution of Caracalla he fled to Palestine where he expounded the Scriptures. He returned to Alexandria for the most productive years of his life. He had previously traveled extensively and visited Antioch. Now his friend and student, Ambrose, supplied secretaries, stenographers, and all the means needed for scholarly work.

The last phase of Origen's life brought unhappiness and suffering. Bishop Demetrius had objected to Origen's lectures on Scripture during his stay in Palestine. Around 230 Origen took a trip to Achaia and here friends of his, Alexander of Jerusalem and Theopistus of Caesarea, ordained him a priest. Upon Origen's return to Alexandria, Demetrius had him condemned in two synods (230-231) because of the irregularity of this ordination and probably also because of some of his teaching. After this, Origen returned to Caesarea and there founded the school that was to become one of the greatest of ancient Christianity, renowned for its library, scriptorium, and graduates. He visited Bishop Beryllus of Bostra and converted him from Patripassianism. During the Decian persecution he was imprisoned and tortured. He died in Tyre (253–254), it is said of the effects of his torture, and his grave is still venerated there.

A survey of his life, his literary production and his influence on subsequent years are proofs of Origen's greatness. Eusebius (*H.E.* 6,23,2) called him Adamantius (the man of steel) because of his resolute character but the name also recalls how his influence for a time split asunder Christian ranks in the East. The "Origenist controversy," as it is called, broke out shortly after his death and reached the height of its first fury around 300 when Methodius of Philippi and Peter of Alexandria were leaders of the opposition, while Pamphilus of Caesarea was Origen's great defender. The controversy died down after this only to flare up anew towards the year 400. Whereas the fight had been previously only in the literary domain, it now entered the ecclesiastical sphere. Origen was condemned by Epiphanius of Salamis in a synod held at Constantinople and by Pope Anastasius in a Paschal letter. Besides these actions, Theophilus of Alexandria vigorously attacked Origen's teaching. The last phase of the controversy ended when a council at Constantinople anathematized fifteen points in Origen's teaching. This condemnation was approved by the Emperor Justinian I, Pope Vigilius, and all the patriarchs.

"Origenism" as condemned in II Constantinople in 553 taught erroneous ideas on the divine processions, the angels, the soul, and on the last things. Some of these errors were the misinterpretations of Origen's followers. Others were attributed directly to Origen. Two things about his literary activity must be remembered in evaluating Origen's teaching. Many of his books were destroyed by his enemies. Others have come down to us in Latin translations that were not of the greatest accuracy. Other writings of his were mere notes taken by his auditors and never approved for publication by Origen. Whatever erroneous ideas Origen did teach, he certainly wanted in no way to depart from ecclesiastical and apostolic tradition (*De princ. praef.* 2).

Origen's works that have come down to us cover the whole range of theology. He is the first scientific exegete and, besides his monumental *Hexapla*, he has left us scholia, homilies, and commentaries on Sacred Scripture. His great apologetical work is *Contra Celsum*. In dogmatic theology we have *De principiis*, the *Discussion with Heraclides*, *On the Resurrection*, and the *Stromata*. In moral and ascetical theology he has left us *On Prayer*, *Exhortation to Martyrdom*, and *On Easter*. Only two letters remain of Origen's bulky correspondence. All these works show his mastery in each field.

Origen is the father of Christian textual criticism. In his day the Septuagint was regarded as inspired and he set about establishing a critical text. In his *Hexapla* (or sixfold Old Testament) he lined up in order in six columns the Hebrew text in Hebrew letters, the Hebrew text transliterated into Greek letters (such texts were in use), the translations of Aquila, Symmachus, the Septuagint, and Theodotion. The whole work was outfitted with cross references so that the reader could compare at a glance the different versions with the original. He seems to have published the work in several forms, e.g., a *Tetrapla* containing only the four Greek versions and an *Enneapla* which contained three versions of the Psalms in addition to those found in the *Hexapla*. The whole work is a tribute to the library of the school of Caesarea, no less than to the energy and scholarship of Origen.

Besides his work in textual criticism of the Old Testament, Origen left us scholia, homilies, and commentaries. Scholia are explanations of difficult passages in the Bible and here Origen seems to have covered the entire range of the Bible. Homilies are sermons on select passages used in the liturgy. He preached almost daily, according to Pamphilus, and we have at least fragments of his homilies on all sections of the Bible. Homilies served the purpose of edification but he seems also to have given scientific explanations of practically all of the Bible in his commentaries. Of those that have come down to us the most important, because they illustrate his hermeneutical principles, are his commentaries *On Matthew, On the Gospel of John, On the Epistle to the Romans*, and *On the Canticle of Canticles*. Most of his commentaries fell prey to the Origenist controversy.

It is only in modern times that Origen has come completely into his own as an exegete. Clement of Alexandria had distinguished the literal and the spiritual sense in the Scriptures. However, in his search for the Christian *gnosis* Clement had frequently resorted to mere accommodation in his pursuit of the spiritual sense of a given biblical passage. Origen, his successor, continued seeking out the literal or historical sense of the Bible. However, he attempted to draw a fast line between what is the genuine spiritual or typical sense and what was mere accommodation in the exegesis of the Alexandrian school. Sometimes he missed the mark because he missed the point of figurative language. On the whole, however, he was as much sinned against by his followers as he himself erred. Origen has often been held accountable for errors that he did not in reality hold.

In the field of dogmatic theology, Origen has given us the first handbook of dogma in his *On the Fundamentals* (*Peri archon* or *De principiis*) which has come down to us only in an expurgated Latin translation. In it he treats of the Trinity, the angels and their fall (Book I), of creation, the fall and redemption of man (Book II), of the principles of moral theology (Book III), of Sacred Scripture as a source of revelation, and of the senses of the Bible (Book IV).

Origen's polemic *Contra Celsum* (Against Celsus), the greatest apologetic work of the third century, is important today because of its detailed and able refutation of Celsus. The latter had charged that Christ was a low deceiver and that the extraordinary spread of Christianity could be explained naturally. Origen refutes Celsus in detail and quotes him extensively. The work is invaluable to the Church historian.

His ascetico-practical writings best reveal the soul of the man,

Origen. His work, *On Prayer*, is a gem and the oldest scientific discussion of prayer. The first part speaks of prayer in general and the second part explains the Lord's Prayer. The *Exhortation to Martyrdom* is the best theological analysis of the "Baptism of Blood" and a magnificent expression of love of Christ.

The missing letters of Origen are in a way our greatest loss. We have only his letter to Gregory Thaumaturgus, in which he explains how his student is to use pagan philosophy, and the letter to Julianus Africanus defending the deuterocanonical parts of Daniel. Other small fragments of his letters give a taste of their rich theological and spiritual fare.

Origen outdid his predecessor and succeeded in producing a systematic theology by beginning with the triune God as its center. However, his teaching on the Trinity is not easily established. Often his exposition of the docrine is clear and unequivocal but other statements of his seem to subordinate the Son to the Father, and the Holy Spirit, in turn, to the Son. But he clearly and precisely explains the *communicatio idiomatum*. It is Origen who gave theology the terms God-man, *homoousios, physis, hypostasis, ousia*, and *theotokos*.

Origen's Christology is vibrant with love for Christ the God-man and for His mother, the Theotokos, who is also the mother of us all. In his writings about the Church are to be found some of the finest passages of all his works. Original sin, baptism (of infants, also), the Eucharist as sacrament and sacrifice, all are discussed. Besides baptism and the rigorous penitential discipline of his day he lists six other ways of obtaining forgiveness and it is in the light of all this that the seeming extreme statement about the unforgivable sins in *De orat.* 28 must be taken.

Origen's errors that had the greatest repercussions among those who came after him were in the field of Eschatology. He believed in the pre-existence of another creation prior to the present one. The souls of men are spirits who fell away from God and were placed in this world in their present bodies to work out their salvation. For this each receives grace according to the extent of the fall. Thus in the end will come the final restoration or recapitulation (*anakephalaiosis*). Since Origen conceived punishment as able to effect cleansing, there must come a time when all souls will have been cleansed and restored. Such thinking leads to a denial of the eternity of hell.

Patterned along this thinking but entirely orthodox are Origen's principles of the ascetical life and they have greatly influenced later theologians. Perfection consists in restoring the image of God in one's soul and in becoming as like God as possible. To do this requires self-knowledge and self-discipline; self-knowledge makes plain the need to do battle against sin, while self-discipline by ascetical practices provides the training for this battle. Thus, the soul begins the mystical ascent to union with the Logos. Hence, Origen is also the first mystical theologian among the fathers.

3. MINOR ALEXANDRIANS

The school of Alexandria and the daughter school at Caesarea produced some of the greatest churchmen of the time. The men listed here are called "minor" only because they have left sparse literary remains. Some engaged in little writing because of the press of administrative duties or other distractions. Others wrote extensively but their works have been lost. Many of them were graduates of the school of Caesarea, but they opposed forms of Origenism when they encountered it. All, however, followed Alexandrian teaching. The chief men are Ammonius, Dionysius of Alexandria, Firmillian of Caesarea, Gregory Thaumaturgus, Julius Africanus, Peter of Alexandria, Pierius, and Theognostus.

4. EARLIER ANTIOCHIANS

The school of Antioch did not reach its peak until the end of the fourth century. Here are listed some followers of the Antiochian school who, though relatively unimportant as literary men, yet play a part in Church history. All of them were anti-Origenists. Dorotheus of Antioch, Lucian of Antioch, Malchon of Antioch, Methodius of Olympus, Paul of Samosata, and the unknown author of *De recta fide in Deum* (On the Correct Faith in God).

PART TWO

The Golden Age of Patrology

Introduction

The Edict of Toleration of 313 marked the end of Christianity's struggle for existence in the Roman Empire. It was not long after the conversion of Constantine and the favorable legislation of the emperors Constantius, Gratian, and Theodosius I, that Christianity ultimately crushed paganism so completely that the efforts to revive it by Licinius and Julian the Apostate collapsed before they had made a good start. Thus there came to full bloom the Golden Age of patristic literature. Were one to attempt to establish the foremost cause of this phenomenal growth, it should be attributed to the irresistible internal vitality of the Church. But there were also external forces at play.

The Peace of Constantine, as it is called, permitted the young Church to flex her muscles as it were, and begin the divine commission to Christianize on a vast scale. The Church could begin the reform of the social structure of the Empire through legislation by a favorable state. She could come into the open to champion the cause of the poor and downtrodden. Churches and elaborate temples of worship, often remodeled and refurnished pagan temples, were built, and the liturgy, no longer a matter of furtive action, was enhanced. There was greater freedom and chance to pursue learning for Christians, and a more literate and educated Christian public made for greater demands on the writers of this age. Paganism was dead, and its tools, the arts and sciences, its literary forms could be put to serve Christianity without fear. In short, all the things that made for the spread of the Church during these years also contributed to the growth of patristic literature.

Even the very evils that rose from the turmoil of this growth contributed no little in an indirect way. The protection given the youthful Church by the state often led to a form of attempted union of Church and state or a Caesaro-papism that was intolerable. In this struggle the practical principles of Church-state relationship were clarified, at least in fundamentals. The missionary activity of the Church brought huge numbers into her fold and there resulted a deterioration of discipline and of the theological thinking in some circles. The former inspired great ascetical writings. The latter produced heresies, but the discussions and controversies precipitated by these errors brought forth the keenest theological thinking. Porphyry, Julian the Apostate, and Manichaeism caused some little trouble and elicited a few apologies, but the chief heresies were Arianism, Apollinarianism, Macedonianism, Monophysitism, and Nestorianism in the East. Donatism, Pelagianism and Semi-Pelagianism plagued the West. It is significant, too, that as these heresies burned out, patristic literature began to decline.

The Golden Age produced the greatest variety of writings, apologetic, polemical, dogmatic, exegetical, liturgical, historical, moral, homiletic, disciplinary, and ascetical as well as letters, many of which were really treatises. In fact, the systematic foundations of practically all the ecclesiastical sciences were laid during these years. If we compare the East and the West and except Augustine, there is small comparison except in the field of poetry. The Eastern writers are, as a whole, far superior to the Westerners. The former seldom use the works of Western writers and show little acquaintance with them. On the other hand, the Westerners made great use of the Greeks in translations.

The Greek Writers of the East

When we turn to the East we immediately think of the great schools of Christian antiquity. However, there are great names popping up in any number of places, many unheard of before this and even unexpected. The schools, too, have undergone some change. For the most part they are no longer so extreme in their exegesis and the Alexandrians of Caesarea should, in fact, be referred to as Neo-Alexandrians. Neither should the designation Alexandrian or Antiochian be applied carelessly. Many exegetes, warned by the heresy into which a rigid application of the earlier principles of each school had led some contemporaries, set out on their own.

Geographically we find the Greek writers of this period distributed throughout the East, in Alexandria, Egypt, Antioch, Asia Minor, Thrace, Syria, and Palestine. Distributed among them also are to be found all types of literature. We shall treat them as follows:

I. History, Biography, and Chronicles
II. Ascetical Literature and Lesser Writers
III. Heretical Writers
IV. Alexandrians and Egyptians
V. Asia Minor, Syria, and Palestine

I. History, Biography, and Chronicles

1. EARLY CHRISTIAN BIOGRAPHIES

This type of literature, which properly belongs to the field of hagiography, should receive at least brief mention here. It flourished during the Golden Age and long after. With the Peace of Constantine the Age of the Martyrs came to an end, but Christians would not be denied heroes. To replace the martyrs in popular fancy and interest came anchorites, hermits, and the great ecclesiastical figures of the age. Accounts of their lives and deeds were published everywhere, so great was the popular demand.

These "Lives" were for the most part an outgrowth of the *Acta* and *Passiones* of the martyrs, but most of them displayed greater imaginative detail. In fact they were written predominantly to edify and to amuse. Their immediate reading public was little interested in historical accuracy. All follow a certain pattern. The author begins with protestations of incompetence for the task and follows by citing his authorities for what he is about to tell. Then come accounts of the hero's birth with properly unusual events, of his life and deeds filled with miracles, visions, prophecies, and encounters with demons, and of his demise with the miracles that ensued. All these things are told with charming simplicity. Only the harsh cynic will be repelled by them.

How are we to evaluate these "Lives"? Some would find them absolutely worthless, while readers of a gullible and uncritical attitude would accept all of the tales. Romancing and story telling lie most close to the human heart. Before their conversion many of the Christian readers had enjoyed pagan romances. Others had avidly read the Apocrypha and folk tales dealing with New Testament personages and early Christian heroes. Glorification and idealization were what readers wanted and they reveled in the rich imagery that presented the lessons of the "Lives."

Athanasius' *Life of St. Anthony* served as a model for practically all these writings. Best known to us in the West and most readily accessible to the average reader were the hagiographical works of such Latin writers as Jerome and Sulpicius Severus. These works should be studied. Though they show a considerable variety in content and form, they all follow much the same general pattern.

Palladius is probably the greatest of the Greek hagiographers. Others are Anthony, a disciple of Simeon Stylites, Callinicus, Chrysippus, Cyril of Scythopolis, Gerontius, James the Deacon,

John of Ephesus, John Moschus, Leontius of Neapolis in Cyprus, Mark the Deacon, and Sophronius. Most of the great writers of the East also left some hagiographical works. Besides these there are collections of anecdotes and sayings of the fathers, such as the *Apophthegmata Patrum, Verba Seniorum,* and *Vitae Patrum,* all based on Greek writings. A few other Greek "Lives" have come down to us in Syriac.

2. DIARIES OR TRAVEL-BOOKS OF PILGRIMS

The Peace of Constantine threw open the Empire to Christians for free travel, and the practice of making pilgrimages to the Holy Land started, although Melito of Sardis and Origen seem to have been the earliest such pilgrims. Some of these travelers have left us a *Peregrinatio* or *Itineraria,* that is, accounts of their trips that are of value to the student of history and the liturgy. Such are the *Aetheria peregrinatio, Breviarius de Hierosolyma,* the *Itinerarium Antonii Placentini,* the *Itinerarium Burdigalense* and the *De situ terrae sanctae* by Theodosius the Archdeacon.

3. EUSEBIUS OF CAESAREA (339)

Eusebius is one of the earliest fathers of the Golden Age. He died before it got well under way and he must be judged as the child of a period of transition. Born around 265, the greater part of his life belongs to the pre-Nicene period and the charges of heresy and worldliness directed against him, though well founded, must be weighed against the background of the turbulent times in which he lived, and in the light of his close association with Constantine and the emperor's court. He seems to have been a slave of the famed Pamphilus of Caesarea who gave him an excellent education. Eusebius began his literary activity early. This literary career was interrupted by the persecution of Diocletian in which Pamphilus was martyred, but Eusebius escaped first to Tyre and thence to Egypt. By 313 he had become bishop of Caesarea and was very influential at court. He was present at the Council of Antioch (330) that deposed Eustathius, at the Council of Tyre (335) that deposed Athanasius, and at the Council of Constantinople (336) that condemned Marcellus. Previously he had been excommunicated by a council at Antioch (325) for Arianism and, though he signed the profession of faith drawn up at Nicea (335), he did so with reservations and later ridiculed it. All in all he seems to have been busier with secular affairs and his studies than with ecclesiastical things. He preached for the dedication of Constantine's Church of the Sepulchre (335) and for the thirtieth anniversary of Constantine's rule. Whether he preached the sermon opening the Council of Nicea is not certain. He died about 339 shortly after Constantine.

Eusebius was not a great ecclesiastic. In fact, he loved peace and the quiet needed for study so much that he was always ready to compromise. He has been called the earliest of the worldly-minded bishops who have afflicted the Church. He was, however, a prodigious scholar, even if he cannot be reckoned a great theologian. He was the father of Church history and an outstanding apologist. He also pioneered in several fields of Scripture study, but he followed Origen in his exegesis.

Eusebius' greatest work is his *Ecclesiastical History* (*H.E.*). It reports the history of the Church to Constantine's victory over Licinius in 324. First published in seven books in 303, it was enlarged and continued by the author. Its present form in ten books was published after 324. The work is a collection of facts and includes many excerpts from earlier Christian writings. All these are critically evaluated in such an objective way that Eusebius is justly called the father of Church history. In contrast to all other historical notices of earlier date, he shows himself a master of the science of history. Thinking of the work in terms of the art of history or the philosophy of history is another matter. The work lacks synthesis, and the closest Eusebius comes to a philosophy of history is in his apologetical thesis that Christianity's history and victory over paganism are proof of divine origin. It remained for Augustine to give us a Christian philosophy of history. But for all its shortcomings Eusebius' *Ecclesiastical History* is priceless for its store of information about the early Church and earlier writings.

Eusebius has also left us a *Chronicle*. This is a history of the world from Abraham to the year 323. Another most valuable work is *On the Martyrs of Palestine*. His *A Life of Pamphilus* and a collection of the *Acts of the Ancient Martyrs* have been lost except for meager fragments.

The *Evangelical Preparation* and *Evangelical Demonstration* are Eusebius' greatest apologetical works. Written about 315–325, the former proves the superiority of the Old Testament to paganism and the second shows that the Old Testament was but a preparation for the New Dispensation. *A General Elementary Introduction* and *On the Theophany* were explanations of the Messianic prophecies. A long work against the Neoplatonist Porphyry, another against Hierocles, who compared Apollonius of Tyana to Christ in his *Philaletus*, and two books of *Responses* and *Apology* have been lost except for small pieces.

In biblical studies Eusebius pioneered in archaeology and geography. He wrote four books on the geography of Palestine, a treatise on the peoples of the Bible and an *Onomasticon* discussing names of places in the Bible. He has also left commentaries on Isaias and the Psalms in which the exegesis is Origenistic, despite the author's historical bent. He also published important studies on the Gospels that influence later Gospel harmonies, *Gospel Canons*, and *On Problems and their Solutions in the Gospel.* Not much is known of his works *On Easter* and *On Polygamy and the Patriarchs.*

Two dogmatic writings, *Contra Marcellum* and *De Ecclesiastica theologia* are no great credit to Eusebius as they are tainted with Origenism and directed against Marcellus of Ancyra, a forerunner of Nicean Orthodoxy.

Eusebius must have written many letters but not much is left of them, as is also the fate of his sermons. A sermon on the dedication of a church in Tyre is important for the study of ecclesiastical architecture. The *Laus Constantini* (Panegyric for Constantine) contains Eusebius' jubilee sermon for Constantine (1–10). The rest (11–18) is apologetic, an introduction to Christianity. The *Vita Constantini* (Life of Constantine) in four books is an exaggerated panegyric of Constantine.

Eusebius erred in his conception of the Trinity even to the extent of regarding the Holy Ghost as a creature and the Son, though divine, as inferior to the Father. He condemned the veneration of images in a letter to the emperor's sister Constantia. But he wanted to be orthodox and he loved the Church, as his intense interest in her history and his great love for her martyrs amply show. Next to the Church he loved his studies and the peace indispensable to study. In a sense he was a worldly ecclesiastic, but he never used his position nor his influence at court to further his own end.

4. OTHER CHURCH HISTORIANS

Two students of Eusebius were his successor, Acacius of Caesarea, and Eusebius of Emesa. Other historians who followed the path of Eusebius were Basil of Cilicia, Epiphanius the Monk, Evagrius Scholasticus, Gelasius of Caesarea, Gelasius of Cyzicus, Hesychius of Jerusalem, John Diakromenos, Philip of Side, Philostorgius, Socrates, Sozomen, Theodore the Lector, Theodoret of Cyrus, and Zacharias Rhetor.

5. CHRONICLERS

The missionary activity of the Church and the spread of Christianity aroused great interest in the peoples and countries beyond the Roman Empire. The number of historians already mentioned are evidence of this. This interest in foreign countries induced many literary men to publish chronicles, works that were content to throw together the most varied historical facts without any endeavor to tie them together or to coordinate them. The author simply gathered as much data as he could about a country or some geographical area which might interest his readers. He gave these facts some chronological order and let it go at that. The works of Julius Africanus, Hippolytus, and Eusebius along these lines seem to have served as models. Such works appear to have been very popular in both East and West. The chief chroniclers and chronicles of the East, including some who wrote in Syriac, are Anianus, *Chronicles of Arbela*, *Chronicles of Edessa*, *Chronicon Paschale*, Dionysius of Tell-Mahre, *Excerpta Latina Barbari*, Hesychius of Miletus, John of Antioch, John of Ephesus, John Malalas, John Nikiotes, Josua Stylites, and Panodorus.

6. COLLECTIONS FOR HISTORY
AND CANON LAW

Brief reference should here be made to the earliest collections of documents of importance to the historian and to the student of ecclesiastical discipline. The earlier period in the history of the Church had seen some collections of related materials, such as the letters of Ignatius, of Dionysius of Corinth, of Origen, and the correspondence of Cyprian. In the Golden Age such activity increased because there were more materials available. Only the chief collections will be mentioned here, and for convenience those of the East and the West will be listed together.

The chief collectors of such general documents in the East were Sabinus of Heraclea, the *Chronographer of 354*, the *Collectio Avellana*, and John Malalas. In the West we find the beginnings of such a collection under Pope Julius I (337–352), when the Latin version of the Canons of Nicea was joined to the Canons of Sardica to form the oldest of Latin collections. Another collection, the *Prisca canonum editio Latina* originated under Pope Gelasius I (492–496). Around 500 appeared the important collection of Dionysius Exiguus. A century later came the *Collectio Isidoriana*, giving special importance to Spanish conciliar decrees. Other later collections are of too late a date to be mentioned here.

More specialized collections are the following: for Nicea see Theodosius the Deacon; for Donatism see Optatus of Mileve and Augustine (*Breviculis collationis cum Donatistis*); for Ephesus and Chalcedon look up the respective Acts; for Constantinople, John Maxentius and *Collectio Sabbaitica*. Finally for collections of civil codes check *Codex Justinianus* and *Codex Theodosianus*.

II. *Ascetical Literature and Some*
Minor Writers

The Golden Age produced a vast amount of ascetical literature. There are any number of "Lives" and collections of anecdotes and sayings of the ascetics. There are manuals of asceticism, rules of discipline, monastic regulations, and apologies for the ascetic's way of life. If all of these had been preserved, the literature would be quite bulky. Monachism as a movement is certainly older than Anthony. The numerous devotees to monachism and the eremitical way of life fired the imagination to produce a whole flood of this type of literature, which has already been referred to in an earlier chapter.

Asceticism is a phenomenon common to all religions to a greater or less extent. It has sometimes been carelessly said that monasticism was the natural outgrowth of the secularization and corruption of the Church in the fourth century. Nothing could be more wrong, though conditions in that century did give no little stimulus to this way of life. The ascetical life has its foundation in the teaching of Christ. The apostles left all things. The four daughters of the deacon Philip renounced marriage to live an ascetical life. The early Christians of Jerusalem led some kind of common life, and Christ has promised great rewards for the renunciation of all things. The early writers of the Church are witness to the prevalence of lives of "single blessedness," and virgins were the special solicitude of the bishop in the early Church. Out of this asceticism, monasticism grew by natural steps. Two factors contributed directly to the organization of monasticism. The Decian persecution (c. 250) drove many Christians into the desert. When the persecution had passed they had come to love solitude and remained in the desert. Then, with the freedom of the Church, morality and ideals of sanctity did deteriorate somewhat. As a consequence many earnest souls fled from the world. Finally, with the passing of the age of the martyrs, new heroes, the ascetics, came to fire the imagination of Christian folk.

The study of the Scriptures occupied all these ancient ascetics. Two books of John Cassian, his *Institutes* (*De institutis coenobiorum*) and his *Conferences* (*Collationes*), should be read for information on the scriptural studies of the ascetics. The Golden Age was one of astounding development in the study of the Sacred Writings. All the great ecclesiastical writers of this age produced important exegetical studies. Only the lesser writers will be mentioned here. The great men will be discussed separately.

Another literary form that engaged the talents of the great writers of the Golden Age is the funeral oration. It was taken over and adapted from pagan oratory. There were four kinds: the encomium, the epitaph, the modony, and the consolatory oration. The last was most prominent in the literature of the Golden Age and Gregory Nazianzen was probably its most notable exponent. It followed a strict pattern and comprised the following parts: the exordium or introduction, the encomium which told of the family, birth, way of life, and achievements of the deceased. After comparing the accomplishments of the deceased with other great figures of the past, it concluded with a final exhortation and prayer.

The other three forms of funeral oration are not frequent in the literature of this period. The encomium was an oration in praise of one long dead. The modony was strictly a lament for the dead. The epitaph combined elements of both the encomium and the lament for the dead.

The chief writers to be mentioned in this chapter aside from the great figures of the Golden Age are the following: Acacius of Miletene, Ammonas, Anthony, Amphilochius, Asterius, Basil of Seleucea, Dalmatius of Constantinople, Diodochus of Photice, Evagrius Ponticus, Firmus of Caesarea, Gennadius I, Patriarch of Constantinople, Hadrian, Hesychius of Jerusalem, Horsiesi, Isidore of Pelusium, Macarius the Egyptian, Macarius Junior (see also Macarian writings), Marcellus of Ancyra, Mark Erimeta, Memnon, Nilus of Ancyra, Pachomius, Proclus of Constantinople, Proclus Cyzicus, Serapion of Thmuis, Shenute, Symeon of Messala, Synesius of Cyrene, Theodore the Abbot, and Theodotus of Ancyra.

1. EVAGRIUS PONTICUS (346–399)

Evagrius Ponticus, ordained deacon by Gregory Nazianzen, became a popular preacher in Constantinople but retired to the Nitrian desert to become a disciple of Marius. He earned his living as a copyist. Most of his original writings have been lost because he was condemned in 553, together with Didymus the

Blind. Some of his works have, however, come down to us in translation. He endeavored to popularize the asceticism of Origen. To what extent he subscribed to the latter's errors cannot be known. Evagrius is the first monk to develop a comprehensive literary activity, and his influence on the development of Christian spirituality can hardly be overestimated. Such men as Palladius, John Cassian, and Maximus Confessor are extensively dependent upon him. His works that have come down to us are:

1. *Antirrheticus* in eight books, containing Scripture texts to be used in time of temptation against the eight vices. Evagrius is one of the first writers on the theory of eight vices which later developed into the teaching on the seven capital sins.

2. *The Monk:* a manual for monks, part one for the novice and part two for the seasoned monk.

3. *Problemata Gnostica,* a collection of 600 ascetic, dogmatic, and moral questions.

4. A collection of *Maxims* for monks and another for nuns.

5. *Letters,* sixty-seven in number.

6. *Commentaries* on the Psalms and Proverbs.

7. Two works ascribed to Nilus of Ancyra, *De oratione* (On Prayer) and *De malignis cogitationibus* (On Evil Thoughts) are now known to be from the pen of Evagrius.

2. HESYCHIUS OF JERUSALEM (after 450)

Hesychius of Jerusalem, a monk and later (after 450) a priest in Jerusalem, is important as an exegete of the allegorical Alexandrian school. He is said to have commented on the entire Bible. He was strictly an exegete and biblical theologian, distrusting philosophy. He followed Cyril of Alexandria in his Christology, but he did not use his terminology. He comes suspiciously close to Monophysitism in some of his statements. He is an important witness to the teaching on original sin. Of his great literary output there remain: a commentary on Leviticus, twenty-four homilies on Job, glosses to Isaias, the Psalms, and remains of an extensive commentary on the Psalms. Hesychius has also left some famous Marian sermons, two on the Annunciation and one on the Purification. He also has explanations of thirteen hymns of the Old and New Testaments and some sermons. Much of his extant literary work still awaits editing. He wrote a Church history of which only the section dealing with Theodore of Mopsuestia remains.

3. ISIDORE OF PELUSIUM (c. 435)

Isidore of Pelusium (c. 435) is one of the best letter writers of the Greek church. He was a rhetorician and philosopher, later a monk and disciple of Chrysostom of whom he wrote (*Epistle* 5, 32) that if Paul had chosen his own interpreter he would have taken John Chrysostom. Most of his some 2,000 letters are short and treat of exegetical and ascetico-moral matters as well as current problems. He was very popular and greatly admired in his own day and afterwards. An Antiochian in his exegesis, he was also the most prolific and cultured letter writer of his time.

4. PROCLUS OF CONSTANTINOPLE
(middle fifth century)

Proclus of Constantinople, bishop of Cyzicus (426), became in 434 the second successor to Nestorius as patriarch of Constantinople, whose heresy he was one of the first to attack in his Marian Sermon. He was an effective peacemaker in the controversies over Chrysostom and Theodore of Mopsuestia. The *Trisagion* (thrice Holy) was introduced into the liturgy by him. He did not come out openly against Theopaschism but neither did he coin the phrase, "one of the Trinity was crucified." He was one of the greatest preachers of the East, and there are twenty-seven sermons and seven letters current under his name though not all of certain authenticity. Some of the *Spuria* of Chrysostom have also been ascribed to him. Best known of his letters is the *Tomus ad Armenios* (Memorandum for the Armenians) on the two natures in Christ. His best known sermon is Sermo I, *De laudibus Mariae* (In Praise of Mary) preached against Nestorius in 429.

III. Heretical Literature

Three great heresies plagued the Church in the fourth century, all outgrowths of earlier erroneous speculation on the Incarnation.

They are Arianism, Apollinarianism, and Nestorianism. Though native to the East, all, especially Arianism, had wide repercussions in the West.

1. ARIANISM

Arius (336), though an Alexandrian, studied at Antioch under Lucian of Antioch, who, though he died a martyr's death, held strong subordinationist convictions. Arius developed these teachings and proposed a Christology based on these three fundamental propositions: 1. God is not generated and cannot communicate His nature to creatures; 2. God generated the Word in order to create the universe and, therefore, since the Word had a beginning He is not divine but an intermediary creature between God and the universe; and 3. it follows, therefore, that the substance of the Word differs from the substance of God, the Father. The Son is a son only in an adoptive sense. These fundamental propositions are an outgrowth of earlier errors of Gnosticism, Subordinationism, and Adoptionism.

Arius wrote a work called *A Banquet* composed of popular verses to propagate his errors. Most of it has been lost. There are three letters, one to Eusebius of Nicomedia asking help, another containing a profession of faith to Alexander of Alexandria, and a third, a profession of faith to Emperor Constantine.

A study of the life of Arius will throw clear light on the course of the bitter battle that he started. Some refer to the time as the period of "galloping bishops" because of the many gatherings held to condemn now this ecclesiastic and then another. The Council of Nicea condemned the teachings of Arius, but so vicious were his errors and so much had the evil personality of the man attracted followers, that the heresy continued to spread and persist far and wide, long after his unhappy death.

After Nicea (325) and the death of Arius a little later, his followers split into roughly three groups. The Anomeans or pure Arians taught that the Son is unlike (*anomoios*) the Father. The Homeans were mostly a group swayed by ecclesiastical politics. They were content to agree that the Son is like (*homoios*) the Father. The Semi-Arians approached close to orthodox Christology by admitting that the Son is like (*homoiousios*) the Father in all things (in substance also), but they stopped short of accepting the con-substantiality (*homoousios*) of the Son with the Father. Since the chief theological disputes later centered about the question whether the Son is con-substantial (*homoousios*) or only like (*homoiousios*) the Father, Cardinal Newman could justly say that the great Athanasius spent his entire life in a fight over the one single letter *iota* (ι).

It is, indeed, significant that all the great theological writers of the day who encountered Arianism in any form were arrayed against the error, both in the East and in the West. Even Diodore of Tarsus, who was condemned in Constantinople (499) as the father of Nestorianism, was a vigorous opponent of Arianism in all its forms. The anti-Arian phalanx could call the roll of the following names: Alexander of Alexandria, Ambrose of Milan, Athanasius, Basil the Great and his fellow Cappadocians: Gregory of Nazianzus and Gregory of Nyssa, Cyril of Alexandria, Cyril of Jerusalem, Diodore of Tarsus, Eusebius of Vercellae, Eustathius of Antioch, John Chrysostom, Hilary of Poitiers, Theodoret of Cyrus, Phoebadius, and Vigilius of Thapsus. Eusebius of Caesarea, though he accepted Nicea, seems to have made a turnabout. Anyway, he cannot be reckoned a great theologian.

Among the followers of Arianism appear the following names: Acacius of Caesarea, Aetius, Asterius the Sophist, Basil of Ancyra, Eudoxius, Eunomius, Eusebius of Emesa, Eusebius of Nicomedia, Euzoius, George of Laodicea, Philostorgius, Photinus, Potamius, Sabinus, and Theodore of Heraclea.

2. APOLLINARIANISM

Apollinaris of Laodicea (310), son of a priest of the Nicean congregation of Laodicea, became bishop (c. 361) and died about 390. A friend of Athanasius and an exceptionally gifted man, he fought the Arians but, defending orthodox trinitarian theology, he fell into the Christological error that paved the way for Monophysitism. To defend the Incarnation, he taught that the Second Person of the Trinity took to Himself an incomplete human nature consisting only of body and a sensitive soul. The Logos supplied the place of the intellectual soul. His error found, as was the case in Arianism, varied expression and shades of teaching. He was deposed and condemned by Pope Damasus in 377 and again in 382. He did not hesitate to forge false statements, attributing them to Athanasius, but his followers were of negligible stature, e.g., Timothy, Valentine, Vitalis, and others too unimportant to mention. The chief writers to combat his errors were Diodore of Tarsus, the Cappadocian Gregorys, later Leontius of Byzantium, Theodoret of Cyrus, and others.

Practically all the writings of Apollinaris except those formerly attributed to orthodox writers have perished. He published extensive commentaries on both Old and New Testaments, of which larger parts of a commentary on Romans have been recovered from Catenae. He wrote thirty books against Porphyry, a work against Julian the Apostate, and some dogmatic treatises against Origen, Dionysius of Alexandria, Eunomius of Cyzicus, Marcellus of Ancyra, Diodore of Tarsus, and Flavian of Antioch. He wrote, mostly on biblical themes, many poetical works for use in teaching religion. The following works have come down to us among the writings of other fathers: a profession of faith found among Gregory Thaumaturgus' works, treatises ascribed to Athanasius, viz., *Quod unus sit Christus* (That Christ is One) three books *De Incarnatione Dei Verbi* (On the Incarnation of God's Word), a profession of faith to Emperor Jovian. There are three works that were current under the name of Pope Julius I (337–352): *De unione corporis et divinitatis in Christo* (On the Union of Humanity and Divinity in Christ), *De fide et Incarnatione* (On Faith and the Incarnation) and a letter to a Presbyter Dionysius. A dogmatic work, *Demonstration of the Incarnation of God in the Image of Man,* can be reconstructed from the *Antirrheticus* of Gregory of Nyssa. Another small work can be partially reconstructed from a Dialogue, formerly attributed to Athanasius (*Dialogus de S. Trinitate*).

3. NESTORIANISM

Nestorius, born of Persian ancestry (c. 381), became a monk and priest in Antioch. There he studied under Theodore of Mopsuestia. A brilliant orator, he became Patriarch of Constantinople in 428 and vigorously attacked the Jews and all heretics except the Pelagians whom he treated kindly. In the controversy over the title *Theotokos* (God-bearer) he projected himself in the midst of the strife. The council of Ephesus (431) condemned him. The emperor confined him to a monastery and later banished him to Egypt in 436, where he died sometime after 451.

Nestorius was the author of one of the most devastating heresies in the Church. There are Nestorians even today. He reduced the Incarnation to a mere moral union between a human being and the Second Person of the Trinity. According to Nestorius, Jesus Christ is a mere human being in whom the Son of God was present as in a house. So, morally Christ is one person, but in reality, there are two persons and their union is merely accidental. Hence a strict distinction has to be made between the two. Therefore, Mary is not the mother of God (*Theotokos*) but the mother of the man, Christ. And it is not the Son of God who redeemed us but the man, Christ. This is the pivotal error of Nestorius, but he also leaned to Pelagianism, denied transubstantiation and the reality of justification.

Only fragments are left of his works, fifteen letters and thirty sermons. The *Liber Heraclidis*, attacking Ephesus and Cyril of Alexandria is doubtful, and the twelve Counter-Anathemas against Cyril of Alexandria are the work of followers of Nestorius.

Theodore of Mopsuestia was Nestorius' teacher. Among his followers were, Acacius of Miletene, Cosmas Indicopleustes, Diodorus of Tarsus who fought all the other Christological heresies, Eutherius of Tyana, and Gennadius I of Constantinople.

There were many friends of Nestorius whose position is not entirely clear. Thus Acacius of Miletene was at first a close friend, then a bitter opponent. Others whose stand is not beyond question in the matter are Irenaeus Comes, Julian of Eclanum, Severus of Antioch, and Theodoret of Cyrus.

The following writers are important for the history of Nestorianism: the Chronicler of Edessa, Evagrius Scholasticus, John of Antioch, and Liberatus the Deacon.

The chief writers against Nestorianism were Anastasius Sinaita, Boethius, Pope Celestine I, Cyril of Alexandria, John of Damascus, Justinian (see Theodore Askidas), Leontius of Byzantium, Mark Eremita, Marius Mercator, Proclus of Constantinople, and Vincent of Lerins.

Out of Arianism, Apollinarianism, and Nestorianism grew other heresies that troubled the Church later, chiefly Monophysitism and Monothelitism.

IV. *Alexandrians and Egyptians*

Alexandrians and Egyptians already mentioned among the ascetical writers are Anthony, Evagrius Ponticus, Horsiesi, Isidore of Pelusium, Macarius, Pachomius, and Theodore the Abbot. The Arianist controversy raged hottest in Alexandria at first and evoked an immense amount of literature. The resolute Alexander of Alexandria was the first to attack Arius. Lesser Alexandrians are Eusebius of Alexandria, Nonnus of Panoplis, Serapion of Thmuis, and Theophilus of Alexandria. The most important of the Alexandrians are Athanasius, Cyril of Alexandria, Didymus the Blind, and Synesius of Cyrene.

1. ATHANASIUS (295–373)

Athanasius is one of the most imposing figures in all Church history. He has been justly called the "Father of Orthodoxy," the "Champion of Truth," and "Pillar of the Church." His life deserves close study because of his position on Church-state relationship and his accomplishments as an ecclesiastic administrator. His writings are of greatest importance in theology, but as literature they cannot be called great. They often lack order and are frequently characterized by digressions and repetitiousness. Many of them may have been written in a hurry. But they all show penetrating, precise thought and clarity of expression.

Born in 295, he received an excellent education, and as a young deacon served Alexander of Alexandria as secretary at Nicea. In 328 he was unanimously chosen to succeed Alexander, and almost at once the storm broke because he refused to accept Arius. Five times he was exiled, spending altogether seventeen years away from his see. It was only during his last seven years that he enjoyed a measure of peace in administering his see with its suffragans. He died May 2, 373. Read the panegyric on Athanasius by Gregory Nazianzen.

His writings cover a wide field but can be classified into three groups: 1. apologetic and dogmatic works; 2. historical and polemical treatises and letters, many of which are in reality treatises; and 3. exegetical and practical or ascetical writings.

1. Apologetic and Dogmatic Works

The earliest works of this group are *Oratio contra Gentes* (Against the Greeks) and *Oratio de Incarnatione Verbi* (On the Incarnation of the Word). Written around 318, they form a unit of which the first part is directed against polytheism and demonstrates the truth of the Incarnation against Jews and pagans. An abridged edition was published in anti-Apollinarist circles in Antioch.

Athanasius' most important dogmatic work, the three *Orationes contra Arianos* (Against the Arians), appeared between 335–356. Book I defends the doctrine of Nicea on the unity of nature of the Son with the Father and His eternal generation. Books II and III explain the texts of Sacred Scripture, which Arians had abused to bolster their teaching. A fourth *Oratio* was later added by an anonymous hand.

A number of spurious works have also been attributed to Athanasius. These need not be listed here but there is a *De Incarnatione et contra Arianos* (On the Incarnation and Against the Arians) that was long questioned because of the phrase, "One God in Three Hypostases." The work has been established as genuine and the phrase is an interpolation.

2. Historical and Polemical Works

These treatises and letters were written either to defend himself or to attack heresy. The *Epistola ad episcopos encyclica* (Encyclical Letter to the Bishops) protests his deposition in 340. The *Apologia contra Arianos* (Apology Against the Arians) reports on the proceedings and decisions of the various synods and councils before 357. The *Epistola de decretis Nicaenae synodi* (Letter on the Decrees of Nicea), written about 351, defends the terminology approved at Nicea. In 356 appeared *Epistola encyclica ad episcopos Aegypti et Libyae* (Encyclical Letter to the Bishops of Egypt and Libya). The *Apologia ad Constantium Imperatorem* (Apology to the Emperor Constantius 357) refutes the charge that Athanasius had stirred up Constans against his brother, the emperor. An *Apologia de fuga* (Apology for His Flight [357]) defends his flight to the monks of Egypt a year earlier. The *Historia Arianorum ad monachos* (History of the Arians for the Monks [c. 358]) reports on Arianism for the years 335–357. A letter to Serapion of Thmuis reports the death of Arius. An *Epistola de synodis Arimini in Italia et Seleuciae in Isauria celebratis* (359) reports on these two synods. Three letters were written at the instance of synods: *Tomus ad Antiochenos* (to the Antiochians [362]), *Epistola ad Jovianum imperatorem* (to Jovian, the Emperor [363]) and *Epistola ad Afros* (to the Africans [369]) to the bishops of West Africa. There are four letters to Serapion of Thmuis (358–362) that are most important, on the Third Person of the Trinity. Lastly there are three important Christological letters, *Epistola ad Epictetum episcopum Corinthi*, *Epistola ad Adelphium episcopum*, and *Epistola ad Maximum philosophum.*

3. Exegetical and Ascetical Works

The Catenae have preserved fragments of some exegetical works, among them an allegorical explanation of the Psalms. Best known of the ascetical works of Athanasius is the *Life of Anthony* which was translated into Latin by Evagrius of Antioch. Athanasius also wrote a work *On Virginity* which was long thought lost but can now be reconstructed.

We have thirteen festal letters covering the years 329–348. Written shortly after the Epiphany, they are pastoral letters fixing the date of Lent and Easter. They treat of other matters also. Most important of these is letter 39, of the year 367. It fixes a canon of the Bible as we know it today except that Athanasius rejects the Deuterocanonicals of the Old Testament, though he recommends that they be read for edification.

The *Quicumque* or Athanasian Creed is not the work of Athanasius. The author is not known though it is frequently attributed to Ambrose. Only since the seventh century has it been associated with Athanasius.

Athanasius is beyond question a landmark in theology. It was his contribution to theology to give a clear, scholarly, and scientific exposition of Catholic teaching on the Trinity and on the

Logos. Far more precisely and with greater clarity than any earlier thinker, Athanasius developed the doctrine of the unity of nature of the Trinity, of the generation of the Son, and the procession of the Holy Spirit. On the latter point, however, he erred with other theologians of the East in holding the Son to be the immediate source of procession of the Holy Spirit. He proceeds from the Father through the Son, according to Athanasius.

Athanasius' next great contribution to theology was his Christology. He clearly analyzed the Incarnation and the implications of this union of two natures in one person. It is as God-man that Christ redeemed us and elevated our fallen nature. Because of the Incarnation it is the person that acts and Mary is God's mother (*Theotokos*).

Protestants have claimed some statements of Athanasius for a symbolic interpretation of the Real Presence, but he is quite emphatic in teaching transubstantiation. He challenged the validity of Arian baptism on the ground that these heretics could not baptize in the name of the Trinity.

2. CYRIL OF ALEXANDRIA (444)

Cyril, the nephew of Theophilus of Alexandria, succeeded his uncle in that see in 412. He was a resolute character and the vigorous action he brought against the Novatians and the Jews made him many enemies. But the charge of complicity in the murder of Hypatia is sheer calumny. Cyril was a most vigorous champion of orthodoxy against Nestorius, whom he denounced as early as 429 in a Paschal letter. A Roman synod (430) condemned Nestorius, and Cyril was authorized to draw up twelve anathematisms. Cyril presided at Ephesus (431) and Nestorius was again condemned. But a rump synod decreed the deposing of Cyril. Theodosius II, the emperor, approved both decrees and imprisoned both men. By 433 the opposing factions were reconciled; Nestorius was sent to a monastery in Antioch, and Cyril returned to his see. Until his death in 444 Cyril was often attacked for errors he did not hold.

Cyril's writings are of the greatest theological importance, even though of rather inferior literary quality. They are, however, characterized by deep penetration and clarity of thought.

He was a great preacher but only twenty of his numerous sermons have come down to us. The best known is the panegyric on the *Theotokos*, the most famous Marian sermon of antiquity. His exegetical works cover a wide range. On the Old Testament he has left us *De adoratione et cultu in spiritu et veritate* (On Adoration and Worship in Spirit and Truth) in seventeen books, and a sequel in thirteen books entitled *Glaphyra* (Select Pieces), which explains selected passages of the Pentateuch. There are commentaries on Isaias and the minor prophets and the Catenae have fragments of studies on other Old Testament books. There is part of a commentary on John, 156 homilies on Luke, and fragments on Matthew, Romans, Corinthians, and Hebrews. In his Old Testament exegesis, Cyril is an allegorist, but he adheres more to the literal sense in his New Testament exegesis.

Cyril's chief dogmatic and polemical works are directed against the Nestorians. The Twelve Anathematisms have already been mentioned. Cyril wrote three *Apologia* in defense of these propositions (c. 431). There are five books *Adv. Nestorii blasphemias* (Against the Blasphemies of Nestorious [430]), criticizing the sermons of Nestorius. The *Apologeticum ad Imperatorem* (Apology to the Emperor) defends Cyril's conduct in the Council of Ephesus, at which he presided. There are also three books on Christology warning the royal household against Christological errors and explaining correct doctrine. They are *De recta fide ad Imperatorem Theodosium* (On the True Faith to the Emperor Theodosius) and *De recta fide ad Reginas* (On the True Faith to the Queens), the latter, in two books, addressed to the emperor's wife and his two sisters. The *Quod unus sit Christus* (That Christ is One) was widely read and very popular. Finally there are *Scholia de Incarnatione Unigeniti* (Scholia on the Incarnation of the Only-Begotten), a treatise, *Adversus nolentes confiteri s. Virginem esse Deiparam* (Against Those Who Refuse to Confess that the Virgin is Mother of God) and fragments of works against Diodorus of Tarsus and Theodore of Mopsuestia.

Cyril's bulkiest apologetical work is the *Adversus libros athei Juliani* (Against the Books of Julian the Atheist) in thirty books of which only the first ten are extant. Julian the Apostate had published three books against the "Galileans." The first of these can be reconstructed from what is left of Cyril's work. Of no less importance are the following two works that deal with the Trinity: *Thesaurus de sancta et consubstantiali Trinitate* (Thesaurus on the Holy and Consubstantial Trinity) expounding, in thirty-five propositions, the whole range of Trinitarian doctrine and a *De sancta et consubstantiali Trinitate* in seven Dialogues.

Besides Cyril's twenty-nine festal letters of the period 414–442 there are ninety letters of dogmatic import which are valuable also for the study of Church history and canon law.

3. DIDYMUS THE BLIND (c. 398)

A layman who had been blind from his fourth year, became the most illustrious headmaster of the Alexandrian school and served in that capacity for fifty years. Jerome and Rufinus were among his students. A brilliant teacher and an indefatigable writer, practically all of his works have either been lost or destroyed, because the fifth general council (II Constantinople, 553) condemned him together with Origen and Evagrius Ponticus in the Three Chapters controversy. Though orthodox in his teaching on the Trinity, he had followed Origen in his doctrine of the pre-existence of souls and the *Apocatastasis*.

All of Didymus' exegetical work has been lost except for what can be rescued from the *Catenae*. He seems to have commented on all the Bible and followed the principles of the Alexandrian school in his interpretation. Fortunately his most important dogmatic work has been preserved. Between 381 and 392 he wrote his *De Trinitate* in three books against the Arians and Monarchians. We have also three books *De Spiritu Sancto* (On the Holy Spirit) preserved for us by Jerome's translation, and there is a short work *Contra Manichaeos* (Against Manichaeans). Two books *De dogmatibus et contra Arianos* (On the Dogma against Arians), circulated as an appendix to Basil's *Adversus Eunomium* (Against Eunomius), have been identified as also the work of Didymus.

4. SYNESIUS OF CYRENE (414)

Synesius of Cyrene, born between 370 and 375 of noble extraction in Cyrene in Libya, studied under Hypatia in Alexandria and served as ambassador to Constantinople, 399–402. In this post he greatly aided his impoverished people at home by reduction of taxes. When the Berbers threatened his native city he led the defense. As a reward for this he was elected bishop of Ptolemais and metropolitan of the Pentapolis. He hesitated to give up his life of leisure, but finally accepted on condition that he could continue married life and retain his ideas on the pre-existence of souls, the eternity of the world, and his allegorical interpretation of the resurrection. He tried to become thoroughly Christian, but he never quite succeeded. He died young (413 or 414), and has left some treatises, orations, ten hymns in Doric dialect, and 156 letters valuable for the light they shed on the times. An oration on kingship holds up the ideal king to young Emperor Arcadius. Among his treatises are: *On Providence, Dion Chrysostom,* or, On His Way of Life, *In Praise of Baldness,* and *On Dreams.* All his writings show how defective was his Christian training and how steeped he was in pagan culture and learning.

V. Asia Minor, Syria, and Palestine

Turning from Alexandria and Egypt to the north and east, to Asia Minor, Syria, and Palestine, great churchmen, theologians, and writers seem to spring up everywhere, many in places that have dropped from memory. Here we encounter the great Cappadocians—Basil the Great, Gregory of Nyssa, Basil's brother, and Gregory Nazianzen, their friend. There are Cyril of Jerusalem, Epiphanius, the metropolitan of the island of Cyprus, Theodoret of Cyrus, the incomparable John Chrysostom of Constantinople, and the much maligned Theodore of Mopsuestia. All these call for more detailed treatment but before directing our attention to them mention should be made of other writers.

Many of the following men were important figures in the Church of the day but have left insufficient literary legacy to warrant special study. They will be listed alphabetically with little regard for their place chronologically in the Golden Age. They are: Acacius of Berea, Acacius of Melitene, Adrian the Priest, Aetius of Antioch, Amphilochius of Side, Antiochus of

Ptolemais, Antipater of Bostra, Apollinaris of Laodicea, Asterius of Amasea, Basil of Ancyra, Dalmatius of Cyzicus, Eustathius of Antioch, Evagrius of Antioch, Firmus of Caesarea, Gelasius of Jerusalem, Hegemonius, Hesychius of Jerusalem, John of Jerusalem, Macarius of Magnesia, Marcellus of Ancyra, Marcus the Deacon, Marcus Eremita, Memnon of Ephesus, Nemesius of Emesa, Nilus of Ancyra, Philo of Carpasia, Proclus of Cyzicus, Severian of Gabala, Sophronius, Theodotus of Ancyra, Theophilus of Alexandria, Titus of Bostra, and Triphyllius, bishop of Ledra in Cyprus.

1. BASIL THE GREAT (379)

The three great Cappadocians, Basil and the two Gregorys were bound together by ties of country, of schooling, of friendship, and by common cause against the errors that harassed the Church. Basil and Gregory of Nyssa were brothers. Basil, however, was easily the greatest of the three. Yet each Gregory has his own genius. Basil outdistanced them in the range of his accomplishments and was pre-eminent in every field. It may be said, however, that Gregory Nazianzen was the greater orator and that Gregory of Nyssa was the more penetrating thinker. Basil was above all else a man of action. He fought the emperor, heretics, schismatics, and aided by the Gregorys triumphantly vindicated the teachings of Nicea and Constantinople in the East, especially in his native Asia Minor. The father of Eastern monasticism, he profoundly influenced Western monasticism also.

The accomplishments of Basil are all the more astounding because of the little time he had. Born into a Catholic family of several generations about 330, he studied in the best schools including Athens, then retired to solitude with some friends around 356. He was in public affairs only nineteen years (360–379) and a bishop only nine years (370–379). Furthermore, his great work as bishop of Caesarea, metropolitan of Cappadocia, and exarch of Pontus, is even greater because of the sadness of his last years. In 372 began his estrangement with Gregory Nazianzen. His close friends, Athanasius and Gregory Nazianzen the Elder, died in 373 and 374 respectively. His friend, Eusebius of Samosata, was banished and his brother, Gregory of Nyssa, was deposed. Bishops

Anthimus of Tyana, Apollinaris of Laodicea, and Eustathius of Sebaste became his violent enemies. Through all this he was in frail health and died at the age of forty-nine.

Basil had been ordained about 364 and practically at once administered the affairs of Eusebius, bishop of Caesarea. After the latter's death in 370 Basil succeeded him, although not without violent disturbances. Despite all opposition he went his way preaching, instructing, and looking after the material needs of his flock. Few bishops have so fearlessly excoriated the rich and pointed out their obligations as stewards of their wealth. He established the famous Basileiad or Ptochotropium, a combination home for the aged, the poor, and strangers; a hospital, and an industrial school to train the unskilled in the trades. He founded similar institutions throughout his jurisdiction.

Outside his diocese he rallied the forces of orthodoxy. His influence in composing the Meletian schism in Antioch was great, even though he failed to induce Pope Damasus to take decisive action. In Epistle 239 he pours out his disappointment to his friend Eusebius of Samosata. However, Basil always looked to Rome and was more farseeing than most ecclesiastics of his day in his endeavors to bring East and West closer together.

Gregory Nazianzen delivered a brilliant funeral oration for Basil. This is one of the best sources for many details of his early life; but to get acquainted with the man one must read Basil's own many letters. They tell the story of a life of tremendous and varied activity and they reveal the many facets of the personality of Basil. He has time to write letters of condolence, to intercede in tax matters and other legal affairs. His letters to his clergy reveal the disciplinarian and executive. He can be stern and unyielding, but his letters to a fallen monk and a fallen virgin reveal the great heart of the man. All his writings disclose the soul of an ascetic solitary who pursued his task in many restless necessities, always with a devoted and dedicated sense of duty. Small wonder that almost immediately after his death Basil was acclaimed "the Great" and venerated as a saint.

In a relatively short public life of intense and violently distracting activity, Basil has left us a comparatively large number of writings. There are three books against Eunomius of Cyzicus, a treatise *De Spiritu Sancto*, and a *Philocalia* of Origen's writings which he edited together with Gregory Nazianzen. These are all dogmatic works. His most important ascetical writings are the *Moralia*, eighty rules of the ascetical life based on New Testament passages and his two monastic rules. The longer or *Regulae fusius tractatae* comprises 55 sections, and the shorter or *Regulae brevius tractatae*, 313 sections. In the form of question and answer, these discuss all phases of monastic life. Much of their materials are of earlier origin and profoundly influenced Western monasticism.

Basil was a polished orator. There are nine homilies on the Hexaemeron, eighteen homilies on the Psalms, twenty-three sermons on various topics, and panegyrics on martyrs. These are valuable for the study of the times. There is a sermon on fasting, another excoriating the rich, and one on drunkenness. Among the homilies is usually found also a treatise on the study of pagan classics and what benefit a young student may derive therefrom (*Hom.* 22).

Basil has left us 365 letters as far as we know, covering a wide range of interests. The Liturgy of St. Basil, still in use in the Orthodox Greek Church on certain days, owes much to him. However, it is difficult to tell what is his contribution and what is a matter of normal growth. Gregory Nazianzen tells of Basil's interest in the liturgy.

Basil is the greatest doctor and theologian of the East. One may also call him one of the greatest of the early canonists because, in his capacity of metropolitan and exarch, he was called on to settle many questions of discipline and custom. His letters are filled with such decisions. Above all he was the ascetic and monk, but paradoxically almost no less the ecclesiastic executive and administrator.

Basil's greatest contribution to dogmatic theology is his writings on the Godhead and the Trinity. His three books against Eunomius may, in a way, be said to be the earliest handbook of theodicy. Though the earlier apologists did deal with the problem of attaining a knowledge of God by unaided reason, Basil explores farther what reason can come to know of God and His being. It is his further achievement to bring out clearly the unity of nature and the Trinity of Persons in the Godhead. Up to his time, the terms for nature (*ousia*) and person (*hypostasis*) were used interchangeably to the confusion of all. The Meletian schism had its origin in what Paulinus had taught about one divine hypostasis, and Meletius had said concerning three hypostases. Basil saw clearly through the confusion and acrimony of the schism to point out the individuality of each divine Person, which is rooted respectively in fatherhood, sonship, and sanctification.

Some contemporary bishops attacked Basil for not teaching the divinity of the Holy Spirit as clearly as they expected him to do. Gregory Nazianzen explains that Basil at times spoke in a restrained fashion because of the hostility of the Arians. Gregory explains further that as long as the divinity of Christ was still not unchallenged, Basil did well not to emphasize the divinity of the Third Person. Such procedure might have resulted in Basil's deposition and loss to the Church of this great champion of orthodoxy. That the Holy Spirit is one with the other divine Persons in nature and a Person of the identical divine nature, is a teaching that permeates all of Basil's dogmatic writings. However, he is in line with most of the great Greek theologians in teaching the procession of the Holy Spirit from the Father through the Son. But he emphatically attacks the opinion of Eunomius, that the Holy Spirit proceeds only from the Son.

The theological writings of Basil cover almost the whole range of dogmatic theology. His works are important for the study of the fall and the redemption, of grace, baptism, the Eucharist (here he places the transubstantiation in the Epiclesis), penance, matrimony, and the last things. The substance (*ousia*) of angels he conceives as a tangible breath of air of immaterial fire. He urges frequent Communion and what he has to say about penance and marriage is of great importance to the Church historian and the canonist.

Whether Basil clearly recognized the primacy of the bishop of Rome is not altogether clear from his writings, but his dealings with Damasus would seem to indicate that he saw more than a *Primus inter pares* (Primate among Equals) in the bishop of Rome. All his writings must be taken into consideration before one tries to give an exposition of Basil's thinking.

Basil was a solid exegete. He avoided the extremes of both Alexandrians and Antiochians. For him Scripture is the first rule of faith but, equally important is tradition. Those who reject it are in error.

2. GREGORY OF NYSSA (394)

Basil's younger brother was most unlike him, and was a deeper and keener thinker. Gregory of Nyssa was an introvert who hated the bustle of executive tasks and the turmoil of the world. He gave up a promising career as a rhetorician and, at the instance of his friend, Gregory Nazianzen, entered upon the life of an ascetic and solitary to devote himself to the study of theology. He was rudely hauled out of his seclusion by his brother Basil who induced him, against his will, to become bishop of Nyssa in 371. Administration was too much for Gregory, and in 376 he was deposed by a synod in Nyssa composed chiefly of Arians and court prelates. He had been falsely accused of misappropriating funds. When the Emperor Valens died, Gregory was recalled to his see in 378. A synod of Antioch sent him as visitator to the diocese of Pontus (c. 379) and during this time he was chosen metropolitan of Sebaste, an assignment that he regarded as a kind of Babylonian Captivity. He was an outstanding champion of orthodoxy at the Council of Constantinople in 381. Shortly after attending another council at Constantinople in 394, he died.

Details of his early training by Basil, his choice of a rhetorician's career after he had been ordained a deacon, of his marriage, and of events of his episcopal career are found scattered through his own work and in the letters of Basil and Gregory Nazianzen.

Gregory of Nyssa was widely known as an orator. He preached the panegyrics for the Empress Flacilla and her daughter Pulcheria in 386, and was much in demand as a preacher in court circles. His greatest contribution is, however, in the field of theology, in the philosophical exploration of Christian dogma. As a philosopher and theologian he far outstripped his fellow Cappadocians.

Gregory's most important dogmatic work is the *Oratio catechetica magna* (Great Cathechesis). It is an exposition and defense of the chief dogmas of Christianity against heretics, Jews, and pagans. The first part treats of the one God in three Persons (1–4); the second covers the fall, original sin, the Incarnation, and the redemption (5–32). The final section treats of baptism and the Eucharist (33–40). There are also two Dialogues from his pen. The *Dialogus de anima et resurrectione* (On the Soul and Resurrection) is dedicated to his sister Macrina whom he visited on her deathbed as he returned from the synod of Antioch (379). It treats of the soul, of death, immortality, the resurrection, and the final restoration of all things. This last section very definitely shows the influence of Origen. The other Dialogue, *Contra fatum* (Against Fate), combats fatalism and astrology.

Among Gregory's dogmatic works are the following which are more polemical in tone than the above. The most famous of these is that known as the XIII Books *Adversus Eunomium*. In reality this work is made up of four independent writings. Book II is a refutation of an *Expositio fidei* (Exposition of Faith) by Eunomius. The other three treatises are directed against Eunomius' attacks on Basil. The first comprises Book I, the second takes in part of Books XII and XIII, and the third covers the remaining ten books. Besides these polemical works Gregory has left us the following: *Antirrhiticus adv. Apollinarem*, the most important of the anti-Apollinarist treatises of the time, *Adversus Apollinarem* (a smaller work directed to Theophilus of Alexandria) and the *Adversus Macedonianos et Pneumatomachos*. Finally there are these important treatises on the Trinity: *Ad Eustathium de Trinitate, Ad Abladium, Ad Simplicium,* and *Adversus paganos*.

In his exegesis Gregory of Nyssa is the greatest representative of the Alexandrian school of the fourth century. His *De opificio mundi* (On Creation) and *In Hexaemeron* (On the Hexaemeron) are rather restrained, and do justice to the literal sense of Scripture, but his other works are almost extreme in the allegorizing tendency of his exegesis. The former works were meant to supplement Basil's writings on the same subject and to defend them against misinterpretation. In *De vita Moysis* (Life of Moses) he develops the theme of the mystical ascent of the soul to God in his interpretation of the life of Moses. In *Psalmorum inscriptiones* he finds in the Psalm titles and in the divisions of the Psalms lessons that man can use to achieve perfection. He comes close to saying that man can do this of himself alone. Typical of Gregory's exegetical methods is the treatise *On the Witch of Endor.*

The exegetical writings show Gregory to have been a master of mystical theology. His ascetical writings evidence this even more clearly. His homilies may well be placed in this group also. There are fifteen homilies on the Canticle of Canticles which develop the theme that God is the groom and the human soul the bride of the Canticle. There are eight homilies on Ecclesiastes, on the Beatitudes, and another eight on the Lord's Prayer. But the greatest ascetical work of Gregory is the *De virginitate*, a sublime exposition of the soul's bridal with Christ. He has also left smaller treatises on perfection, on the monastic life, and on monastic penance. We can include here also a little book on the premature death of little children. Finally, there is the *Vita sanctae Macrinae*, the life of his sister written after the pattern of the early Christian biographies.

Gregory was a great preacher and he has left many sermons on the greatest variety of topics. There are moral and dogmatic sermons, panegyrics of the saints, discourses for the great feasts, and some funeral orations. These sermons show that Gregory was a zealous pastor and they give us many valuable insights into his times. However, there is a certain artificiality in them and they lack a certain straightforwardness. Among these sermons may be mentioned those on usury, on the postponement of baptism, on Gregory Thaumaturgus, and on the divinity of the Son and the Holy Spirit.

Finally, mention must be made of Gregory's correspondence. He has left us thirty letters, though he must have written more. These are mostly casual letters dealing with the things of everyday life and therefore have great value for the study of the times. The letter (no. 2) referred to as *De iis qui adeunt Jerosolymam* (On Those Who Travel to Jerusalem), is of great interest because it inveighs against many abuses connected with pilgrimages. Gregory himself had made a pilgrimage to the Holy Land, as we learn from letter three.

It is not easy to distinguish in Gregory the philosopher, the theologian, and the mystic. Aside from his brother Basil, his friend Gregory Nazianzen and other contemporaries, the great influences on his thinking were Philo, Plotinus, and Origen. He seems to have held that man's unaided intellect can come to that knowledge and vision of God that can be achieved only by grace. So too, though he rejected Origen's teaching on the pre-existence of souls, he followed the master in accepting the doctrine of the final *Apocatastasis* and restoration of all things.

Aside from some inexactness of expression and use of terms, Gregory is sound in his Trinitarian teaching, except that, like his contemporaries, he holds the procession of the Holy Ghost from the Father through the Son. He resolutely defends the divine maternity of Mary and is clear in his Christology. He is an important witness to the validity of tradition. In fact his writings are important in the study of all dogmatic theology. He presents a unique theory on the image of God in man, by placing it not in the individual but in human nature as a whole.

3. GREGORY NAZIANZEN (c. 329–390)

The third great Cappadocian, Gregory Nazianzen, reveals himself as a man of contrasts in his life and in his writings. He had small love for theological speculation, just as his friend Basil, and yet he came to be referred to as Gregory the Theologian in the Eastern Church. Greek theologians after him constantly quote him and comment on his writings, and he was no less esteemed in the West where, among others, Augustine speaks of him in the highest terms. It was his strict adherence to Scripture and tradition that earned him this respect. Unlike Basil he had a violent distaste for the active life, and yet his efforts in defense of orthodoxy earned for him a place with Basil and Chrysostom, as the "Three Great Hierarchs of the Eastern Church." Above all Gregory was an orator and a poet. He was a master of style and a man of magnificent imagination. His orations give us a deep insight into the soul of the man.

His father was bishop of Nazianzus and his mother dedicated the infant Gregory to the priesthood. However, he was not baptized until he was about thirty and he spent these years in study in Caesarea and Athens where his friendship for Basil grew deep.

He returned home about 357 and after his baptism was inclined to become a monk. However, in 362 he was ordained priest seemingly against his will, and he fled to solitude. He soon came back to assist his father who had become embroiled in the Arian controversy. Gregory restored peace and showed no little executive ability. Next Basil had him appointed bishop of the little see of Sasima and he was consecrated in 372, again against his will, it seems. He fled into solitude a second time and the estrangement with Basil dates from this time. He soon returned to assist his father again and administered the diocese for some time after the latter's death in 374. Thereupon he returned to his beloved solitude. In 379 he was called to the metropolitan see of Constantinople, a hotbed of Arianism. There was much wrangling about his appointment and even though the second Ecumenical Council held at Constantinople in 381 solemnly confirmed him in his office, he resigned. The next two years he spent in administering the diocese of Nazianzus. Then he retired to his quiet estate to live in ascetical solitude until his death somewhere around 390.

Gregory has left us 45 orations, 245 letters, and a number of *Carmina*, or long poems. The letters and poems are for the most part from his later years. The letters deal chiefly with personal matters of his own or of his friends. Some are short notes of recommendation but all are carefully and interestingly written. Three of them (nos. 102, 103, and 207), are dogmatic in content and combat Apollinarianism. The *Carmina* were written chiefly in answer to the charge that Christians were literary paupers. The *Poemata dogmatica et moralia* are doctrinal in content and to a great extent little more than versified prose. It is in the *Poemata historica* that Gregory reveals his poetic gifts. Many of these are autobiographical and let us look into the fine sensitive soul of the author. His longest poem, *De vita sua* (Of His Life) deserves to rank with the *Confessions* of Augustine. The poem *Christus patiens* (Christ Suffering), though associated with Gregory, is not his work.

Of his orations, nos. 27–31 are the great dogmatic orations. They are directed against the Eunomeans and Macedonians and defend orthodox teaching on the Trinity. It is these orations that earned for him the title, "the theologian." Most of his other orations are panegyrics, some for ecclesiastical feasts and others for some of the saints or his friends. Among these are panegyrics which eulogize the Machabees, Cyprian, and Athanasius; and funeral orations for his father, his brother, and sister, and Basil the Great. He wrote orations against Julian the Apostate; other orations deal with situations in his life, e.g., one in apology for his flight and one of resignation from the see of Constantinople addressed to clergy and laity of that city. The Orations are, except his *De vita sua*, the best source for the study of the man.

Gregory adheres strictly to Scripture and tradition in his theology. Of philosophy he says that its introduction into the Church is like the plagues of Egypt. In his exposition of the doctrine of the Trinity and the Incarnation, he is far clearer and more exact than his fellow Cappadocians. He is a great champion of the divine maternity of Mary. He teaches the value of the veneration of Mary and the saints. He says, "Rome presides over the whole world." In speaking of original sin, he seems not to be sure that the soul of an infant is stained. He seems uncertain, too, about the eternity of hell. He is severe about remarriage. He is clear and unequivocal about transubstantiation and Mass as a sacrifice.

4. CYRIL OF JERUSALEM (d. 386)

Cyril was born around the year 315; he was educated in his native Jerusalem, ordained about 345, and consecrated bishop of Jerusalem in 348 by Acacius of Caesarea, with whom he soon came into conflict. A staunch defender of Nicea, Cyril was deposed and exiled by synodal decree in 357 and 360, and again by the Emperor Valens in 367. The last term of exile lasted until 378. In 381 he attended the Council of Constantinople. He died March 18, 386.

Cyril was not a great theologian, nor an accomplished writer or orator. His claim to fame rests on his famous twenty-four *Catecheses* which were taken down by one of the auditors and thus preserved for us. These show Cyril to have been a master catechist, an expert at lucid exposition. Besides the *Catecheses* there is a homily on the dropsical man of John (chap. 5), and a letter to Emperor Constantius telling of a remarkable apparition of the Cross in Jerusalem. There are also four small fragments of homilies.

The *Catecheses* consist of an introductory lecture or *Protocatechesis*, followed by eighteen *Catecheses* to those to be illuminated or baptized and five mystagogical *Catecheses*. All these lectures were given in Lent and Easter of 348–350, as closely as the matter can be determined. The *Protocatechesis* is an introductory lecture addressed to all who aspired to baptism. It stresses the need for repentance and due preparation for the step to be taken. The next eighteen lectures were given during Lent. The first five deal with general matters such as sin, repentance, and faith. Lectures six to eighteen are an explanation of the Jerusalem Creed or *Symbolum*. The five mystagogical *Catecheses* were delivered during Easter week after the catechumens had been baptized. They treat of baptism (19–20), confirmation (21), the Eucharist (22), and Holy Mass (23). There is no evidence that originally there was a sixth lecture. Despite some manuscript evidence that ascribes the mystagogical *Catecheses* to John of Jerusalem, the successor to Cyril (386–417), the twenty-four lectures seem to be an organic whole and the work of one man, Cyril. The lectures are of the greatest importance doctrinally and for the liturgy.

5. EPIPHANIUS (c. 315–403)

Epiphanius was born near Eleutheropolis in Palestine. He visited the monks of Egypt in his youth. At the age of twenty he founded his own monastery in Eleutheropolis and served as its abbot for thirty years. In 367 the bishops of Cyprus elected him bishop of Salimina (Salamis) and metropolitan of the island. In 376–377 he was engaged in the fight against the error of his friend Apollinaris. Next we find him in Rome visiting Jerome and Paula. In 392, while preaching in Jerusalem, Epiphanius attacked Origen and thus began the bitter and acrimonius fight that arrayed Epiphanius and Jerome against Rufinus and John of Jerusalem. About the year 400 things grew worse when he was duped by the wily Theophilus of Alexandria, who stirred him up against the monks of the Nitrian desert and John Chrysostom. However, Epiphanius saw his error and left Constantinople before the Synod of the Oak had issued its condemnation (403). On the way home to Salamis he died.

Epiphanius was a learned and widely read man. He had the command of five languages: Greek, Syriac, Hebrew, Coptic, and even Latin to a considerable extent. His fiery temperament and unreasonable impetuosity, which his long and strict asceticism failed to conquer, made the calm objectivity necessary for scholarly work impossible for him. His narrow-mindedness is apparent in the part he played in the Origenist controversy and the violence with which he attacked the veneration of images. He considered this idolatry, and in his testament he anathematized anyone who would even gaze upon a picture of the Logos-God. His temperament made him suspicious of heresy everywhere, and he made capital of even the smallest inaccuracy of statement. It appeared impossible for him to see any viewpoint but his own. Since he lacked critical acumen and was a poor, even a tiresome writer, his works would be of little value if it were not for his use of many quotations. He thus saved much that would otherwise have been lost to us. He despised philosophy and theological speculation, but adhered rigidly to traditional doctrine. His writings are diffuse, verbose, and inaccurate.

In his lifetime, Epiphanius was regarded as a miracle worker and saint. His reputation for learning was widespread. He was a great devotee of the Blessed Mother and a witness to the universal belief in her perpetual virginity. He attacked the veneration of images with unreasoning vehemence, and his Trinitarian doctrine followed Basil's teaching of the procession of the Holy Spirit from the Father through the Son.

So popular were the writings of Epiphanius and so great was his reputation for learning that quite a number of spurious works were circulated in his name. Genuine works of Epiphanius are the *Ancoratus* or The Firmly Anchored Man, the *Panarion* or The Medicine Chest, *On the Weights and Measures of the Jews*, and *On the Twelve Precious Stones*. The first two are his most valuable writings and the last are respectively a biblical encyclopaedia and an allegorical interpretation of the twelve gems in the breastplate of the Old Testament highpriest. Recently there have been discovered fragments of three writings, a treatise, a letter to Theodosius I, and a testament addressed to his diocese, all of which violently attack the veneration of images. Only two letters have come down to us in Latin. Everything else attributed to him is apocryphal.

The *Panarion* is the most valuable. It treats of eighty heresies, including accounts of pagan schools of philosophy and Jewish sects. It has preserved many and extensive quotations. It concludes with a summary, the *Expositio fidei*. Another summary of the *Panarion* called the *Recapitulatio* is not genuine.

The *Ancoratus* is an elementary exposition of Catholic dogma containing many polemical digressions attacking heresies of the time. The work concludes with two creeds or baptismal symbols. The first is the Creed of Salamis (also called *Constantia*) and the other is a composition of Epiphanius himself. The former was adopted by Constantinople and thence spread through the East.

6. THEODORE OF MOPSUESTIA (428)

Theodore and John Chrysostom were fellow students under the pagan rhetorician Libanius and the great Diodorus of Tarsus, headmaster of the school of Antioch at its zenith. Theodore was born in Antioch, and he and Chrysostom spent some time together as ascetics. He left the solitude but his friend Chrysostom induced him to return. Later Theodore was ordained priest and exercised his office in Antioch until in 392 he was made bishop of Mopsuestia in Cilicia, at the instance of his old teacher Diodorus. He died in 428. At his death he was, like his teacher Diodorus, highly esteemed and regarded as orthodox. However, when his student Nestorius began to preach his errors, the storm broke over Theodore also. Cyril of Alexandria bitterly attacked him, and the fifth Ecumenical Council held in Constantinople in the year 553 condemned his writings together with the "Three Chapters." The result was that practically all his literary output was destroyed or lost.

Today it is impossible to evaluate Theodore's teaching objectively. How much he has been the victim of association with Nestorius and of misconstruction of his teaching by others can perhaps never be established. It has been shown, however, that he was an effective defender of orthodoxy against Apollinarianism and a staunch defender of the teachings of Chalcedon on the two natures in Christ. It has also been demonstrated that many of the writings on which his condemnation in 553 was based, were not his work or were interpolated so that they did not express his true position. During his lifetime and for some time after his death, he was regarded as the greatest exegete of the school of Antioch. The Nestorian Church still speaks of him as the exegete par excellence.

Theodore, it appears, wrote commentaries on practically all the books of the Bible and also published a considerable number of theological treatises. A commentary on the minor prophets is the only work preserved in its entirety in the original Greek. Other works that have come down in translation or that can be reclaimed in great part from *Catenae* are commentaries on the Psalms, on the Fourth Gospel, and on the Pauline Epistles. Of his theological treatises there remain in Syriac translation only a *Disputatio cum Macedonianis* and some catechetical lectures after the pattern of the *Catecheses* of Cyril of Jerusalem. A work entitled *De Incarnatione* was destroyed in World War I.

The verdict of the Council of Constantinople was that Theodore was the originator of Nestorianism together with his teacher Diodorus of Tarsus. As an exegete Theodore has generally been tagged as a rationalist but it has never been clearly established to what extent he made extreme application of the exegetical principles of the Antiochian school.

7. THEODORET OF CYRUS (c. 460)

Theodoret is another victim of association with Nestorius. Though it cannot be established that he and Nestorius were fellow students under Theodore of Mopsuestia, his personal loyalty to his friend Nestorius got him into various troubles. Some of his writings, notably his attack on Cyril of Alexandria and the Council of Ephesus, as well as several letters and sermons were condemned by the Council of Constantinople in 553, along with the "Three Chapters." His orthodoxy and his personal holiness of life were never questioned. He was a prolific writer, accomplished orator, and one of the last great theologians of the East.

Born in Antioch about 393, he received his early training there and in 423 he was, against his will, made bishop of Cyrus, a small city near Antioch. He was busy with the zealous care of his diocese until 431 when he entered the Christological controversies in defense of his friend Nestorius by attacking the "Twelve Anathematisms" of Cyril of Alexandria. This work has been lost. The next year he again attacked Cyril and also the Council of Ephesus in five books. Theodoret never subscribed to the teachings of Nestorius. In fact, he himself drew up the formula of union in 433 but did not sign it until the next year when he knew that Nestorius would not then be condemned. When Eutyches appeared on the scene Theodoret attacked his error resolutely. For this he was then deposed by the so-called "Robber Synod" of Ephesus (449). He appealed to the pope and after declaring his position in opposition to the errors of Nestorius, he was seated at the Council of Chalcedon as an "orthodox teacher." Nothing is known of his last years.

Theodoret was regarded by many as one of the greatest exegetes of his time, though his work is not characterized by any great originality. He combined exegetical principles of both Antioch and Alexandria in his work. He has left complete commentaries on the Psalms, on all the Prophets, on the Canticle of Canticles and on the Pauline Epistles. Besides his commentaries he wrote treatises (*Quaestiones*) on various problems in the historical books of the Old Testament.

Most of Theodoret's polemical works have been lost. But, some of his attacks on Cyril can be reclaimed from the latter's work. The same source preserved a two part work of Theodoret *On the Holy and Vivifying Trinity* and *On the Incarnation*. Two treatises, *Expositio rectae fidei* (Exposition of the True Faith) and *Quaestiones et responsiones ad orthodoxos* (Questions and Answers to the Orthodox) have been salvaged from among collections of the writings of Justin. The *Eranistes seu Polymorphus*, or simply *The Beggar*, is a dialogue in four books between a Monophysite, who is the beggar because he has gathered his teachings from earlier heresies, and an orthodox teacher who easily refutes the beggar. Theodoret has also left us the last great and most elegant apology for Christianity against paganism, *Graecorum affectionum curatio* (The Art of Treating Greek Distempers) in twelve books. More than a hundred pagan writers are cited and the pagan teachings on all points of philosophy and theology are confronted with Christian truth.

Theodoret enjoyed a great reputation as an orator but only a few fragments of his sermons remain. Of these we have only his ten "Orations on Providence" given in Antioch in 431. He has left 209 Greek and twenty-seven Latin letters. These are very valuable for a study of the fifth century. However, his greatest contribution to Church history is his *Historia ecclesiastica*, covering the years 325–428 in five books. The work is of an anti-heretical and apologetic bent. His presentation is often sketchy and marred by inaccuracies. He must have often used the same sources as Socrates and Sosomen, as similarities with their work show. He has left also a *Historia religiosa*, an history of mona-chism similar to the *Historia Lausiaca* of Palladius and a short history of heresies in five books (*Hereticarum fabularum com-pendium*), of which the last book is valuable for the history of dogma. It is a systematic exposition of Catholic dogma.

8. JOHN CHRYSOSTOM (354–407)

Chrysostom is the greatest father of the East. The West can match only Augustine with him. His literary output was greater, as far as literary remains show, than all the other Greek fathers in range and perhaps in volume also. One of the greatest ec-clesiastics of the Church, he distinguished himself as an ad-ministrator, as pastor, as preacher, and as a champion of the true faith. His outstanding ability as an orator gained for him the appellation Chrysostom, the Golden Mouthed. He has been so called since the sixth century. He is the outstanding exegete of the East by all odds. Isidore of Pelusium remarks that if Paul could have selected his own interpreter he would unhesi-tatingly have chosen John. He stood as a towering oak through the turmoil and turbulence of his times and had few equals in learning and sanctity.

The astounding thing in the career of Chrysostom is the gigantic accomplishments of his comparatively short life. He died in his early fifties, spent about twelve years in the priesthood at Antioch, and served seven years as patriarch of Constantinople. His life falls into five periods. Born around 354, he lived as a layman until 372 when he was baptized. During these years he was trained by his saintly mother, a widow. He studied under the philosopher Andragathius and under Libanius, the last and greatest of pagan rhetoricians. For his Christian studies he had Diodorus of Tarsus, the famed teacher of Antioch. Here he was a fellow student of Theodore of Mopsuestia. After his baptism he devoted himself to an ascetical life, first at home, then for four years under the direction of an ascetic and finally two years alone. During this period Theodore of Mopsuestia was with him for a time. The third period began when in 381 he was ordained deacon, followed by ordination to the priesthood in 386. It lasted until his call to Constantinople in 397. The period of his episcopate is the most important of his life and lasted until his exile, Sept. 6, 404. The last years of his life were spent in dreary exile, first in Cucusus in the valley of the Taurus in Armenia. He did not reach his second point of exile, Pityus on the eastern shores of the Black Sea. He died Sept. 14, 407, while en route. And now it should be added, to throw full light on what Chrysostom accomplished, that he was physically not very robust and that there are many references to his ill health in his orations and letters. In fact, had his health allowed, Chrysostom might never have taken holy orders but remained an ascetic solitary.

Aside from Chrysostom's orations and letters, the best sources for information about his career as priest and bishop are Palladius who wrote his life, Jerome (*Vir. ill.*) and the ecclesiastical histories of Socrates, Sosomen, and Theodoret of Cyrus. They reveal that Chrysostom's Antiochian period was almost as important and fruitful as his years in the episcopate and patriarchate of Constantinople. Flavian, bishop of Antioch, held John in high esteem and entrusted many tasks to him. It was Chrysostom who resolved the Miletian schism, shouldered many of Flavian's burdens and became the leader of the Antiochian Church, although at first he was only a deacon. As priest he brought about many reforms and it was he who quelled the disorders attending the erection and destruction of the emperor's statues in 387, when he preached the famous discourses "On the Statues." During this period he produced much of his distinguished exegetical work and wrote many of his orations. He preached every Sunday and often during the week, especially in Lent. By his blameless life and by his eloquence he effected a great change in the Christian living of Antioch, which had been notoriously bad. Even in exile in far-off Cucusus, he maintained contact with the city and was a great influence for good.

Called to Constantinople by popular demand, in spite of great intrigue and opposition in some circles, Chrysostom at once set about, as Palladius says, to sweep the stairs from the top down. He cut all expenses in the patriarchal household. He took vigorous and decisive action to eliminate abuses in the life of the clergy. He brought order into the monastic life at Constantinople and corrected abuses among the widows of that city. Then he turned his attention to his flock. The rich and upper classes heard things that only Chrysostom was unafraid to tell them. He cared for the poor, and with what he himself had saved built hospitals and other institutions for the care of the underprivileged.

All this time his enemies were busy. The Empress Eudoxia was constantly trying to undermine his influence but John did not hesitate to liken her to Jezebel. The unscrupulous minister Eutropius was always trying to cause Chrysostom trouble but in the end had to crawl to him for protection. No less active were his enemies among the ecclesiastics, such as Acacius of Berea, Antiochus of Ptolemais, Severian of Gabala, and Macarius Magnes. They were always in bitter opposition because of the prominence and authority Constantinople had under Chrysostom. However, they failed to find a leader for concerted action and a pretext or occasion for a public and outright attack on the Patriarch. Both pretext and leader presented themselves when the wily Theophilus of Alexandria became involved with the monks of the Nitrian desert in the incipient Origenist controversy. Theophilus put the blame on Chrysostom and dared to summon him to account, a summons which was three times ignored. Thereupon in 402 Theophilus met with thirty-six of his followers and deposed

Chrysostom at the so-called synod of "The Oak," so named after the country estate where the meeting was held. The emperor confirmed the decree and banished John. That same night, it seems, some disaster befell the city and, within a few days, Chrysostom the exile was recalled and received in triumph.

The ensuing peace was a troubled one and did not last long. Things took so bad a turn that the emperor again took a hand in the matter. There had been rioting on Good Friday and the baptism of three thousand catechumens was violently stopped. The emperor banished Chrysostom again and the saint left the city on Sept. 6, 404. From his place of exile John kept in close touch with Antioch and his friends in Constantinople. It was therefore decided to change his place of exile. But he died on the way to the Black Sea, Sept. 14, 407. On Jan. 27, 439, the Emperor Theodosius II had Chrysostom's remains brought back in triumph to Constantinople; kneeling in prayer, Theodosius II publicly asked God's forgiveness for the wrong done the saint by his parents, the former emperor and Eudoxia.

Chrysostom's death did not end the fight. His followers, called Johannites by their enemies, had to suffer much until Pope Innocent I intervened. He ordered John's name restored to the diptychs of the cathedral and stopped the trouble by recognizing Atticus as the legitimate successor of Chrysostom.

Chrysostom's literary output was staggering and covered so wide a range that it is best to mention only the most important works and to group these roughly under three heads, viz., exegetical writings, sermons, and theological treatises. His letters naturally form a separate group. There are 236 letters directed to more than a hundred addressees. Most of them are short and were written during his exile. They give information about their author and are an attempt to bring comfort to his friends. Perhaps the most noteworthy are the two addressed to Pope Innocent I and the seventeen sent to the widow and deaconess Olympias, one of John's most staunch followers. It might be mentioned that so great was Chrysostom's literary reputation, that the number of apocryphal works attributed to him is colossal. There are any number of series of homilies on the Old Testament books attributed to him that are of doubtful authenticity, to say the least. There are several hundred printed sermons under his name and another five to six hundred that have not yet been edited and published. Finally, the divine liturgy of St. John Chrysostom, which is still in frequent use in the Eastern Churches, stands as a tribute to the man though it certainly is not his work.

The exegetical works of Chrysostom apply the principles of the Antiochian school in sober fashion. They are marked by a clarity of exposition and a practicality of application of Scripture. This makes them of great value to both the trained exegete and to the ordinary reader. He has left numerous series of homilies on Genesis, on the Psalms, and on Isaias. The New Testament however, was Chrysostom's favorite and here it was St. Paul who elicited his greatest enthusiasm. There are more than 250 magnificent homilies on all the Pauline Epistles. Of these the homilies on Romans are his greatest work. Besides this there are ninety homilies on Matthew, seven homilies on Luke, eighty-eight homilies on John, and three series on the Acts of the Apostles.

John's sermons and discourses are too numerous to mention by title. They cover the widest range. There are more than a hundred. Some are occasional discourses such as the twenty-one *On the Statues*, two *On the Occasion of the Fall of Eutropius*, and a stirring sermon on the invincibility of the Church preached by Chrysostom just before going into exile. There are numerous panegyrics. These eulogize the saints of the Old Testament, the martyrs, and great bishops of the Church among whom Paul (there are seven in honor of him) and John's beloved teacher Diodorus are not missing. The majority of Chrysostom's discourses concern ascetical and moral topics, such as repentance, superstition, the circus and theaters, almsgiving, etc. There are sermons for the great feasts of the liturgical year, Epiphany, Easter, and the Ascension. A Christmas sermon mentions that this feast had come to the East from the West within the past ten years. There are also some dogmatic and polemical discourses: twelve on the incomprehensibility of God, against the Anomoeans, and on the unity of nature between Father and Son, and eight sermons warning against the customs and practices of the Jews. There are also two Catecheses.

The most important treatise of Chrysostom is the *De sacer-*

dotio (On the Priesthood), written in 386 in the form of a dialogue to extol the priesthood, in six books. It is the most popular of all his writings and, though imitated by others, it has never been matched. Treatises *On Vanity* and *On How Parents Should Rear Their Children* deal with the disorders in Antioch. The second part could be read by parents today with great profit. There are three works in defense of monasticism, viz., *On the Enemies of Monasticism*, in three books, *On Compunction*, in two books and two *Paranaeses ad Theodorum lapsum* (Exhortations to the Fallen Theodore) which induced his friend Theodore of Mopsuestia to return to the ascetical life. On virginity Chrysostom wrote: *The Virginal State, To a Young Widow*, and *De non iterando conjugio* (On Perseverance in Widowhood). Two disciplinary treatises dealing with abuses indicated by their titles are: *Ad eos qui apud se habent virgines subintroductae* (To Those Who have Dedicated Virgins with Them) and *Quod regulares feminae viris cohabitare non debeant* (That Deaconesses should not live with Men). He deals with the problem of suffering in three books: *Ad Stagirium a daemone vexatum* (To Stagirius, a Monk afflicted by a Demon), *Quod nemo laeditur nisi a se ipso* (That no one is hurt except by Himself), and *Ad eos qui scandalizati sunt ob adversitates* (To Those Who are shocked by Adversities).

Turning now to the theology of Chrysostom, it should be observed at once that a minute perusal and detailed scrutiny of each and every statement of so voluminous a writer must turn up some unsatisfactory or even questionable utterances. It must be called to mind also that many of his works were taken down in shorthand and were not meant for publication, or were not given the benefit of a final revision by the author. So it is not surprising that statements of Chrysostom have been taken from their context and misconstrued. The Pelagian, Julian of Eclanum, has done this in his controversy on original sin with Augustine. Some theologians have been dissatisfied with what John did not say about the Blessed Mother. Others have depreciated his attitude about the primacy of Rome. Statements of his emphasizing the necessity of interior contrition and confession to God have been cited against the Catholic teaching on the sacrament of penance.

Chrysostom can be evaluated as a theologian only if one makes a coherent analysis of all his writings. Moreover, each statement of his must be taken in its remote and proximate context. Then there emerges one of the greatest theologians of the Church. After him the East seemed to produce only inferior theologians. On one thing the centuries are agreed—John Chrysostom is the "Eucharistic Doctor."

Syriac and Armenian Writers

As Christianity spread throughout the East, there gradually developed a vernacular literature in each country. At first there were naturally translations of the Bible. Next followed translations from Greek ecclesiastical literature and later there developed original writings. Coptic, Ethiopic, Georgian, and Arabic Christian literature came to bloom after our period. The early years of Christianity produced only translations for the most part in these languages. The Bible, of course, liturgical, disciplinary treatises and some exegetico-heretical works were translated from the Greek to meet the most immediate needs of the early Church in these tongues. We shall consider Syriac and Armenian literature.

1. SYRIAC WRITERS

Christianity was established in Mesopotamia by the middle of the second century. It grew and developed normally until the outbreak of Nestorianism and Monophysitism in the fifth century. In the middle of the seventh century the Arabs took over. We are interested here only in the first six centuries of Syriac literature. The second and third centuries produced only a few original works outside of translations of the Bible. See Tatian and Bardesanes. But the succeeding centuries show considerable literary activity, chiefly Nestorian and Monophysite. We shall give Ephraem separate treatment and list the other Syriac writers alphabetically with no regard for their chronology.

Aphraates the Persian Sage, Babai the Great, Balaeus (Syr. Balai), Bar Chatar, Barsauma, Cyrillonas, Dionysius of Tellmahre, George, bishop of the Arabs, Henana of Adiabene, Ibas, Isaac of Amida, Isaac of Antioch, Isaac of Edessa, Isaac of Nineveh, James

Baradaeus, James of Edessa, James of Sarug, John of Asia, John Bar Cursus, Mar Aba, Maruthas, Miles, bishop of Susa, Narsai, Paul of Tella, Paulonas, Philoxenus of Mabug, Rabbulas, Sahdona, Simeon Bar Apollon, Simeon Bar Sabbae, Stephen Bar Sudaili, Thomas of Edessa, Thomas of Heraclea, Zenobius the Deacon. Besides these writers the following anonymous works should be mentioned. These are biographies of Alexius (reproducing the legend), of Eusebius of Samosata, of Peter the Iberian, and the life of Rabbulas by a cleric of about 450.

2. EPHRAEM (373)

Ephraem is the greatest writer of the Syriac Church. He was born near the year 306, and was ordained a deacon about 338. When the Persians took Nisibis in 363, he fled to Edessa and brought that famous school to its heights. In 373 he died and, in 1920, he was proclaimed a Doctor of the Universal Church. His countrymen had already come to speak of him as the "Lyre of the Holy Spirit," the "Prophet of the Syrians," the "Syriac Chrysostom," the "Eloquent Mouth" and the "Column of the Church." There are stories about his travels and other tales but we know little of his life.

Ephraem was a voluminous writer but most of his literary remains still await critical editing and publication. He wrote many and extensive commentaries, treatises, orations, and hymns. A large number of these are in poetical form. Others have been left us in translation only. This fact and the large number of works falsely circulated under his name are proof of Ephraem's great popularity and importance. His writings are all permeated with moral and ascetical exhortation.

Ephraem's chief prose compositions are exegetical. Sections of these have been preserved in the *Catenae*. The only larger exegetical work of Ephraem is his commentaries on Genesis and parts of Exodus in Syriac, on the *Diatessaron of Tatian*, on Acts and the Pauline Epistles in Armenian translation. As an exegete Ephraem strove to elucidate the literal sense, though his Old Testament work does much moralizing.

Ephraem is the greatest poet of the Eastern Church and most of his writings are in poetical form. They are either *Mimre*, i.e., poetical homilies and discourses, or *Madrasche*, i.e., instructions in the form of hymns. The form of the *Mimre* is characterized by having the same number of syllables to the line, generally seven. The *Madrasche* has a recurring refrain as its distinctive feature.

Ephraem attacked the Gnostics, Arians, Mani, Bardesanes, Marcion, and Julian the Apostate in his polemical writings. There are fifty-six *Madrasche* and three prose works against Marcion, Mani, and Bardesanes. He has left a number of homilies on individual passages of Scripture and there are numerous penitential sermons and panegyrics on martyrs and for holydays. There are fifty-one hymns *De virginitate* and many hymns composed for processions and funerals. He also composed a large number of hymns meant to be used in the liturgy. Finally, there are seventy-seven *Carmina Nisibena*, most important for the history of the Syriac Church. The collection is complete except for numbers 8 and 22–24. The *Carmina* covers the ravaged years 338–363 and narrates the history of two noted hermits, Abraham of Kidun and Julian Sabas. There is also a Testament of Ephraem which would seem to be substantially genuine.

Ephraem is important in the study of sacramental dogma. He is an exponent of the traditional and orthodox teaching on the Trinity and the Incarnation. However, his greatest contribution is in the field of Mariology. He has been called the Bard of Mary. There are twenty homilies and twelve prayers to the Queen of Heaven in which he treats all the essential points of Mariology. It is in these that Ephraem brings all his brilliant gifts as a poet into play, especially in the prayers.

3. ARMENIAN WRITERS

Christianity came to Armenia toward the end of the third century. Gregory the Illuminator (c. 332) is regarded as the apostle of Armenia. The Armenians used the Greek, Syriac, and Persian alphabets until Mesrop (440) invented the Armenian alphabet and script. Mesrop and the patriarch Sahak the Great (390–439) gathered together a group of clerics and set them to the work of translating the most important Greek and Syriac writings. Later these men became known as the "holy translators." Thus came the beginning of Armenian Christian literature. Before this the Bible, the Gospels first, and some liturgical works had been translated into Armenian. Here follows an alphabetical list of Armenian writers with no regard for their dates.

Agathangelos, Ananias, Chosrowig, David the Armenian, Eliseus the Doctor, Eznik of Kolb, Faustus of Byzantium, Sahak (Isaac) the Great, John Mandakuni, Korium, Lazarus of Pharp, Mambre Versanogh, Mesrop, Moses of Chorene, and Wardapet.

4. MESROP (440)

Mesrop, also called Mashtots, royal secretary, monk, and missionary was the inventor of the Armenian alphabet and with Sahak (Isaac) the Great, the founder of Armenian Christian literature. Under the guidance of Mesrop and Isaac a group of scholars called the "holy translators" made available to Armenian readers the outstanding works of Greek and Syriac writers. An Armenian liturgy was produced, the New Testament was translated from a Syriac text dependent on the *Diatessaron*. Gradually the whole Bible was made available in Armenian and under the impetus of Mesrop and Isaac, an original Armenian literature appeared. There are twenty-three orations and letters, formerly attributed to Gregory the Illuminator, left of Mesrop's work. His life was written by his disciple, Korium.

- SECTION III -

The Western Writers

Introduction

The fourth century is the age of the great fathers in the West no less than it was in the East. The same factors contributed to the growth of Christian literature in both spheres. The Church came to find peace and official recognition externally. Internally the West was not troubled nearly so much by the bitter and acrimonious battles of schism and heresy as the East. Donatism was confined to Africa and the Western invasion of Arianism was by no means so protracted and vicious as its onslaughts in the East.

The patristic literature of this period in the West follows the pattern of history. In Africa it is to a considerable extent controversial, but elsewhere it is for the most part undisturbed by heresy and schism. Generally it is positive. Moral questions, points of dogma, and ascetical matters are treated according to the interests of the Western Church. These interests are cosmopolitan. The writers of this period are in constant touch with the East and, though few of them read Greek, they all are acquainted with the great works of the Eastern Church in translation.

Four great figures, Hilary, Ambrose, Jerome, and Augustine dominate the West. Each is surrounded by a circle of friends and, it goes without saying, each had also his enemies and antagonists. Of these Augustine is simply unsurpassed. Ambrose and Augustine were in constant communication with the East; Jerome spent most of his life at Bethlehem, and Hilary was exiled to the East. It may be that had the East been equally close to the West, the great schism might not have happened.

We shall survey the period in eight chapters:

I. Heretical and Anti-Heretical Writers

The great Christological and Trinitarian controversies of the East did not go without repercussions in the West, but the heresies native to the Western Church were more of a practical nature than a matter of erroneous speculation. The Eastern, chiefly the Greek theologians, were preoccupied with the philosophical and theological exploration of the triune Godhead and the Incarnation, while the West concentrated on anthropological questions. The Greek theologians wrestled with the questions, who and what is God and what did He do for man and how did He do it? The Western group grappled with the questions, how did God save man; how do God's grace and human effort work together in man's salvation? The Easterners were engrossed in theoretical theological speculation, while the Westerners devoted their efforts to practical moral problems. These trends are reflected in the heresies that beset the West.

It is of interest to note that these heresies developed first in the land where ancient Christian moral theology has its beginnings, the land of Tertullian, North Africa. Here Montanism had gained a foothold and ensnared the great Tertullian himself. Here the controversy over the rebaptism of heretics and the question of the readmission of sinners to the Church raged violently. Fundamental to these controversies was the question: What is the relationship of the sanctity of the Church to the overall and average weakness of man? Out of this ferment rose Donatism and the error of Priscillian and his followers. Pelagianism, though it originated in Rome and later spread to Africa and Europe, is related to the same problem. Pelagius, however, answered the question by an extreme and pure naturalism.

Donatism began as an ecclesiastical schism and its historical development belongs to Church history. The name derives from Donatus, called the Great. Donatism answered the question concerning the holiness of the Church by maintaining that this sanctity exists only when and where the members of the Church are holy. The Donatists insisted that all public sinners must therefore be excluded from the Church. They insisted on rebaptism and declared that all sacraments administered by sinful ministers are invalid. Claiming to be the only true and sinless church, they set up their own ecclesiastical organization and devastated the Catholic Church of Africa for decades, until the mighty Augustine broke their strength.

Priscillian gathered a band of fanatics and formed a secret group that assembled only in secret meetings. These were characterized by an unreasoned, emotional pietism and claimed to have attained perfection through their extreme and fanatical rigorism. They condemned all sense pleasure and earthly goods. They indulged in all manner of violent mortification, including intolerable fasting, even on the Lord's Day. Some members claimed special illumination and the gift of prophecy. Priscillian was put to death in 385 but his error persisted after him.

Pelagius was an Irish lay monk who came to Rome in the fifth century. Here he proposed his solution to the problem of man's cooperation in his salvation. Though he led an austere and blameless life and is called a saint by Augustine, his system is anything but Christian. It is pure naturalism. He maintained that human nature such as it is can avoid sin and gain merit for heaven. A life led in conformity with nature will lead man to salvation, he said. Hence, grace is unnecessary, redemption is not needed, and the result of all his teaching is that Christianity is nothing. He came to his conclusion by a denial of the effects of original sin. The sin of Adam, he taught, was a purely personal matter and in no way affected human nature. Pelagius was condemned at the Synod of Carthage in 416 to which Pope Innocent subscribed. His error had also spread to the East and was there condemned in 431 by the ecumenical Council of Ephesus. Before Pelagianism died out, it had been modified to Semi-Pelagianism which taught that grace was indeed necessary to man but not for the beginning of conversion, nor for his perseverance. Many saintly theologians of the West were attracted to this modified form of the error but Augustine, the Doctor of Grace, had already administered the deathblow.

Three lesser heretics are the following: Helvidius, against whom Jerome wrote, Jovinian, and Vigilantius. Helvidius denied the perpetual virginity of Mary and the superiority of the celibate state over marriage. Jovinian also taught the inferiority of celibacy, although he was a monk. He also propounded some ideas condemned by a Roman synod in 390 that seemed to imply salvation by faith alone and the uselessness of good works. Vigilantius denounced the monastic life and the homage paid to the saints. Jerome wrote against him also.

All the important fathers of the West dealt with these errors in some way or other. They will be studied in detail. Here we shall list first the heretical writers and next the defenders of orthodoxy.

The chief heretical writers were: Adimantus, Auxentius, Cresconius, Dictinius, Donatus the Great, Emeritus, Fastidius, Faustus, Felix, Gaudentius, Germinius of Sirmium, Helvidius, Instantius, Jovinian, Julian of Eclanum, Latronius, Macrobius, Maximinus, Parmenianus, Pelagius, Petilianus, Potamius of Lisbon, Priscillian, Secundinus, Sympronianus, Tychonius, Vigilantius, Vitellius, and Wulfilas or Ulfilas. The anonymous author of the *Opus imperfectum in Matthaeum* belongs to this group also.

The chief orthodox writers are: Audentius, Bachiarius, Eusebius of Vercelli, Eutropius, Faustinus, Gregory of Elvira, Hilary of Rome, Hosius of Cordoba, Hydatius or Idacius of Emerita, Ithacius, Lucifer of Calaris, Marcellinus, Olympius,

Optatus of Mileve, Pacian of Barcelona, Pastor of Galicia, Philastrius, Phoebadius, Syagrius, Turribius, Zeno of Verona, and C. Marius Victorinus.

II. The Popes of the Fourth and Fifth Centuries to Leo the Great

Damasus I and Leo the Great are the only popes of the fourth and the first half of the fifth century who have left any literary remains other than letters. Damasus I was the author of numerous metrical compositions, as mentioned earlier. Leo has left a varied literary legacy. The other popes of this period are: Anastasius I, Boniface I, Celestine I, Innocent I, Julius I, Liberius, Siricius, Sixtus III and Sosimus or Zosimus I.

LEO THE GREAT (440–461)

Leo is the greatest pope of these early centuries. His reign is characterized by the zeal he shows for the papacy. He laid the foundations for the powerful influence of the papacy in the West and throughout the world, later. Leo saved Rome from Attila in 452 and from Geiserich in 455. He was even more resolute in directing the internal affairs of the Church. He proceeded against the Pelagians and the Manichaeans in Italy, the Priscillianists in Spain, and straightened out ecclesiastical affairs in Gaul, Illyria, and North Africa. Even more important was the stand he took in the Monophysite controversy. When the heresy of Eutyches sprang up he at once supported Flavian and outlined the correct Catholic teaching in his famous *Epistola dogmatica ad Flavianum* (ep. 28) in 449. He condemned the proceedings of the rump synod held that year under Dioscorus, the friend of Eutyches. It was Leo who called it the "Robber Synod." At Chalcedon (451) the greatest ecumenical council up to that time, he sent his legate to preside and unhesitatingly rejected its Canon 28 which tried to give the patriarch of Constantinople a position equal to the pope in honor, if not in authority. There is much more in the records to show his firm rule over the universal Church and his vindication of the jurisdiction of the bishop of Rome.

The *Epistola dogmatica* is Leo's greatest work, but he has left us five other dogmatic epistles. When the "Dogmatic Epistle" was read at the Council of Chalcedon the assembly cried out: "This is the faith of the fathers and of the apostles. . . . Peter has spoken through Leo." The other dogmatic epistles are numbered 59, 124, 129, 139, 165. There are altogether 173 items in the collection of his letters. Of these twenty are not genuine and some thirty are letters sent to Leo. All these letters show a clear picture of the reign of this pope who was the first to proclaim so often, so plainly, and so unequivocally the primacy of the bishop of Rome inherited from Peter.

There are ninety-six sermons. Most of these are short but all are marked by simple, majestic style, and sonorous eloquence. Though short they are full of thought because of their conciseness of composition. They deal with varied topics, dogmatic and moral. Many of them were delivered on feasts of our Lord and the saints. Others deal with Christological questions. Then there are sermons on fasting, almsgiving, the powers of the papacy, and eighteen (nos. 52–70) on the Passion.

The *Sacramentarium Leonianum* is not Leo's work. It is our earliest *Missale Romanum* and dates from about 550, but it is based on older materials from the fourth and fifth centuries.

The importance of Leo in theology for Christology and the papacy should be evident from what has been said. He is important equally for the development of Catholic teaching on Church-state relationship. The state, he taught, must aid the Church in maintaining discipline and true doctrine. He conceded the emperor the right to call a council but always insisted on the supremacy of the Church in the spiritual domain. In disciplinary matters, it is interesting to note that Leo decreed that baptism should be administered only at Easter and Pentecost, except in cases of necessity. He was also obliged to correct an abuse that required privately confessed sins to be made the object of public penance. Leo seems also to have been the first of the fathers to make mention of the Ember Days, observed four times a year.

III. Gallic and Italian Writers

In this chapter Ambrosiaster, Hilary of Poitiers, John Cassian, Nicetas of Remesiana, Vincent of Lerins, and Peter Chrysologus will be discussed. Other writers of Gaul and Italy will be listed. They are: Arnobius Jr., Eucherius of Lyon, Evagrius Priest, Firmicus Maternus, Hilary of Arles, Maximus of Turin, and Salvian of Marseilles.

1. AMBROSIASTER (c. 370)

Ambrosiaster is so named because of his commentaries on the thirteen (Hebrews is missing) epistles of Paul which were handed down among the works of Ambrose. The author is unknown and wrote around 370. Augustine believed him to be Hilary of Poitiers. A Decimus Hilarianus Hilarius, prefect of Rome in 408, and Evagrius of Antioch have been proposed as the author. More generally he is thought to be a convert Jew who relapsed into Judaism after he had written a short treatise on the Trinity and Incarnation entitled *Fides Isaatis ex Judaeo*. Whoever he was, Ambrosiaster was an excellent exegete and the author of another good exegetical study entitled *Questiones Veteris et Novi Testamenti* (Questions on the Old and New Testament). He is an important witness to the pre-Hierominian Latin text of Pauline letters and to the pre-Augustinian interpretation of those letters.

2. HILARY OF POITIERS (c. 315–367)

Hilary is justly called "the Athanasius of the West." He was like Athanasius in firmness yet goodness of character. It was he who stopped the inroads of Arianism and broke that heresy's power forever in Gaul and throughout the West. Born about 315 of a rich and prominent family, he received a good education. His philosophical and rhetorical studies introduced him to the Scriptures and as a result of this study he was baptized and entered the Church. In 350, although recently married, he was unanimously chosen bishop of Poitiers by both clergy and people. He remained aloof from the synods of Arles (353) and Milan (355) which condemned Athanasius, but instead he rallied the orthodox bishops of Gaul against Saturninus of Arles, the leader of the Arians. For this Emperor Constantius banished him to Asia Minor where he spent the years 356–359 and wrote his monumental *De Trinitate*. He attended the synod of Seleucea (359) and next asked Constantius to be allowed to debate publicly with Saturninus. His request was refused and by this time the Arians had quite enough of him in the East. He was returned to his homeland. In 361 he again excommunicated Saturninus in a synod at Paris. This broke Arianism in Gaul. Next he presided at a synod in Milan (364) which would have deposed Auxentius of Milan, the leader of the Arians in Italy, had not the emperor intervened. But by this time Hilary had routed the Arians in the West. He died the next year, 367.

Hilary is the first great dogmatician and exegete of the West. As his early training would suggest he was a master of style and determined to express the sublime truths of Catholic dogma in language that befits these truths. His works are not easy reading because of the profundity of his thought. A distinctive characteristic of his writings is the knowledge of Scripture evident in them. He furthermore brought to the West the best of the theological speculation of the great minds of the East. Pius IX declared him a Doctor of the Church in 1851.

Besides being the first dogmatician and exegete of the West, Hilary is also its first hymnologist. Unfortunately only three hymns of his Hymn Book, the *Liber hymnorum* have been preserved. He must have found his inspiration to engage in hymnography during his stay in the East where this art and practice were far advanced. We have two acrostics, one on the Trinity, the other on baptism. The third hymn has as its theme Christ battling the devil.

The *De Trinitate*, in twelve books, is written with great enthusiasm and stamps Hilary as an original and independent thinker, but it is plain that he was influenced by the thinking of his Greek contemporaries. Strictly speaking it is more a work on Christology than the title would indicate and in fact its original title was *De fide* or *De fide adv. Arianos* (On the Faith Against Arians). Attached to the *De Trinitate* is usually found another work (c. 359) the *De synodis seu de fide Orientalium* (On the

Synods and the Faith of Orientals). The first part (1-65) seems to have been a memoir or memorandum for the bishops of Gaul and Britain, explaining and commenting on the various Christological formulas current in the East. The rest (66-91) is an appeal to Semi-Arians. It was irenic in tone and most conciliatory. For this he was attacked especially by Lucifer of Calaris, and in defense he wrote *Apologetica ad reprehensores libri de synodis responsa* (Apologetical Answers to the Critics of the *De synodis*), most of which has been lost.

Though Hilary adheres strictly to the literal sense in his use of Scripture in the *De Trinitate*, what remains of his extensive exegetical writings would seem to betray an inclination to allegorize. In these his chief purpose appears to have been the edification of his readers. All that is left is a commentary on Matthew, *Tractatus super Psalmos* (Treatise on the Psalms), covering more than half of the Psalms, and a *Tractatus mysteriorum* (Treatise on the Mysteries), a discussion of the types of the Old Testament.

What is perhaps Hilary's most valuable polemical and historical work for us today is the small *Contra Arianos vel Auxentium Mediolanum* (Against the Arians or Auxentius of Milan). As the title indicates, it is an account of Hilary's efforts to depose Auxentius and destroy Arianism at the synod of Milan. *Liber ad Constantium Augustum* (A Book for Constantius Emperor) asked permission of the emperor to debate with Saturninus, and the *Contra Constantium imperatorem* is Hilary's answer to the emperor's refusal to grant the permission. Hilary's *Opus historicum adversus Valentem et Ursacium* (Historical Book against Valens and Ursacius) is of little value because of its fragmentary condition.

3. JOHN CASSIAN (c. 435)

John Cassian is often called the "Father of Monasticism" in Gaul. The religious and cenobitical life had been introduced into that country before his time, but John Cassian gave the movement fresh impetus by his rules and by the monasteries he founded, one for men, another for women. Born in Scythia, modern Rumania, about 360, he got his early religious training in a monastery in Bethlehem and during ten years stay with the monks of Egypt. Chrysostom ordained him a deacon and sent him to Rome as his representative to Pope Innocent I in 404. Ordained a priest, he proceeded to Marseilles where he founded his two monasteries in 415. Through his writings, in elegant Latin, he gave a powerful stimulus to the monastic life in Gaul and became known as a spiritual director and trainer of monastics. But he also fathered Semi-Pelagianism in his writings. He died between 430 and 435 and soon was venerated as a saint.

Cassian has left only one dogmatic work, *De Incarnatione Domini contra Nestorium*, a refutation of the heresiarch in seven books written at the request of Leo I (c. 430) when the latter was still a Roman deacon. Cassian's principal works are *De institutis coenobiorum et de octo principalium vitiorum remediis* (On the Institutes of Monks and on Remedies for the Eight Chief Vices) in twelve books, and the twenty-four *Collationes Patrum* (Interviews with the Fathers). The former (written 419–426) reports on the monasteries of Egypt and Palestine in the first four books. It tells of the way of life and the rules and regulations that obtained in these monasteries, going into details of dress, of prayer-practices, of Psalm-singing, of conditions for the reception of members, and the daily pursuits of the monks. Books five to twelve, as the title indicates, discuss the eight capital sins and the measures to combat them.

The *Collationes* (402) in three parts is John's most important and popular work. Masters of the spiritual life have always held it in high esteem and strongly recommended its reading. Thus did Benedict, Gregory the Great, Cassiodorus, John Climachus, and many others. It relates interviews, most of them probably fictitious, with the most illustrious and best known figures of Egyptian monasticism. Cassian points out that mere seclusion from the world does not alone make for perfection. The virtues must be cultivated and brought to fruition. Perfection consists in perfect charity which is a gift of God. Charity and cleanness of heart are prerequisites for contemplation which in turn is the prelude to the vision of God. The eight capital sins, gluttony, lust, avarice, anger, sadness, sloth, vanity, and pride are the great obstacles to perfection. Cassian, along with Evagrius Ponticus and Augustine, is among the earliest fathers to engage in an analysis of sins according to their species and gravity.

What Cassian has to say in *Collatio* XIII fathered Semi-Pelagianism and made him regarded as the father of that error. This heresy infected his whole monastery of St. Victor and plagued the West until its condemnation at the council of Orange in 529. Cassian taught that man's free will and God's grace work together to man's salvation, but that the beginning or initial act of faith and the good disposition of the human will are purely the work of man. The error developed into a system which may be summed up briefly in these points. Man does not need grace to begin faith and sanctification, but only for their completion. God grants grace only according to man's merits and his good disposition to receive them. Final perseverance, therefore, is the fruit of man's own merits. The error attracted such men as Gennadius of Marseilles, Faustus of Riez, and even Vincent of Lerins.

4. NICETAS OF REMESIANA (c. 414)

Nicetas of Remesiana, a good friend of Paulinus of Nola whom he twice visited, was an hymnographer and did much to promote ecclesiastical chant. He wrote Latin, though he was an Easterner. His chief work is the six books of *Libelli instructionis* (Instructions for Catechumens). Book V is extant and is important for the history of the Apostles' Creed. The rest of the work has come down only in fragments of which *De ratione fidei* (On the Nature of Faith) and *De Spiritus Sancti potentia* (On the Power of the Holy Spirit) seem to belong to Book III. A work *Ad lapsam virginem* (To a Fallen Virgin), two sermons *De vigiliis* (On Vigils), *De utilitate hymnorum* (On the Use of Psalms), and a short treatise *De diversibus appellationibus Christi* (On the Names of Christ) also seem to be from his pen. The *Te Deum* has also been associated with his name.

5. VINCENT OF LERINS (c. 450)

There is nothing known of Vincent except that he was a monk and priest of the famous Monastery of Lerins, that he attacked Augustine's teaching on grace and that he was a Semi-Pelagian. But he is known to every theologian through his *Commoni-*

torium. In fact, he wrote two such works but the second is lost. However, the first contains an outline of the lost one. The title of the book indicates its nature. It is a memorandum, written as an aid to memory, setting forth the rule to be followed in establishing the true Catholic teaching in the dogmatic controversies of the time. This rule is the principle of tradition developed by Hippolytus, Irenaeus, and Tertullian earlier. From the summary of the second memorandum, this work seems to have been an application of this principle of tradition to Nestorianism and some other heresies. Vincent, though he does not mention his name, seems to be attacking Augustine's teaching on grace in chapters twenty-six and twenty-eight of this book.

An elementary summing up of Vincent's principles would be this. Scripture and tradition are the rule of faith. Scripture alone is insufficient because the Sacred Books are so profound in meaning that the Church and tradition are needed to establish the true sense of the Bible. The fact that there are as many and varied interpretations as there are interpreters proves the point, he says. He then gives us what has become the classic statement of the principle of tradition: *Magnopere curandum est, ut id teneamus, quod ubique, quod semper, quod ab omnibus creditum est, hoc est etenim vere proprieque catholicum* (2:5). (Above all we must see that we hold that which is always and everywhere believed by all, for this is truly and properly Catholic.) This is, indeed, a clear and basic statement but Vincent did not succeed in drawing out all the implications contained in it as dogmaticians can do today after centuries of history of dogma.

An earlier writing of Vincent, *Objectiones,* has been lost. It set forth Semi-Pelagian teaching and was refuted by Prosper of Aquitaine. In 1940 there was recovered a collection of anti-Nestorian statements by Vincent from the writings of Augustine. They are mostly Trinitarian and Christological texts. Some of them may have played a part in the development of the *Quicumque.*

6. PETER CHRYSOLOGUS (c. 450)

Peter Chrysologus, archbishop of Ravenna under Pope Sixtus III (432–440), died around 450. Little else is known of his life.

His feast is celebrated December 4 as a Doctor of the Church. He was very close to Leo I, and when Eutyches appealed to Peter Chrysologus in 449, the latter curtly assured him that nothing could be settled without the Roman Pontiff. He has left some 170 sermons, six in explanation of the Creed and five on the Our Father. Peter was a popular and eloquent preacher. His sermons cover a wide range of subjects and are characterized by a lively and colorful style. They are generally short but clear, practical, and to the point. There are sermons on the Creed, on the Mother of God, on John the Baptist, on the Incarnation, and on varied other topics.

IV. Historians and Chroniclers of the West

Most of the great writers of the West during the Golden Age engaged in some kind of historical writing or other. Thus Jerome continued the work of Eusebius and published his own *De viris illustribus*. Augustine gave us his monumental *De civitate Dei*. Historical writers to be given separate treatment in subsequent chapters of this book are Cassiodorus, Gregory of Tours, Isidore of Seville, and Prosper of Aquitaine. Other historians, histories, and chronicles are: *Catalogus Liberianus*, *Chronicon Horosii*, the *Chronographer of 354*, *Depositio episcoporum*, *Depositio martyrum*, Hilarianus, the Easter Table for the years 312–411, Hydatius, John of Biclaro, Marcellinus Comes, Marius of Avenches, Orosius, Paulinus of Milan, Sulpicius Severus, and Victor of Tunnuna.

V. Poets of the West in the Golden Age

The Church did not produce any significant or even worthwhile poetry before the fourth century. Even then the East had no poet worth noting except Gregory Nazianzen. Though it was ahead of the West in all other forms of Christian writing, the East lagged far behind in the output of poetical works. In the West the rise of liturgical poetry brought in its wake a general flowering of poetry. Poets found their themes chiefly in Sacred

Scripture, especially in the historical books of the Bible. The lives and sufferings of the saints and martyrs were frequent topics of poetry also. Lyric poetry developed rapidly. Even dogmatic and polemical writings were cast into verse; so were letters and epigrams. Other poetic forms also flourished. Yet, when all is said, the poetical output of the Golden Age is not too exciting. Certainly Prudentius was a true and gifted poet. Perhaps Paulinus of Nola and Sedulius could be ranked with him or near him. The majority of the poetry that has come down to us is, however, just average. Poets and poems of this period are: Ausonius, Claudius Claudianus, Commodianus, Cyprianus Gallus, Pope Damasus I, *De Jona, De Sodoma*, Endelechius, Hilary of Poitiers, Juvencus, the *Laudes Domini*, Paulinus of Beziers, Proba, and Claudius Marius Victor.

1. PAULINUS OF NOLA (353-431)

Paulinus of Nola was a member of a rich senatorial family. Through the influence of his teacher and friend Ausonius he became governor of Campania in 379. He was baptized in his native Bordeaux in 390 and soon thereafter decided to retire from the world. In 395 he and his wife Teresia moved to Nola in Campania, the burial place of Felix, his protector. Here they led a strict monastic life. Later he was ordained a priest in Spain and in 409 consecrated bishop. He died in 431, generally revered as a saint. He has left us thirty-five poems that show his refined taste and rare poetic ability. Fourteen *Carmina natalicia* (Feastday Poems) are dedicated to St. Felix. *Carmina* X and XI, both dedicated to Ausonius, contrast pagan and Christian culture. His some fifty letters are addressed to the greatest variety of persons. They are valuable for the study of the history of the liturgy and for the light they shed on the times.

2. PRUDENTIUS (348-c. 405)

Aurelius Prudentius Clemens was probably born in Calahorra, Spain, in 348. He studied rhetoric and law, served two terms as governor of a Spanish province, and rose to high office. He was close to Theodosius I, but at the age of fifty he left public life and went into retirement to use his talents for Christ. In the years 402–403 he made a pilgrimage to Rome to visit the graves of the martyrs. He died sometime after 405 in Spain. This information is to be found in a preface to an edition of his works that he prepared and published in eight books. His writings are arranged as follows in this edition:

I. *Cathemerinon liber,* i.e., Songs for the Day, contains twelve long, mostly lyrical poems in different meter. The first six are for the hours of the day, *Ad galli cantum* (At Cockcrow), *Matutinas* (Morning), *Ante cibum, Post cibum* (Before and After Meals), *Ad incensum lucernae* (Lamplighting), *Ante somnium* (Before Retiring). There are two Lenten hymns and one each for Christmas and Epiphany. The breviary hymns for Holy Innocents are taken from this last poem.

II. *Apotheosis* defends the doctrine of the Trinity.

III. *Hamartigenia,* as the title indicates, discusses the origin of sin and refutes Gnostic dualism.

IV. *Psychomachia* (The Battle for the Soul) is the oldest Latin Christian allegorical poem. It depicts a battle for a man's soul between the virtues and the vices.

V. *Contra Symmachum* attacks paganism in general.

VI. *Contra Symmachum* attacks the efforts of Symmachus, leader of the pagans in the Senate. Symmachus had written a *Relatio Symmachi* in which he petitioned the emperor to restore an altar to *Victory* in the senate chambers. Ambrose thwarted these efforts and Prudentius bases his argument on Ep. 17 and 18 of Ambrose.

VII. *Peristephanon* (On the Crown of Martyrs) contains fourteen poems of high literary quality in varied meter. Dramatic, lyrical, and epic strains are found in all of them. Their subject matter is the lives and sufferings of Spanish and Roman martyrs (Cyprian is included), described in vivid and highly realistic fashion. This is perhaps Prudentius' greatest work. Certainly it was the most popular. It served many later writers as a mine of material.

VIII. *Dittochaeon* (Double Nourishment) is a collection of descriptions of scenes from the Old and New Testaments. There are forty-nine, each in four hexameters. They seem to have been meant to be placed under paintings of these scenes and are of inferior quality.

3. SEDULIUS (fifth century)

Sedulius, a priest of southern Gaul, was one of the most gifted poets of his day. About 431 he published his *Paschale carmen* (Easter Hymn) in five books. It celebrates the heroic deeds of God in both the Old and the New Testaments. Later he enlarged the work and published it under the title *Paschale opus*. He has also left us two hymns. The first, "Elegy," draws parallels to Christ from the Old Testament and commemorates events and miracles in His life in fifty-five distychs. The other is an acrostic life of Christ in twenty-three verses of four lines each. From this work are taken the hymns *A solis ortus cardine* (Christmas) and *Crudelis Herodes Deum* (Epiphany) still used in the Roman Breviary.

VI. *Ambrose of Milan* (339–397)

Ambrose has left us ninety letters, and Paulinus of Milan, his former secretary, wrote his *Vita s. Ambrosii* in 422. These are the chief sources for the life of the great churchman. He was born in 339, probably in Treves where his father was *Praefectus praetorio Galliarum* (Governor of Gaul). After the early death of the father, his mother took her three children to Rome. Marcellina entered the convent, Satyrus died in 378 after a brief public career, and Ambrose, after an excellent training in rhetoric and law, became Consul of Liguria and Emilia with headquarters in Milan. When Auxentius, bishop of that city, died, a violent battle ensued between Catholics and Arians over the choice of a successor. When the governor, Ambrose, intervened he was unanimously chosen to succeed Auxentius. He was immediately baptized and eight days later ordained and consecrated bishop (Dec. 7, 374) despite all his remonstrances. His first step was to give his possessions to the poor and begin a strict ascetical life. Then he began the study of theology under the direction of Simplicianus, later to be his successor, and mastered especially the works of the Greek fathers. He died April 4, 397, and his influence lived long after him.

Jerome well said that with the installation of Ambrose as bishop of Milan, all Italy returned to the faith. He broke the efforts of a resurgent paganism and routed heresy, especially that of Arius. He put Church-state relationship on an even keel and crushed Caesaro-papism. The rhetorician Symmachus, leader of the pagan party in the senate, tried to restore the altar to the goddess of *Victory* in the senate chambers. Ambrose put swift stop to that. The Empress Justina attempted to procure a church in Milan for the Arians to restore their stature, but was thwarted by the bishop. Three emperors were his friends, sought his advice and help. One day the two greatest figures of Italy met, the one the emperor, the other a bishop. Theodosius I, justly called the Great, had in 390 ordered 7,000 citizens of Thessalonica massacred for participating in a revolt. The bishop, Ambrose, had at once pointed out the heinousness of the act. When the two met, the bishop remanded the emperor to the ranks of the public penitents, and the emperor, showing his claim to greatness, magnanimously confessed his guilt and did penance. Theodosius died in 395. Ambrose preached the funeral oration.

Ambrose had a genius for administration. The grandeur of his character and the loftiness of his view made any stand that he took impregnable. The Italy that he brought back to the faith had not long before been swept by Arianism; a synod at Milan had condemned Athanasius in 364. The emperor had come to think himself above the Church. Ambrose put him in his place saying "The emperor is within the Church, not above her." His accomplishments in the internal affairs of the Church are no less notable. His eloquent preaching stirred up Catholic living. It converted Augustine. Notable are Ambrose's contributions to the liturgy and ecclesiastical chant by means of both literary and musical compositions. The Rite of Milan still bears his name.

Ambrose was eminently the practical pastor, but Jerome was intemperate when he called him a scholar of second rank. Even his dogmatic writings show this practical bent. Against the Arians he directed, at the instance of the Emperor Gratian, *De fide ad*

Gratianum in five books (381) and *De Spiritu Sancto*. His *De Incarnatione Dominicae* is also against Arianism. He left three works for catechumens. *De mysteriis* treats of baptism, confirmation, and the Eucharist. *De sacramentis libri VI* treats of these same sacraments of initiation and explains the Lord's Prayer. The genuineness of the *Explanatio symboli ad initiandos* has been challenged. A last work *De paenitentia* is directed against the rigorism of the Novatians.

The most extensive literary legacy of Ambrose is his exegetical work. Here his masters were Philo and Origen, though he was also influenced by Basil the Great. His exegesis is chiefly moral exposition and, using the principles of Origen, he finds the most unsuspected lessons in Sacred Scripture. An illustration of this is his exposition of the history of Noe. For him the ark is man's body, the members of the body are found in the parts of the ark, and the animals within the ark are the passions of man.

Ambrose's exegetical work is concentrated on the Old Testament, though his only work on the New Testament is his most comprehensive. It is a commentary on Luke in ten books. Here his dependence on Origen can be noted especially in the first two books. The influence of Basil is discernible in the six books on the Hexaemeron. Other treatises that seem to have developed from his homilies are: *De Paradiso, De Cain et Abel, De Noe, De Abraham* (two books), *De Isaac et animo, De Jacob et vita beata* (two books), *De Joseph, De Patriarchis, De Helia et jejunio* (On Elias and Fasting), *De Nabuthe* (On Naboth), *De Tobia, De interpellatione Job et David, Apologia Prophetae David, Enarrationes in 12 psalmos* and *Expositio in Psalmum 118*. These works show his great interest in the Old Testament.

His chief moral-ascetical work is *De officiis ministrorum* in three books, an exposition of Christian ethics patterned after Cicero's work of the same title. The contents of the following works are indicated in their titles: *De virginibus ad Marcellinam sororem* (three books), *De viduis, De virginitate, De institutione virginis, Exhortatio virginitatis*. They are all inspiring expositions of the excellence of the unmarried state.

We have left only ninety-one letters of Ambrose. They are mostly of an official nature. Ambrose's orations are all valuable for a study of his times. There are two funeral orations for his brother Satyrus, a funeral oration for the assassinated Emperor Valentinian II (382) and the famed oration for the burial of Theodosius I (395). Another notable sermon is the *Sermo contra Auxentium de basilicis tradendis* (386), a sermon on the queen's plan to turn over a basilica to the Arians.

Ambrose introduced antiphonal singing into the liturgy and he may be called the father of ecclesiastical chant. He composed both words and music, being influenced in the latter by the liturgical chant of the East. By 386 ecclesiastical chant was in full bloom in Milan and thence spread throughout Europe. The label "Ambrosian" has been attached to so many hymns that it is not easy to sift out the spurious work. See the *Te Deum* and the Athanasian Creed. The *Exultet* of Holy Saturday is ascribed to him by some. Of certain Ambrosian authorship are the following well-known hymns: *Deus Creator omnium, Aeterne Rerum Conditor, Jam surgit hora tertia, Intende qui regis Israel.* The number of other hymns ascribed to him by scholars varies from eight to eighteen.

Finally, it should be mentioned that Ambrose composed a number of inscriptions in verse such as that in the baptistery of the church of St. Thecla in Milan. Other writings credited to Ambrose whose authorship cannot be established need not be listed here. The amazing thing is that a man as busy as he should have produced so large a literary output, and, furthermore, that the theology of his writings should be so consistently clear. Although his dogmatic writings are characterized by a dependence on the Greek fathers, the moral and ascetical writings of Ambrose display his individuality and independence of thought. He seems to have had little time or zest for philosophical and theological speculation, but his penetrating intellect is evident from the clarity of his theological conceptions. He is, for example, far ahead of his predecessor, Hilary of Poitiers, in his exposition of Christological teaching and Trinitarian doctrine. Ambrose may be said to be the best and most representative spokesman for both East and West among the fathers. He traversed the whole range of patristic theological writing before his time and, amazingly, sifted what he studied and came up with the best. This he gave to the universal Church and to posterity. It will be well to survey Ambrose's teaching point by point, but not in detail, in the following summary:

1. Faith is above reason and error comes through philosophy.

2. Ambrose is the great Trinitarian and Christological teacher of the West. Though Hilary is the outstanding champion of Nicea in the West, Ambrose surpassed him in some points. With crystal clarity he taught the union of two complete natures in the one person, Christ, and the procession of the Holy Spirit from Father and Son.

3. Original sin is universal and therefore children need to be baptized. In adults baptism of desire can replace the sacrament. Sometimes he seems to identify concupiscence with original sin, and there are statements by Ambrose that might appear to indicate an opinion that original sin will not be punished on Judgment Day.

4. The angels are mediators of heavenly aid and war against evil. The Church, each human being, and each state of life have a guardian angel. Angels belong to the City of God and war against the City of the Devil and this world.

5. Grace makes the soul the spouse of Christ, just as original sin makes us a partner of the devil. Faith alone, without baptism and devotion, avails nothing. Sometimes Ambrose appears to ascribe the beginning of salvation to ourselves, but all such statements must be taken in the framework of his general teaching. The same is true of what he says, at times, on original sin.

6. The Church is more than the external assembly of the faithful. She is the mother of the living, Eve raised to life from the wound in Christ's side. She is the channel of all grace. The bishop of Rome is the head of the Church and anyone not in communion with him is outside the Church.

7. Holy Mass is a true sacrifice. Ambrose coined the term *Missa* to designate the Sacrifice of the New Law.

8. Private penance seems not to be alluded to in Ambrose's works. Ambrose chides those who resort to public penance repeatedly. Even private or occult sins, though confessed privately, should be submitted to the discipline of public penance.

9. Mary is the object of Ambrose's special devotion. He

describes beautifully her virginity. Her life is a school of virtue. She is sinless. She is the mediatrix of salvation, the conqueror of the devil, the antitype of Eve and Sarah, and the prototype of the Church. But emphatically Ambrose guards against an idolatrous worship of Mary.

10. Ambrose writes enthusiastically about the veneration of martyrs, about pilgrimages and celebrations in their honor. He lays down clear principles for the veneration of relics.

11. Death is followed by judgment. The just straightway enter heaven and sinners will pass into two groupings according to the weight of their sins. Some will go to the cleansing fires (he does not use the term purgatory), others will share the fate of unbelievers. For this latter class he seems at times to hold out hope, but he does not come anywhere near teaching the *apocatastasis* of Origen. The fire of hell is not material.

12. The end of time seemed to be near for Ambrose because he could not dissociate the disintegration of the Roman Empire from the end of the world. He appears to have thought that although the world will be destroyed, a transfigured earth might be re-created to worship Christ.

Three friends and correspondents of Ambrose should be mentioned here. They are Chromatius of Aquileia, Simplicianus, and Vigilius of Trent.

VII. Jerome and Rufinus

The names of Rufinus and Jerome are linked together in a feud that has been blown up by posterity to proportions far beyond its importance. As a matter of historical fact, the quarrel was only a small incident in the greater battle over Origen and his works that occupied Christianity for a long time and in many places. The feud did not last too long, because Rufinus soon withdrew from the scene and certainly came off best as far as his reputation is concerned. It was the fire of Jerome's bitterness and acrimony that kept it alive long after Jerome himself and his gentle antagonist lay in the grave. Even after Rufinus had died, Jerome continued to vilify and ridicule him, calling him a scorpion and a hydra-headed monster. When he heard of Rufinus' death, he remarked that now he might attack his studies of Ezechiel in peace.

Rufinus was highly respected by his contemporaries and Jerome's abuse did not shake the esteem in which Rufinus was held by such friends as Paulinus of Nola, Palladius, Gaudentius of Brescia, Chromatius of Aquileia, Proba, and the two Melanias. John Cassian and Cassiodore spoke well of him. Sidonius mentions difference of opinion on the worth of the work of Rufinus, but Gennadius of Marseilles rates him highly. The Gelasian decree and Isidore gave a good estimate of him, and his works continued to be popular in the Middle Ages. Since the time of Erasmus, historians have divided into two camps, but it is difficult to see how Rufinus deserves the harsh treatment sometimes accorded him by the friends of Jerome. After all it was the bitterness and rancor of Jerome that kept the feud alive initially.

Jerome and Rufinus had been close friends at school and while living an ascetical life together with other mutual youthful friends. Later when both headed their respective monasteries near Bethlehem they were still good friends. The break came in 392 when the controversy over Origen broke out in Palestine. Jerome issued a condemnation of Origen's writings, but Rufinus refused to do so. They patched up their differences and when Rufinus left for Rome in 397, Jerome went with him some distance to escort him. In Rome, Rufinus translated Origen's *De principiis* and referred to Jerome in the preface as his forerunner. Two busybodies, mutual friends, sent a copy to Jerome, who answered with a letter to the two and an enclosure for Rufinus, both moderate in tone. Rufinus did not get this letter and when the two aforesaid friends published Jerome's translation of *De principiis*, Rufinus wrote his first *Apology* in two books. The controversy can be traced by reading the *Apologies*. Rufinus wrote two books and Jerome three. Rufinus did not answer *Apology III* of Jerome and thus withdrew from the controversy. But Jerome would not let the matter rest and one comes away from it all thinking better of Rufinus than of Jerome.

1. RUFINUS OF AQUILEIA (410)

Rufinus was born near Aquileia around 345 and after a good education in Rome returned to enter a monastery in Aquileia where he was baptized. Here, too, he was again associated with Jerome. In 371 he traveled with the elder Melania to Egypt, visited the monks, and studied under Didymus the Blind. In 378 he founded a monastery near the Mount of Olives with subsidies furnished by Melania. John of Jerusalem ordained him a priest. In 397 he returned to the West and lived in Aquileia from 400 to 407, when he was forced to flee before the Visigoths. He died in 410 in Messina.

His translations are Rufinus' greatest literary legacy. It was his endeavor to preserve the best of Christian Greek literature to the West, which had drifted away from an acquaintance with that language. He seems to have followed no particular plan and most of his translations are works of Origen. He also translated Pamphilus' apology for Origen and added an appendix of his own, *De adulteratione librorum Origenis* (On the Adulterations in the Works of Origen). Besides this he translated some of the Clementine Recognitions, *De recta in Deum fide,* works of Basil the Great, Gregory Nazianzen, Evagrius Ponticus, the Christian edition of the sayings of Sextus, and the Church histories of Eusebius of Caesarea and Gelasius of Caesarea. His translations of the two *Regulae* of Basil and of the *Historia monachorum in Aegypto* of Timothy of Alexandria had profound and far-reaching influence on Western monasticism.

The most important original works of Rufinus are his *Apologia ad Anastasium Romanae Urbis episcopum* and the *Apologia in Hieronymum.* The former defends his failure to appear at a synod in Rome and justifies his translation of Origen's works. He added a profession of faith to this work. Another work, the *Commentarius in symbolum Apostolorum* (Commentary on the Apostles' Creed) is based on the *Catecheses* of Cyril of Jerusalem and contains the oldest Latin text of the Apostles' Creed. Rufinus has also left an allegorical interpretation of the blessing of Jacob, *De benedictionibus Patriarcharum.* Unfortunately all his letters have perished.

The importance of Rufinus has come more and more to be recognized in modern times. It may be summed up by adding him to the list of fathers of the Middle Ages.

2. JEROME (419 or 420)

Jerome has been aptly named "the irascible saint," for saint he is despite his irritating irascibility. Few of God's saints have loved God and His Church more than Jerome. Like the Psalmist of old, he made the enemies of God his own personal enemies. Enemies of the Church and purveyors of what he thought to be theological error were all Jerome's personal enemies. Such enemies were to be fought without giving quarter. The most devastating weapons were, in his estimation, to be used against these enemies and none, even the gentle Rufinus whom he thought to be promoting theological error, was to be spared. He fought the world, the flesh, and the devil—all enemies of God—in the same violence of combat. Only with these considerations in mind can this Titan of Christian scholarship be understood.

Paradoxically neither the date and place of birth nor the exact year of death of the incomparable Jerome is known with complete certainty. Born (c. 347) in Stridon in Dalmatia, a place that cannot be identified with certainty, he was sent at an early age to Rome to be educated in rhetoric, philosophy, and the classics. All his life he displayed a great interest and command of the Latin classics. What he insinuates of evil in his student life in Rome must be heavily discounted. From Rome, after baptism at the age of twenty, he went to travel in Gaul and made his first acquaintance with accounts of the monks of the East. Next we find him in the monastery at Aquileia with Rufinus and his companions, though he never became affiliated with the group. Suddenly (c. 373) he set out for the East. An illness detained him in Antioch. He employed the time by attending the lectures of Apollinaris of Laodicea and mastering Greek. From Antioch he went to live as an anchorite in the desert of Chalcis, east of Antioch, and studied Hebrew. In 379 he was ordained priest by Paulinus of Antioch, and shortly thereafter we find him in Constantinople. Here he attended the lectures of Gregory Nazianzen and developed an enthusiasm for Origen's writings. He also got acquainted with Gregory of Nyssa (381) and other outstanding scholars of the East.

In 382 Jerome was back in Rome under the tutelage of Pope

Damasus whom he came near succeeding, it seems, for he was his secretary and confidant. Damasus commissioned him to bring order into the chaos of the Latin Bible, and this definitely shunted all his energies into biblical study for the future. In Rome, too, he became the spiritual director of a large circle of ascetics that included some of the most prominent women of the city. He made many enemies and was much calumniated until in 385 he left Rome with his brother Paulinian and several monks. He stopped in Crete. In Antioch the party was joined by Paula and Eustochium with a group of ascetical women. Thence the party went to Alexandria where Jerome spent a month with Didymus the Blind. Next the pilgrims visited the monks of the desert and thence proceeded to Bethlehem where they arrived in 386. The resources of Paula were used to establish a monastery for women headed by her, and one for men ruled by Jerome. Here Jerome settled with his extensive library to spend the next thirty-four years of his life, until his death in 419 or 420. Nearby, Rufinus also settled with a group of monks.

But the peace of Bethlehem was soon broken. The Origenist strife estranged Rufinus and John of Jerusalem from Jerome. Shortly afterwards the heretics Jovinian (393), Vigilantius (404), and finally Pelagius, who had come East in 415, disrupted the serenity of Jerome's studies and asceticism. In 416 the Pelagians set fire to his monastery and Jerome had to flee for his life. Jerome's last years were sad. Many of his friends died and barbarian hordes both in the West and the East threatened to engulf all that he held dear. But the indomitable man kept busy with his studies. To the very end he continued to teach the classics to the children of the school he had, years earlier, established. He was buried in Bethlehem, but his present resting place, said to be Mary Major in Rome, is uncertain.

Jerome was the most learned scholar of his day and his influence is still great. Naturally, he must be reckoned among the "founders" of the Middle Ages. He was a master of Latin prose, a great spiritual director and protagonist of the ascetical life, a violent controversialist of the old style, a prodigious writer of interesting and eminently readable letters and, though his work in the field of history is not so extensive, he displays a remarkable grasp and understanding of history. Above all he is the Church's greatest doctor in expounding Scripture. He is not the deepest theological thinker, but Augustine, who easily surpassed him here, regarded him with the highest esteem. Chrysostom surpasses him in interpreting Paul, but no exegete has come near to excelling Jerome's overall knowledge of the Bible.

Above all Jerome was an ecclesiastic who loved the Church and Christian Rome where the head of the Church presided. This got him into many controversies that really should not have disturbed the quiet of his studious and ascetical life. In battle he was relentless and gave no quarter. He seems even to have invented a few antagonists to satisfy his sheer lust for battle. His dogmatic writings are all polemical. He vigorously attacked error and championed especially the veneration of Mary, virginity, the monastic state, and the need for good works and asceticism. His *Altercatio Luciferiani et orthodoxi* is a devastating attack on Lucifer of Calaris and defends, among other things, the validity of Arian baptism (379). Against Helvidius, who denied the perpetual virginity of Mary, he wrote *Adversus Helvidium de perpetua virginitate b. Mariae* (383). Jovinian began to teach that virginity is not superior to marriage and that asceticism is of no value. He proposed also that the Devil cannot harm one who has been baptized and that the rewards of heaven are equal for all. At once Jerome wrote *Adversus Jovinianum* in two books. Against Vigilantius, who had belittled the veneration of the saints and their relics, monasticism, and certain liturgical practices, he wrote his *Contra Vigilantium* (406). When Pelagius appeared to disturb the peace in the East in 415, Jerome immediately published his *Dialogi contra Pelagianos libri III*. The Origenist controversy evokes his most mordant and venomous writings, the *Contra Joannem Hierosolymitanum* (396) and the three *Apologia adversus libros Rufini* (401-402).

Jerome never got around to writing the historical work on the Christian era that he talks about in a number of his writings. Had he done so we can be sure that it would have been a first-class work. He had a remarkable historical sense and an unusual appreciation of the value of history engendered by his early classical studies in Rome. However, he has left us only his continuation of Eusebius' History of the Church and his own *De viris il-lustribus* (Of Illustrious Men). More legend than history and following the pattern of early Christian biographies are his "Lives" of Paul of Thebes, Malchus, and Hilarion. The *Martyriologium Hieronymianum* is not his work.

The prodigious accomplishments of Jerome in the study of the Scriptures have eclipsed his work as an ascetic and a spiritual director. He wrote no manuals of asceticism but his homilies and especially his letters, many of which are entire treatises, show him a master of ascetical and spiritual theology. His homilies were mostly preached to the members of his monastic community in Bethlehem and taken down in writing by some of them. There are seventy-three on the Psalms, one on Mark, two on Isaias, and ten on various biblical texts. A large proportion of Jerome's letters deals with ascetical subjects and many of them were written in the interests of spiritual direction. He was the greatest letter writer of the early Church, but only a relatively small number have come down to us. We have a collection of 150 letters of which 117 are genuine. The collection contains twenty-six letters written to Jerome. How many he wrote altogether is a matter of guesswork. For a period he wrote daily to Paula. Jerome is at his best in the letters as a master of Latin style and in giving an unmatched personal touch to what he wrote. The letters cover a period of some fifty years of his life and the widest range of things. Practically all seem to have been written with a view to their publication. He writes about personal things, about asceticism, and any number of scholarly matters. Many of them are polemical. To single out a few, mention may be made of letter 22 to Eustochium on *De conservanda virginitate* (On Preserving Virginity), number 52 to a young priest, Nepotian, and letters 127 and 128, to two noble matrons, Laeta and Gaudentia. These are important for the history of the times as they deal with the education and training of girls. In fact all his letters have great autobiographical and historical value. Jerome's ascetical theology is based on the fundamental principles of renunciation to follow Christ, study, especially of the Scriptures, prayer, and mortification. It will readily be seen how distasteful and abhorrent his teaching must have been to the decadent age in which he lived. It should be apparent also why his contemporaries even among the clergy, to whom he held up the bright mirror of his own heroic life, attacked him viciously and resorted to unspeakable calumnies in an attempt to discredit him and his teachings.

Jerome is best known for his translation of the Bible, but his work as a translator has preserved for posterity and made available to the West also some valuable patristic writings. He translated the following works of Origen whom he esteemed most highly until the unhappy Origenist controversy broke out: fourteen homilies on Jeremias, fourteen homilies on Ezechiel (381), two homilies on the Canticle of Canticles for Pope Damasus (383), thirty-nine homilies on Luke for Paula and Eustochium (390 in Bethlehem), and eight homilies on Isaias (c. 392). The translation of Origen's *De principiis* which he made in 398 during his feud with Rufinus has been lost. Lost also is his translation of a vicious attack on Chrysostom by Theophilus of Alexandria. He translated the second part of Eusebius' History and continued it to the year 378. He has left a free rendering of the same writer's *Onomasticon* under the title *De situ et nominibus locorum Hebraicorum* (Hebrew Places and Their Names). The *Liber de nominibus Hebraicis* (On Hebrew Names) is a free adaptation of an earlier anonymous work. The *De Spiritu Sancto* of Didymus the Blind escaped destruction through Jerome's Latin version. Lastly Jerome translated (404) the monastic Rules and the letters of Pachomius, Theodore, and Horsiesi, to bring these important ascetical writings to the West.

This brings us to Jerome's biblical labors. His greatest work is the Vulgate and his gigantic labors on the text of the Bible. But his exegetical work also stamps him as the greatest scriptural scholar of his day. He was recognized as such by all. His acquaintance with earlier patristic exegesis is astounding and his knowledge of biblical archaeology and other tools for the literal interpretation of the text far surpassed that of any other patristic exegete. His command of the biblical languages was the marvel of his day. He has left us a series of "Prefaces" to the books of the Bible. Many of these are exegetical treatises. Others discuss problems of introduction to some of the books of the Bible.

A large number of his letters also expound exegetical and introductory problems. Though he was concerned primarily with the literal sense of Scripture, he frequently resorted to accommodation and allegorizing when he wished to bring home a lesson for the spiritual life. He commented on Psalms, Ecclesiastes, and all the prophets. In 381 he wrote an allegorical treatment of the visions of Isaias, *De visione Isaiae*, which was followed in 397 by an historical exposition of the ten visions (Isa. 13–23). His *Quaestiones Hebraicae in Genesim* (Problems in the Hebrew Genesis) explain some of his principles of translation. As his work of translating the Bible progressed, he had abandoned the opinion of his contemporaries that the Septuagint was an inspired version and had come to a higher esteem for the original text of the Old Testament (*Hebraica veritas*). He explains his rendering of many passages in Genesis in the *Quaestiones*, and it is too bad that he did not cover the entire Pentateuch in this way. In the New Testament he explained Philippians, Galatians, Ephesians, Titus (387–389), and superficially commented on Matthew (398). He also edited the commentary on the Apocalypse by Victorinus of Pettau, eliminating the chiliastic errors of the work. The chief flaw in all his exegetical work is that most of it was done too hurriedly and therefore lacked thoroughness and completeness.

Jerome began his revision of the Bible at the instance of Pope Damasus. So rapidly had copies of the Latin Bible been multiplied that there existed no little confusion in the textual tradition of some books. Damasus commissioned Jerome to eliminate this confusion. He was to restore and revise the Old Latin text (*Vetus Latina* or *Itala*). Jerome set to work at once and revised the text of the four Gospels. It is generally thought that he also revised the rest of the New Testament. At this time, too, he hurriedly revised the Latin Psalter according to the Septuagint. This has come to be known as the Roman Psalter because of its use in Rome. Next, shortly after his arrival in Bethlehem, he undertook the revision of the Old Testament using the Septuagint text of Origen's *Hexapla* and the original Hebrew as his guide. All that is left of this work are the texts of Job and Psalms. This latter text came to be known as the Gallican Psalter because it was first introduced into liturgical use in Gaul. Later Pius V brought it into the

Breviary and the Missal, but did not completely eliminate some small elements of the Roman Psalter. The Gallican Psalter also was printed in the Vulgate. All this preliminary work gradually led Jerome to the conclusion that the only thing to do was to translate the Old Testament from the original text. This huge undertaking he began in 391 and completed about 406. This is the Vulgate Old Testament. The version is remarkably accurate but not slavish. Jerome explains his method and procedure in several of his prefaces and letters. There was considerable outcry against the version at first, but by the eighth century it was the standard Bible of the West.

VIII. *Augustine and His Friends*

Augustine marks an epoch in Western Christianity. Augustine and his friends, but chiefly Augustine himself, cut down the heresies that remained to plague the Church in the West and opened new avenues of defense against the pagan elements that assailed the Church from without. As he lay dying he could know that he had cracked the wall of darkness that enveloped his beloved Africa as the Vandal was about to engulf it. He could concentrate his gaze on the Penitential Psalms on the wall beside his pallet and prepare to give his soul to God in peace. He had established a legacy for Western Christianity of the future.

The chief friends of Augustine are Aurelian of Carthage, Capreolus, Evodius, Leporius, Marius Mercator, Orosius, Possidius, Prosper of Aquitaine and, Quodvultdeus.

1. AUGUSTINE OF HIPPO (354–430)

Augustine's fabulous life, his towering genius, and his inestimable contribution to Western civilization simply defy assessment in the pages of an elementary patrology. Even volumes and hours of lecturing would fall short of doing justice to the many facets of Augustine's life and work. It will be best to summarize his life, briefly list his writings, and summarily survey his teaching. The student of the great father can then pursue his interest from this point.

The study of Augustine should begin with a reading of Possidius's *Life of Augustine* and his own *Confessions* and *Retractationes*. Possidius was in close contact with his master for nearly forty years and stood by his deathbed. As monk at Hippo, priest, and finally bishop of the important see of Calama in Numidia, Possidius was ranged with Augustine in all his battles against error in the Church. Elected bishop in 397, he was chosen to be one of the seven bishops who took part with Augustine in the debate with the Donatists in 411. In 430 he was driven from his see by the barbarian invasion, and Geiseric finally expelled him in 437. The date of his death is unknown. Thus Possidius was in position to know Augustine well and, though his *Life of Augustine* was written chiefly for edification, he assures us of his sincerity. In thirty-one chapters Possidius gives all the details of his revered master's activities and adds an appendix listing the writings of Augustine.

To meet the man Augustine personally we go to the *Confessions* and the *Retractationes*. The former introduces us to the sensitive soul of the man and his religious development on his way through the gantlet of false values to the final goal of his reunion with God. The latter shows us the intellectual development of one of the great minds of all time.

The *Confessions* introduces a new literary form into the history of Christian literature. Written between 397–400, Augustine in thirteen books bares his soul to his readers. Efforts to dismiss the credibility of the *Confessions* have failed again and again. It is the story of a man who unsparingly bares the turmoil of his soul to the reader. In all literature there is no finer and more penetrating analysis of a troubled soul than that found in Book X. The last three books are unequaled in literature. Here the soul of Augustine soars the heights in praise of the God who has at last filled the desires of his soul.

The *Retractationes* introduces us to the scholar, Augustine, and his intellectual development. The title of the work means not repudiation or disavowal of former opinions but a re-evaluation and revision of his former positions in theological and philosophical matters. Written between 426–428, Augustine lists ninety-three works he had produced to that date. He tells us his purpose, the circumstances, and the main ideas of each. Then he adds any revisions or additions necessary to bring his opinions up to date and to clarify them. Thus the *Retractationes* completes what the *Confessions* tells us about Augustine.

Augustine was born in 354 of a pagan municipal official of Tagaste in Numidia and a Christian mother. His father later became a catechumen but was baptized only shortly before his death. His mother was the great Monica of the annals of Christian motherhood. During a serious illness of the child she had him entered as a catechumen without advancing him to baptism. Augustine received his elementary education in Tagaste and was then packed off by his father to prepare for the career of rhetorician in Madaura and, in 371, at Carthage. Here he led a dissolute life and entered into a common law marriage that lasted till 384 and brought him his son Adeodatus (372) who died 390. He joined the Manichaeans in 373 because he held his mother's religion in contempt and thought to find the answers to his sophisticated inquiries into philosophy. Returning to Tagaste in 374–375 to teach rhetoric, his mother refused him her hospitality. It was then that a bishop consoled Monica with the now famous words, that a child of so many tears could never be lost. He taught in Carthage (375–383). Here the process of his disillusionment with Manichaean teaching began. In 383 he moved to Rome against the wishes of his mother. Early in 384 he received an appointment to teach in Milan. Though he had been reconciled with his mother and now enjoyed a position of great respect, his soul was as restless as ever. Finally the sermons of the great bishop of Milan, Ambrose, the good priest Simplicianus who was to succeed Ambrose, studies in Neoplatonic philosophy and, above all, the reading of Sacred Scripture, brought Augustine to the threshold of the Church. Simplicianus drew his attention to Marius Victorinus, and a friend acquainted him with the great asceticism of Anthony and the anchorites of the desert. On Holy Saturday, 387, he with his son and his friend Alypius were baptized by Ambrose. A few months later Augustine started for home, but the death of Monica and some literary work detained him in Rome.

Augustine arrived in Tagaste in the fall of 388. Here he lived with his friends in retirement until Bishop Valerius of Hippo and his people clamored to have him ordained. In 395 Augustine was consecrated auxiliary bishop to Valerius whom he succeeded shortly after, as bishop of Hippo. He continued his ascetical mode of life and threw all his energies into his episcopal duties of preaching, teaching, and especially looking after the poor. But, most of his time and endeavor was taken up by his literary work. He fought the enemies of the Church in books, sermons, and public debate: first the Manichaeans, next the Donatists who had so long harassed the Church in Africa, and finally the Pelagians. He crushed the Donatists in spectacular public debate at Carthage in 411 in which 286 Catholic and 279 Donatist bishops took part. His victorious leadership against the Pelagians earned for him the title, Doctor of Grace. He died August 28, 430, his dying tear-bedimmed eyes fixed on the Penitential Psalms which he had made his friends affix to the wall next his bed.

Augustine is the greatest philosopher among the fathers of the Church, and there are those who would call him the most important and influential theologian. Certainly he was one of the great "founders" of the Middle Ages. He influenced every division of ecclesiastical and theological science. Some would say that to make another Augustine would require the best of an Aristotle, a Plato, a Tertullian, an Origen, and a Cyprian molded into one. Protestantism has desperately tried to seize Augustine, but an eminent Protestant theologian has conceded that the Church Augustine so loved has always better understood and cherished him than have her enemies or opponents.

The literary output of Augustine was prodigious. He himself tells us of ninety-three writings, comprising 232 books. This enumeration does not include his numerous sermons and letters. A large number of these were in reality long treatises. This almost incredible output did not, however, mean inferior writing. Augustine is ever the master of style and of every literary device of rhetoric. But never, even in the slightest, does he sacrifice truth and fact to fine writing. On the contrary, to get his point over in his sermons Augustine frequently uses the plainest of language. Nothing better evinces his passion for the truth than the many protestations found in his writings that he would welcome any checking on what he had written. Because of the bulk of his works and the wide range of his influence on Christian thinkers since his day, it will be possible here only to survey his most important books.

1. Philosophical Works

Augustine's contribution to philosophy may be succinctly summed up in the statement that he Christianized Neoplatonism as Aquinas later did for the system of Aristotle. We have eight philosophical treatises or dialogues. *Contra Academicos* (Against the Academicians) deals with certitude and is directed against skepticism. *De beata vita* (On the Happy Life) treats of true happiness. *De ordine* discusses the problem of evil and divine providence. The *Soliloquia* is a discussion with his own reason of the immortality of the soul. *De immortalitate animae* (On the Immortality of the Soul) is a kind of supplement to the Soliloquies. *De quantitate animae* (On the Quantity of the Soul) treats of the immateriality of the soul and its functions. *De magistro* is a talk with his son Adeodatus on theories of knowledge. Augustine also published an Encyclopedia of Fine Arts. Of this there remain only *De musica* and fragments of *De grammatica*.

2. Theological Works

The monumental *Civitas Dei* (City of God) is chiefly an apologetical work, but it is of great interest to the philosopher and the historian. It is also of great value to the philologists and to the students of Latin literature because of the many quotations from the lost works of Terence Varro. Alaric took Rome in 410 and at once the hue and cry that Christianity was responsible for the woes of the times echoed throughout the West. Augustine took up his pen to write the "City of God." The first part demonstrates the futility of paganism, which produced good neither here below nor for the afterlife (1-11). There is an unending struggle between the City of God and the City of this World that will not be resolved till the Great Judgment (11-22).

Augustine's greatest dogmatic work is the *De Trinitate* (fifteen books). He spent twenty years (299-419) on it and himself remarks that not many would find it easy reading. He begins with the scriptural proof of the dogma, proceeds to a philosophical and theological exploration of the mystery and concludes with an attempt at an explanation, as far as that is possible, by analogies from created nature. *Enchiridion ad Laurentium sive de fide, spe et caritate* (Handbook for Laurentius, On Faith, Hope, and Charity), written about 423, is a summary of Christian belief based on an explanation of the Creed. Augustine's greatest polemical work *De haeresibus* may be listed here. It was written around 428 at the request of his friend, the Carthagenian deacon Quodvultdeus, and discusses eighty-eight heresies.

The anti-Manichaean writings of Augustine chiefly defend and explain the propositions that God is good, that evil is negative, that the Old Testament is God's Word, and that Christ is true man. Listed chronologically they are: *De moribus Ecclesiae Catholicae et de moribus Manichaeorum* (two books on Catholic Morality and the Morality of Manichaeans, 387–389); *De libero arbitrio* (three books on Free Will, 388–395); *De Genesi contra Manichaeos* (two books on Genesis against the Manichaeans, 388–389); *De vera religione* (On the True Religion, c. 390); *De utilitate credendi* (On the Value of Faith, c. 381); *De duabus animabus* (On Two Souls, c. 392, against the teaching of the Manichaeans on two souls, one emanating from a good principle, the other from an evil one); *Acta seu disputatio contra Fortunatum Manichaeum* (397); *Contra Faustum Manichaeum,* in thirty-three books (397–400); *De actis cum Felice Manichaeo,* in two books (398); *De natura boni* (On the Nature of the Good, 399); *Contra Secundinum Manichaeum* (399); *Ad Orosium contra Priscillianistas et Origenistas* (415); *Contra adversarium Legis et Prophetarum* (Against the Adversaries of the Law and the Prophets, 421, against an anonymous Marcionite).

In his writings against the Donatists, Augustine develops his ecclesiology and his theology of the sacraments. The Church is a visible society. There are good and evil among her membership but the sacraments are independent of the minister in their efficacy. Eight of Augustine's writings against the Donatists have been lost. There are left: *Contra epistolam Parmeniani* (c. 400, three books Against the Letter of Parmenianus); *De baptismo contra Donatistas* in seven books (400–401); *Contra litteras*

Petiliani, in three books (401–405); *De unitate Ecclesiae* (405, On the Unity of the Church); *Contra Cresconium grammaticum*, in four books (c. 406, Against Cresconius the Grammarian); *Contra Gaudentium Donatistarum episcopum* (412–422, two books Against Gaudentius, Bishop of the Donatists).

Augustine's writings against the Pelagians earned for him the appellation, Doctor of Grace. *De peccatorum meritis et remissione et de baptismo parvulorum* in three books (411, On Original Sin and the Baptism of Infants); *De spiritu et littera* (412, On the Law and Grace); *De gratia Novi Testamenti* (412; is *ep. 140* On the Grace of the New Testament); *De natura et gratia* (415, On Nature and Grace); *De perfectione justitiae hominis* (415–416, On the Perfect Justice of Man); *De gestis Pelagii* (417, On the Carryings-on of Pelagius, when he recanted); *De gratia Christi et de peccato originali* in two books (418, On the Grace of Christ and Original Sin); *De nuptiis et concupiscentia* in two books (419–421, against Julian of Eclanum); another work against the same Julian, *Contra Julianum* in six books (422); *Contra duas Epistolas Pelagianorum* in four books (421, Against Two Letters of the Pelagians); *Contra secundam Juliani responsionem imperfectum opus*, in six books (429–430). Other works that are positive expositions of theology and not polemical in tone were also directed against the Pelagians. *De gratia et libero arbitrio* (On Grace and Free Will, after 426) and *De correptione et gratia* (On the Free Gift of Predestination and Perseverance) were written (426–427) for the monks at Hadrumentum. *De praedestinatione sanctorum* and *De dono perseverantiae* (On the Grace of Perseverance, 428–429) were directed to Prosper and Hilary against the monks of southern Gaul.

Augustine has also left some anti-Arian writings: *Contra sermonem Arianorum* (Against Arian Teaching, 418–419); *Collatio cum Maximino Arianorum episcopo* (Discussion with Maximinus, Arian Bishop) tells of his disputation with a Gothic bishop of that name (427–428). *Contra Maximinum* (in two books) was written a little later against the same bishop.

3. Writings on Moral and Pastoral Theology

Augustine was above all else the zealous pastor and bishop of souls. His greatest catechetical work is the *De catechizandis rudibus* (On Instructing Catechumens, c. 400), written at the request of the Carthagenian deacon Deogratias. In the first part Augustine develops the theory of catechizing. In the second part he submits two models of catechesis. *De agone Christiano* (On Christian Living, 396–397) outlines the Christian's battle against sin and the devil. Other works have titles that are self-explanatory: *De mendacio* (On Lying, 395); *Contra mendacium* (Against Lying, c. 420); *De continentia* (On Continence, 395); *De bono conjugali* (On the Goods of Marriage, 401); *De sancta virginitate* (On Virginity, 401); *De bono viduitatis* (On Widowhood, 414); *De opere monachorum* (That Monks Should Labor, c. 400); *De patientia* and *Speculum* (c. 427, A Mirror of Scripture).

4. Exegetical Works

Augustine is often thought of solely as the philosopher and theologian, and his contribution to biblical studies is often lost sight of. There is scarcely a problem of general and special introduction to Scripture that he did not touch on. His exegetical endeavors cover a wide range of scriptural texts. As a rule he adheres to the strict literal sense, especially in his dogmatic and polemic works, but he does show a marked preference for allegorical and mystical interpretation. He knew no Hebrew but his knowledge of Punic aided him in the appreciation of the Hebrew mentality. His ignorance of Greek has been exaggerated. He was able to check his Latin translations of the Bible, of Plato and Aristotle against the Greek. He used a pre-Hieronymian Bible text and even revised some of it according to the Septuagint which he, as some others, thought to be inspired. It has been stated that more than two-thirds of the Bible could be reconstructed from Augustine's quotations from the Sacred Text. It has been estimated that there are no less than 13,276 Old Testament passages and 29,540 New Testament passages quoted in Augustine's writings.

De doctrina Christiana (396–426) is a synthesis of Christian scholarship and Augustine's most pretentious scriptural work. In four books he surveys the profane and theological scholarship needed for the study of the Bible (1–2), lays down principles of hermeneutics (3), and proceeds to the homiletic use of Scripture in the last book. It is too bad that he did not complete the two projected works on Genesis: *De Genesi ad litteram liber imperfectus* and *De Genesi ad litteram* (twelve books on three chapters of Genesis). He has two works on the *Heptateuch*, each in seven books: *Locutiones in Heptateuchum* (419) and *Quaestiones in Heptateuchum*. The former treats of linguistic difficulties in the Latin text, while the latter is more devoted to archaeological matters. His *Enarrationes in Psalmos* (416) is mostly allegorical and comprises chiefly homilies on the Psalms.

De *consensu Evangelistarum* (On the Synoptic Problem, c. 400) tries to solve the difficulties among the four Gospels and related problems. He gave us the earliest attempted solution of the Synoptic problem in *Quaestiones Evangeliorum* in two books (c. 399). Of particular value are the 124 *Tractatus in Joannis Evangelium* and ten *Tractatus in Epistolam Joannis*. These sermons were preached at various times and the entire collection finally put to writing in 418. He has also left us shorter works, *Expositio quarumdam expositionum ex Epistola ad Romanos* (Explanation of Some Questions on the Epistle to the Romans), an *Inchoata expositio* (Beginning Exposition) on the same epistle, and *Expositio Epistolae ad Galatas*.

5. Sermons

Of all Augustine's varied activities the one most overlooked is his preaching. Valerius, his bishop who was a Greek, commissioned Augustine to do his preaching for him. When Augustine became bishop of Hippo this activity increased. He has left more than 500 sermons, and there may have been twice that number because he sometimes preached daily and even twice a day. Possidius tells us that Augustine did not write his sermons and dictated only a few. The rest were taken down by stenographers when he preached. Possidius writes: "Even heretics as well as Catholics came and listened with great interest, and whoever could do so got himself a stenographer to take down the sermon" (*Vita* 7).

6. Letters and Poems

Augustine wrote letters, many of them long treatises, on the most varied topics. His letter (211) to the nuns of Hippo contains his "Rule." Of great interest also is his correspondence with Jerome. Augustine often wrote poetic prose, but he has also left some poems: *De anima, Psalmus contra partem Donati*. The *Exultet* is not by him. There are some epigrams by Augustine.

2. MARIUS MERCATOR (after 431)

Marius Mercator was probably an African by birth, but lived most of his life in a monastery in Thrace. His writings, directed against Pelagianism and Nestorianism, were designed in great part to clear up the errors of these heresies for the members of his monastery. In 418 he wrote two anti-Pelagianist writings which he sent to Augustine. They have perished. Some of his other writings were preserved in the *Collectio Palatina*. Against Pelagianism we have two treatises or Memoranda (*Commonitorium*) *Commonitorium super nomine Caelestii* (429), and *Commonitorium adv. Pelagium, Caelestium et Julianum*. Against Nestorius he wrote: *Refutatio symboli Theodori Mopsuesteni* (Refutation of the Creed of Theodore of Mopsuestia) and *Comparatio dogmatum Pauli Samosateni et Nestorii* (The Teachings of Paul of Samosata and Nestorius Compared). He translated some of the writings of Nestorius. Of these there are four anti-Pelagian sermons, five sermons on the *Theotokos*, a letter to Caelestius, and some correspondence between Cyril of Alexandria and Nestorius.

3. OROSIUS (after 418)

Paul Orosius was a follower and disciple of Augustine. Born in Braga in Portugal, he fled to Hippo before the Vandals. Here he composed his *Commonitorium de errore Priscillianistarum et Origenistarum* (Memorandum on the Errors of the Priscillianists and Origenists). He then proceeded to Palestine, visited Jerome (415), and composed his *Liber apologeticus contra Pelagianos* (Apologetical Work Against the Pelagians). He returned to Africa and in 417–418 wrote, at the suggestion of Augustine, his *Historia adversus paganos* (History of the Pagans) in seven books. This was meant to be a kind of supplement to the *De civitate Dei* of his friend Augustine. It presents in detail the proposition that Christianity is innocent of the evils of the times and that the pre-Christian era was far more involved in wars and sunk deeper in misery than his own day. He sketches world history from Adam to the year 417 and divides it into four periods according to chapter seven of Daniel. He influenced later historians even to the eighteenth century.

4. PROSPER OF AQUITAINE (after 455)

Prosper Tiro of Aquitaine shows in his writings that he received a splendid education, but we know nothing of his early years except his origin in Aquitaine. Although a layman he was above all else, despite his education and varied talents, a theologian who understood Augustine's teaching on grace and predestination as well as any of that great thinker's followers, and defended it against Cassian and Vincent of Lerins. In 428 Prosper and his friend Hilary reported to Augustine, whom they did not know personally, on the uproar and opposition to his teaching elicited among the monks of Gaul by Augustine's doctrine on grace. This occasioned the latter's *De praedestinatione sanctorum* (On the Predestination of the Saints) and *De dono perseverantiae* (On the Grace of Perseverance). After Augustine's death Prosper journeyed to Rome to get Celestine I to condemn the opponents of Augustine. He failed in this, but did effect a general papal commendation of Augustine's teaching. After 432 Prosper's ardor cooled and he gradually cut off from strict Augustinianism. His last years were spent in the papal chancery of his good friend Pope Leo I (since 440). According to Gennadius, it was Prosper who outlined Leo's letter against Monophysitism (*Ep. 28 ad Flavianum*). The date of his death is not known.

Before his retirement to a monastery in Marseilles, Prosper wrote his *Poema ad uxorem* (Song to His Wife), urging her to give herself entirely to God. Letter 225 among the letters of Augustine was written by Prosper to Augustine. His most pretentious poem, his *Carmen de ingratis* (Song of the Grace-less), contains 1,002 hexameters. The title is a play on words. The "Ingratis" are the Pelagians. Much of the thought of this poem is contained in an earlier letter to a certain Rufinus. *Liber contra collatorem* (Against the Collator) is directed, most probably, against Cassian and his *Collationes*. He wrote three works, *Pro*

Augustino responsiones (Answer to Attacks on Augustine), one to Camillus and Theodore, two Genoese priests, another against the Gallic calumniators (of Augustine), and a third against Vincent of Lerins. They explain and defend Augustine's teaching.

Prosper's later works consist mostly of excerpts and summaries of the works of Augustine. In fact, he made no pretense at original theological exposition but was content to be the mouthpiece of his master. These later writings are: *Capitula Celestini* (Pope Celestine's Approval of Augustine), *Expositio Psalmorum* (Explanation of the Psalms), *De vocatione omnium gentium* (Call of the Nations), *Liber epigrammatum ex sententiis s. Augustini* (Quotations from Augustine), and *Liber sententiarum ex operibus s. Augustini delibatarum* (Sayings of Augustine). The last is an attempt, though unsystematic, at exposition of Augustine's theology. As so many others in this period Prosper also published a chronicle of world history. The section that covers history up to the year 412 is little more than a series of excerpts from earlier works. For the years 412–455, however, Prosper is an independent witness and gives valuable historical information.

PART THREE

The Decline of Patristic Literature

Introduction

Patristic literature shot like a meteor to the heights in the fourth and the first half of the fifth century. Then, during the second half of the fifth century, like a meteor too, its light began to pale and suddenly was no more. There are great fathers in this period, but they are not numerous and they are less great than the towering figures of the Golden Age. In the East men like Pseudo-Dionysius, Severus of Antioch, Leontius of Byzantium, Maximus Confessor, above all John Damascene, and in the West, Fulgentius of Ruspe, were great theological minds. They could move in any company. So could Germanus of Constantinople and Caesarius of Arles among the great patristic preachers. Evagrius Scholasticus was an outstanding historian. Gregory of Tours, though not endowed with high critical ability, is still well worth reading. John Climachus in the East, and Gregory the Great belong in any list of ascetical writers. Gregory the Great has also left us a huge number of letters of more than usual worth. The West produced no poetry of more than ordinary merit, but the East has bequeathed to us some notable liturgical poetry. Romanos Melodos deserves to rank among the best of poets. But now the best has been said.

The period of decline in patristic literature has, however, done posterity a great service by producing a new type of writing. These are the *Catenae*, the *Florilegia*, and the *Parallela*. The *Catenae* are, as the Latin word says, sections or excerpts of scriptural commentaries of an earlier age strung together like a chain. The *Florilegia* are bouquets of literary and theological statements gathered from the writings of earlier fathers. The *Parallela* are

174

in reality also *Florilegia* but of a particular sort. They depict the battle between virtue and vice in the words of the moral and ascetical writings of the preceding age. Though often dull and entirely lacking in originality and creativeness, these writings are priceless because they have preserved many fragments of patristic works that would otherwise have perished. In fact the writings of a number of the fathers are known only from these *Catenae* and *Florilegia.*

Coming now to analyze the cause of this decline in patristic literature, it was in the first place the inferiority of the writers themselves. The four great ecumenical councils of the Church had settled the salient fundamentals of the Trinitarian and Christological controversies of the past. Many theologians of this period seem to have got the idea that there was nothing more to do in the field of speculative theology. The result was that some let theological discussion degenerate into acrimonious political controversy. Others came to lean more and more heavily on their predecessors and were content to quote and follow their authority. This attitude produced the *Catenae* and similar writings already mentioned.

However, it was not only the men of the age who were responsible for this condition. These were terrible years, worse in the East than in the West. The Ostrogoth, the Visigoth, the Frank, the Lombard, and the Vandal swept over the Empire of the West seizing even Rome. But these barbarians were far more amenable to Christian influence than were the Persian and the Mohammedan who devastated Eastern Christianity and even uprooted it in many places. The Byzantine area of the East indeed escaped much of these ravages, but was even worse afflicted by Caesaropapism and by the fanatical doings of the Monophysites, in comparison to which the strifes of Monothelitism and Iconoclasm were but minor skirmishes. In all this turbulence the East and West drifted farther apart. The West came to know less Greek, and the East lost what little it had acquired of Latin. As contacts dwindled the way for the Great Schism was paved. Eastern Christianity went its way to dry up and go sterile.

The West in this age made two monumental contributions to the history of the Church. First of all, she began the process of taming and Christianizing the barbarian. Next, she laid the foundations for the later intellectual flowering of the Middle Ages and Scholasticism. Men like Boethius, Cassiodorus, and Isidore of Seville preserved what was best in the literary tradition of paganism, and Boethius introduced Aristotle to the West in a rudimentary way. All this presaged greater things for the time when the turmoil should subside.

The West

1. The Popes from Leo the Great to Gregory the Great

Pope Leo the Great had many worthy successors in the papacy but their literary legacy is not considerable, except in the case of Gelasius and Gregory the Great. What has come down to us from these popes is almost exclusively letters, but many of these are of great importance to both Church history and theology. The popes are: Agapitus I, Anastasius II, Boniface II, Felix II, Felix III, Hilary, Hormisades, John II, Pelagius I, Pelagius II, Simplicius, Symmachus, and Vigilius. Popes John I and John III have left some literary work done before their elevation to the papacy.

1. POPE GELASIUS I (492–496)

Gelasius I (492–496) is, after Leo I, the most important papal writer of the fifth century. He was a prominent power in papal policy under Felix II, his predecessor. As pope he attacked the Acacian schism, pointing out the primacy of jurisdiction of the Roman Pontiff and establishing the principle that synodal decrees and decisions have validity only when confirmed by the pope. In Church-state relationship he taught that both Church and state have authority of divine origin, but that each is independent and supreme in its own sphere. He has left us about sixty letters, chiefly decretal letters: six theological treatises against Monophysitism, Pelagianism, and on the relationship between Rome and Constantinople. Among them are *De duabus naturis in Christo* (On the Two Natures in Christ). As a writer Gelasius must be rated highly.

Associated with the name of Pope Gelasius are the so-called Gelasian Decree and the Gelasian Sacramentary. Neither of these is genuine. The Gelasian Decree or *Decretum Gelasianum de libris recipiendis et non recipiendis* (Gelasian Decree on Books to be Accepted and Not) is probably the private publication of a cleric of south Gaul in the early sixth century. It reflects views and conditions prevailing in Rome. It comprises five parts: 1. *De Spiritu Sancto* (On the Holy Spirit), decisions of the Roman Synod (381) on the Holy Spirit and the names of Christ; 2. *De Canone Scripturae Sacrae* (On the Canon of Sacred Scripture), listing the books of the Bible; 3. *De Sedibus Patriarchalibus* (On the Patriarchal Sees), setting forth the relationship between Rome and the Patriarchates; 4. *De synodis oecumeniis* (On General Councils), treating of councils and fathers of the Church; 5. *De libris recipiendis* (On Books to be Accepted), lists of apocryphal and theologically suspect writings. Sections one and two may derive from Pope Damasus.

The Gelasian Sacramentary is a Roman *Missale*, the nucleus of which originated before 600 and was very early introduced into Gaul, where it developed to its later form. In its oldest form it is now found in the *Codex Vat. Reg.* 316 which originated after 750. The work has no connection with Gelasius.

2. POPE GREGORY THE GREAT (590–604)

Gregory I, called the Great by posterity because of his tremendous achievements and gigantic activity during fourteen years as pope, was called to the papal throne in years most critical to the Church. Providence selected him to repair the ravages of the sixth century wars and invasions of the barbarians. He became the link between Christian antiquity and the Middle Ages, as he charted the course the papacy was to take on the road to becoming the greatest force in Europe. He laid the foundations of the Papal States of later history. He reorganized the management of the temporal possessions of the Church of Rome (the *Patrimonium Petri*, as he called it) and used the greater revenue for the alleviation of poverty and the repair of devastation done by the barbarians. He saved Rome from the Longobards and later brought about their conversion to the Church. He maintained friendly relationship with the Franks and the Visigoths of Spain—all of these projects of the utmost importance to the Church. He sent Augustine to Britain and fostered the missionizing of the Anglo-Saxon peoples in general. He healed the Milanese schism which had been an outgrowth of the Three Chapters controversy. The East was drifting farther from the West, but Gregory vigorously denied to John the Faster, Patriarch of Constantinople, the title of *Oecomenicus,* that he wanted so much. For himself, when the title *Universalis Papa* (Universal Pope) was urged on him, he chose the famous one, *Servus Servorum Dei* (Servant of the Servants of God). Thus did he bring a leadership to the papacy that the Church has not too often seen. Here are the roots of the powerful papacy of the Middle Ages.

Our sources for the facts of Gregory's life are the writings of his contemporaries, Gregory of Tours and Isidore of Seville, and the *Liber pontificalis.* There are also three legendary "Lives" written by an unknown English monk Paul the Deacon, and John the Deacon.

Gregory, born about 540, was the scion of a rich, noble, senatorial family. He had the best in education available and early decided on a public career. His advance was rapid. In his early thirties he became prefect of the city of Rome (c. 572 or 573). But when his father died in 575, Gregory retired to so strict an ascetical life that his health seems to have suffered. He converted the family palace into a monastery and built six more on the family estates. In 579 Pope Pelagius called him out of retirement and sent him to Constantinople as his *apocrisian* or nuncio. He carried out the arduous duties of this office with great success in most trying years. In 585 he returned to Rome and his beloved solitude, where he was retained by Pope Pelagius as his chief advisor. Pelagius died of the plague in 590 and Gregory, despite his remonstrances, was elected his successor. He died March 12, 604.

The amount of Gregory's literary work is astounding, when one considers the many administrative activities that occupied most of his life. The best picture of this immense activity is gleaned from his letters. There are 854, and we know that he also wrote many letters for Pope Pelagius. These letters are valuable both historically and for their literary quality. His other writings are moral and ascetical. His *Moralia in Job* could be called our oldest Handbook of Moral Theology and Asceticism. Finally, Gregory has left his mark indelibly on the liturgy.

His best known work is the *Liber regulae pastoralis* (Manual of Pastoral Care) in four books. It served the diocesan clergy as a guide throughout the Middle Ages. The work reminds the reader of Nazianzen's apology for his flight and Chrysostom's *De sacerdotio* and, indeed, it was written under similar circumstances, for it was occasioned by Gregory's election as pope. In Book I Gregory discourses on the office of the priesthood, its requirements, and the difficulties of the pastoral office. Book II describes the interior and exterior life of a good pastor. Book III is a discussion of the principles of catechetics, and Book IV points out how the busy pastor must often return within himself for contemplation to regather his strength.

The *Moralia in Job* has already been mentioned. It is a thirty-five book commentary on the Book of Job, filled with observations on moral theology drawn from Gregory's rich experiences with human nature and his full philosophy of life. His exegesis adheres to the literal sense, but he is not at all reluctant to indulge in allegorizing and to make copious accommodations of the text to moral questions. Here are some examples of this. Job is a type of Christ; his wife symbolizes carnal living; and the friends of Job represent heretics. Again, the seven sons are on the one hand symbolic of the seven principal virtues, but they also become the apostles by the following ingenious trick. The seven sons are broken down into units of four plus three. Then by multiplying three by four he gets twelve apostles.

Gregory was a zealous preacher. There are forty homilies, mostly short ones on the pericopes of the Sunday Gospels. Of these he preached twenty himself and dictated the others to be read by his notary. They are serious, fatherly talks, many of which have found their way into the Roman Breviary. There are also twenty-two longer homilies on Ezechiel and two homilies on the Canticle of Canticles 1:1–8.

Gregory's most popular work among the laity of the Middle Ages was his *Dialogi de vita et miraculis patrum Italicorum* (Dialogues on the Lives and Miracles of the Italian Fathers). Gregory says he wants to answer his friend the deacon Peter who had observed that Italy had hardly any miracle-working ascetics in comparison to the East. Whether this is fact or a literary device is not certain, but Gregory proceeds to tell in dialogue form all kinds of miracles, prophecies, and visions that are reported about Italian monks. He devotes the whole of the second book to Benedict of Nursia and Paulinus of Nola. Most of the ascetics mentioned in the other books are totally unknown. Book IV tells of many apparitions of the dead. Gregory presents these as proofs for the immortality of the soul. In Book IV, 55, he speaks of the Masses, called "Gregorian Masses" after him.

Gregory is most important for the study of the liturgy. He revised the Missal and reformed the ceremonies of the Mass. The Canon of the Mass in its present form derives from him. His Missal, the *Sacramentarium Gregorianum*, gradually replaced all others in the West. He also revised the liturgical songs of the Church and published them in an Antiphonarium. How much Gregory had to do with the chant that bears his name is not altogether clear.

Gregory was no original thinker in theology and is not of great importance for the history of dogma, except for the doctrine of the primacy of the bishop of Rome. He did contribute to Christology in his writings against the Agnoetae in which he clarified points on the knowledge of Christ. Gregory took over the angelology of the Pseudo-Areopagite which became the basis for all western angelology. It is interesting to note that Gregory had to declare heretical baptisms valid and to censure the bishops of south Gaul for forcing Jews to be baptized. He came out to approve not only the veneration of the saints themselves but their relics and images also. What evidence for the penitential discipline there is in his writings marks no advance or change from the time of Augustine. Gregory seems to be one of the earliest to attempt to prove the existence of purgatory from Matthew 12:32. He was also compelled to insist on the indissolubility of marriage.

II. Writers of Gaul

The monastic centers of Gaul were also the heart of whatever literary activity there was in the Church of that country. The chief monasteries were those of St. Victor and Lerins. Unfortunately the Semi-Pelagian thinking of John Cassian had great influence here. The chief writers of Gaul during this period are Avitus, Caesarius of Arles, Faustus of Riez, Gregory of Tours, and Salvianus of Marseilles. Less important are Aurelianus, Mamertus, Cyprian of Toulon, Ferreol of Uzes, Gennadius of Marseilles, Massianus, Julianus Pomerius, Remigius of Rheims, and Sedatus of Beziers.

1. AVITUS OF VIENNE (c. 494–518)

Avitus of Vienne, bishop of that city, labored to bring the Arians back to Rome and succeeded in converting Sigismund, heir to the throne of the Burgundians. Alcimus Ecdicius Avitus was himself of senatorial, if not royal, lineage. In early life he embraced the monastic life and later succeeded his father in the see of Vienne (494). He has left us eighty-six letters, some on doctrinal matters. Epistle thirty-four contains the statement: *"Si papa urbis vocatur in dubium, episcopatus jam videbitur, non episcopus, vacillare"* (If you doubt the pope, the whole episcopate and not merely a single bishop will totter). Epistles two and three are against Eutychianism and Epistle four is directed against Faustus of Riez and Semi-Pelagianism. Only three of his thirty-four homilies have come down to us. Two of these are for the Rogation Days before the Ascension, recently introduced by Bishop Mamertus of Vienne (c. 470). His other works are five *Libelli de spiritualis historiae gestis* (On Biblical History), a biblical epic in 2,552 hexameters, and *De consolatoria castitatis laude* (In Praise of Chastity), in 666 hexameters for his sister Fuscina. His verse is elegant and theologically sound. He was an outspoken defender of the primacy of the pope.

2. CAESARIUS OF ARLES (542)

Caesarius of Arles (542), student of Julian Pomerius, monk of the celebrated monastery of Lerins, and archbishop of Arles (502–542), was the most important churchman, pastor, and preacher of his day. Arles was the "Gallic Rome" of those turbulent times, and Caesarius reformed ecclesiastical discipline and presided at several councils, notably the two Councils of Orange which condemned Semi-Pelagianism with the approval of Pope

Boniface II. He is best known as a zealous pastor and preacher. He has left us 238 Sermons on the greatest variety of subjects. These reflect his times and are valuable for a study of his age. There are, furthermore, two treatises against Semi-Pelagianism, three pastoral letters, a work *De mysterio S. Trinitatis,* a *Regula ad monachos* (Rule for Monks), a *Regula ad virgines* (Rule for Nuns), and a number of letters on monastic life.

3. FAUSTUS OF RIEZ (died between 490–500)

Faustus, a Briton by birth, became abbot of Lerins in 433 and bishop of Riez in the province in 458. He was a vigorous opponent of Arianism and Macedonianism. For this he was banished from 477 to 485 by the Visigoth King Euric. Upon the death of Euric he could return to his see where he died sometime between 490 and 500. He is venerated as a saint in southern France, but next to Cassian he was the chief protagonist of Semi-Pelagianism.

Faustus has left us ten letters, five of them addressed to Ruricius of Limoges. There is a great bulk of sermons but these have not yet been edited and readied for publication. He is the author also of two books *De Spiritu Sancto* against the Macedonians and two books *De gratia Dei* (On the Grace of God), written at the behest of the synods of Arles and Lyons (473–474) at which Lucidus, a Gallic priest, who was Faustus's chief opponent, was condemned. In his teaching Faustus follows Cassian closely and was a vigorous opponent of Augustine. He thought Augustine's doctrine on predestination entirely extreme.

4. GREGORY OF TOURS (538–594)

Gregory of Tours, a member of a rich senatorial family, became bishop of Tours in 573 and was one of the most important figures of Church and state in the Merovingian Empire. Though Gregory had received little training in grammar and rhetoric, his writings are of great importance in the study of the religious, political, and ecclesiastical history of the sixth century. Gregory is an exponent of the evolution of Latin into the Romance languages. His chief works are:

1. *Historia Francorum* (History of the Franks), in ten books, which is his greatest work. He completed it in 591. It is not very critical and the author's moralizing tendency obtrudes itself.

2. *Miraculorum libri VIII* (Eight Books on Miracles), his greatest hagiographical work, shows Gregory's lack of critical ability even more so that one might accuse him of gullibility. This work contains the following:

a. *In gloria martyrum* (On the Glory of Martyrs) tells the miracles of our Lord, of the apostles, and of Gallic martyrs (Book I).

b. *De virtutibus s. Juliani* (On the Miracles of St. Julian) (304) an account of the miracles at the grave of this martyr at Clermont-Ferrand (Book II).

c. *De virtutibus s. Martini* (On the Miracles of St. Martin) at the grave of Martin of Tours (Books III to VI).

d. *Vitae Patrum* (Lives of the Fathers) contains the lives of twenty-three Gallic saints (Book VII).

e. *In gloria confessorum* (On the Glory of Confessors) tells the miracles of Gallic saints who were not martyrs.

3. *Passio septem dormientium* (History of the Seven Holy Sleepers) preserves the legend of the seven Holy Sleepers.

4. *De cursu stellarum* (On the Course of the Stars), a liturgical treatise to help one compute the hours of the Office.

5. Only fragments of the commentary on the Psalms remain. Of doubtful authenticity are *De miraculis beati Andreae* (On the Miracles of St. Andrew) and *De miraculis beati Thomae* (On the Miracles of St. Thomas).

5. SALVIANUS OF MARSEILLES (c. 400–480)

Salvianus of Marseilles (born c. 400) entered the monastery of Lerins in 425 after a short marriage. Next he was ordained priest and, after moving to Marseilles about 439, he died there shortly after 480. In 440 he published his most important work *De gubernatione Dei* (On the Government of the World), in eight books which is still most valuable for the history of the times. He endeavors to answer the charge that God's providence did not bother about mundane things and that this is the only explanation of the evils of the migration of nations. Salvianus points out how the sins and evils in Catholic Gaul, Spain, and Africa have brought down the punishment of God. He has also left us nine letters and a work, *Ad Ecclesiam libri IV* (Against

Avarice), published pseudonymously, in which he advocated that all property owners, especially the clergy, should at death give their possessions to the poor. The works of Salvianus are most important for a history of the times and for the history of the Latin language. However, he was more the orator than historian or theologian.

III. Italian Writers

Three Italian writers who might have gone unnoticed in an earlier day stand out in this period because the work they did provided a sort of bridge to the Middle Ages. None contributed much that was original, but each made a notable contribution to the Middle Ages. They furnished the material and partially laid the foundations on which the Middle Ages could build. They gathered and preserved for posterity much of the best that had come before. Boethius introduced the *Logic* of Aristotle and many commentaries on this work of the noted philosopher to the West. He also was a pioneer in applying Aristotelian thinking to Christian theology. Cassiodorus was the practical man. He was an encyclopedist. What he gathered of Roman thought and earlier patristic writings was in this way preserved for the monasteries. Thus the light of scholarship that Benedict of Nursia had enkindled could burn brightly in the monasteries in the midst of the darkness of the barbarian devastations. And there was, finally, the humble Dionysius Exiguus. He must certainly be reckoned among the "Founders" of the Middle Ages, because it was he who transmitted what was best in Greek Christian culture and thinking to posterity. To these three should be added Ennodius. His literary remains are a curious mixture of Christian and pagan elements, but his work served as a rich mine of information for subsequent scholars.

Italians of lesser importance are: Arator, Benedict of Nursia, Eugippius, John, deacon of Rome, John Maxentius, Jordanes, Laurentius, the editor of *Liber pontificalis*, Marcellus Comes, Marius of Lausanne, Rusticus Helpidius, and Victor of Capua.

1. BOETHIUS (524)

Anicius Manlius Severinus Boethius was born about 480 at Rome into the ancient noble family of the Gens Anicia. He received a very good education and was then sent to Alexandria for training in Greek philosophy and literature. He returned to Rome and entered politics. At a young age he was appointed consul of the Ostrogothic state in 510. After a little more than a decade of service he was falsely accused by his enemies of too close relations with Constantinople, and the suspicious Theodoric had him executed in 524. Though not specifically a martyr to the Catholic faith, he soon came to be venerated as a martyr, and Pope Leo XIII approved his cult for Pavia in 1883.

Boethius' contribution to the Middle Ages has been mentioned above. His great work *De consolatione philosophiae* (On the Consolation of Philosophy), in five books, was one of the most read books of the Middle Ages. It was frequently translated and commented on by scholars of a later day. He wrote it in prison. It is an artistic dialogue with Dame Philosophy, who appears to him in Book I and asks that Boethius confide his troubles to her. He then tells the story of his imprisonment. Book II develops the theme that fortune is fickle and that true happiness can be found by man only within himself. Proceeding further on this theme, Book III treats of the final end of man and that happiness can be found only in God. Book IV discusses divine providence. This book is an elementary theodicy. The last book discourses on the freedom of the will and its relationship to the divine foreknowledge. God's knowledge transcends all time. God knows the past, present, and future, but this knowledge in no way interferes with man's free will.

It has been alleged that Boethius was a Christian in name only because the *De consolatione* is said to contain nothing specifically Christian. In fact, Christ is not mentioned and there is no reference to the Christian belief in the afterlife. However, only a Christian could have written the work. The sublime and serene thought of the work, the refined conception of the deity and man's relationship to God, could be the product only of a Christian thinker. The whole outlook on life of the work is Christian.

There are thirty-nine exquisite hymns in it that are noteworthy for their artistic perfection of form and for their sublimity of thought.

Boethius' status as a Christian should be clear from the five theological treatises he has left. They are short and relatively unimportant, but they are Catholic. There are two treatises on the doctrine of the Trinity, entitled *De Sancta Trinitate;* a third, *Quomodo substantiae in eo quod sint, bonae sint, cum non sint substantialia bona* (How Substances are Good Inasmuch as They have Being); and a fourth, *Liber de persona et duabus naturis contra Eutychen et Nestorium* (On the One Person and Two Natures Against Eutyches and Nestorius). A fifth treatise, *De fide catholica,* is now also regarded as genuine. These treatises are most important because of the definitions that Boethius coined and gave to philosophy.

In some respects Boethius made his greatest contribution to the Middle Ages in the field of education. His two books on mathematics, *Institutio arithmetica,* and his five books of musicology, *De institutione musicae,* were basic to those two branches of the Quadrivium of the Middle Ages. He furthermore treated problems of logic in *Introductio ad syllogismos categoricos, de syllogismo hypothetico, De divisione,* and *De differentiis topicis.* He had also conceived the grandiose plan of translating and commenting on all the works of Aristotle and Plato. His tragic and early death frustrated this undertaking. He has, however, left us a translation of Aristotle's *Categories* with four books of commentary, a translation of *De interpretatione* with two commentaries, a translation of the *Isagoge* of Porphyry with two commentaries, and a commentary on Cicero's *Topica.* All these works found incalculable use in the Middle Ages.

2. CASSIODORUS (c. 583)

Flavius Magnus Aurelius Cassiodorus, senator, was born around 490 of an old noble family of civil servants in Calabria. In 507 we find him quaestor and private secretary to Theodoric the Great; he became consul in 514 and prefectus praetorio in 533. Shortly after 540, however, Cassiodorus cut short his public career and retired to his family estate in Calabria, where he had established a monastery (*vivarium*) to devote the rest of his days to asceticism, scholarly endeavor, and the education of his monks. He died around 583, a nonagenarian.

Cassiodorus is the opposite of Boethius in many ways. The latter was of a speculative bent and an original thinker. Cassiodorus, on the other hand, was the practical scholar but a profoundly learned one of the widest interests and acquaintance in all fields of knowledge. All his studies were utilitarian and thus he put posterity in his debt more than any other writer of his time. Surrounded by the general ruin brought by the universal barbarism of his day, he salvaged for those who came after him the best of classical and Christian culture in his literary works. It was he who gave the greatest impetus to study in the monasteries, among his own monks and in other houses. The rule of Benedict had laid the groundwork for a monastic life devoted to prayer, study, and work. Cassiodorus gave added stimulus to the movement and furnished many of the necessary tools. His literary activity extends over his whole life, both as a public figure and as an ascetic in the retirement of his monastery.

To the period of Cassiodorus' public life belong his *Chronicle of the World* and his *History of the Goths*. The latter has been preserved in compendious form by Jordanes in his *World History*. The former is mostly a list of consuls and similar data, to which Cassiodorus added some materials from Jerome and Prosper. It covers world history from the beginning to 519, but from the year 496 on he draws mostly on his own personal knowledge. Here the great preoccupation of his public life comes to the fore. It was his great endeavor to bring the Romans and their Gothic conquerors closer together and to a better understanding of each other. Besides these historical works Cassiodorus left twelve books of *Variae* or *Litterae*. This is a collection of rescripts and allied documents that he had prepared for the Gothic kings. To these Cassiodorus added all manner of comment, legal opinions, and observations necessary for the clear understanding of the rescripts and their background. The collection was much used in the chancelleries of the Middle Ages. There were a number of panegyrics on the royal house and some treatises on the family tree or genealogy of the *Ordo generis Cassiodorum*. Of these only small fragments remain.

A little work, *De anima,* written about the time of Cassiodore's retirement from public life, marks the transition from his secular writings to his religious works. It answers a few questions about the soul and is Augustinian in its philosophical outlook. There are some exegetical works of an allegorizing tendency: *A Commentary on the Psalms, Complexiones, In Epistolas et Acta Apostolorum et Apocalypsin,* and an orthodox edition of *Pelagius' Commentary on the Pauline Epistles* that long was circulated under the name of Primasius. Cassiodorus calls these exegetical writings *Complexiones* because it is his practice to explain several verses at a time.

The nonagenarian, Cassiodorus, wrote *De orthographia* for his monks and its mention brings us to his greatest work, of which it is a supplement. This is the *Institutiones divinarum et humanarum lectionum* (Institutes on Divine and Human Letters), which sets forth his educational ideas. Cassiodorus had approached Pope Agapitus (535–536) with a plan to establish a theological school in Rome, but the wars and disturbances of the time frustrated his plans. Accordingly he did the next best thing. He set to writing his program for a well-rounded education in the arts and theology. Book I is an introduction to the study of theology in thirty-three chapters. His purpose is to initiate the reader into the study of theological science, especially the study of the Scriptures. The book is most valuable because it lists authors, books, and other auxiliary materials. Book II, only seven chapters, is designed to be an introduction to the study of the arts.

Finally, Cassiodorus' *Church History* should be mentioned among the religious writings. To produce this Cassiodorus had one of his monks translate the histories of Socrates, Sosomen, and Theodoret into Latin. He then used these works, together with the Church History of Rufinus, to produce his *Historia tripartita* in twelve books. This work became one of the principal source books for the study of ecclesiastical history in the Middle Ages.

3. DIONYSIUS EXIGUUS (middle sixth century)

Dionysius called himself Exiguus in his humility and almost succeeded in reducing himself to anonymity. All that is known of him with certainty is that he lived as a monk in Rome from about 500 to 545. Cassiodore, who knew him well, praises his learning and his sanctity. He distinguished himself for his studies in chronology, as a collector of ecclesiastical documents, and as a translator. His chronological studies on Easter, *Liber de Paschate*, *Argumenta Paschalia*, and *Duae de ratione Paschae*, brought some order into the computation of Easter. Here, too, he made his most celebrated error, though the astounding thing is that the error is so small. He computed the date of the birth of Christ and set it at 754 (A.U.C.), missing the mark by at least four or more years. He translated a *Life of Pachomius*, a *Historia inventionis capitis s. Joannis Baptistae* (History of the Finding of the Head of John the Baptist), some letters of Cyril of Alexandria, and the *Tomus ad Armenos* of Proclus of Constantinople.

Of inestimable value to posterity for the study of law, and particularly canon law, is what came to be called the Dionysian Collection. Dionysius first collected the first fifty of the apostolic canons and added the canons of some of the Oriental councils, both ecumenical and provincial. These he translated himself and then added canons from various councils of Carthage and North Africa. He listed them mostly in chronological order. Next he compiled thirty-eight decretals of the popes from 384 to Pope Symmachus (498–514), omitting several important ones found in earlier collections. There seem to have been three editions of which the third is lost.

4. ENNODIUS (521)

Ennodius, Magnus Felix, born (c. 473) into a noble family of Arles, was reared by an aunt after the death of his parents. In 493 he was appointed deacon in Pavia after having his betrothal dissolved. Some think he had been married. In 496 he moved to Milan to teach rhetoric, but returned to Pavia as its bishop in 514. Twice, in 515 and in 517, he headed a papal delegation to Constantinople in an attempt to heal the Acacian schism. He died in 521. He has left us:

1. 297 letters, mostly of a personal nature and of little importance.

2. Ten *Opuscula miscella*, viz., a life of Epiphanius, his predecessor; a life of Anthony, monk of Lerins; *Libellus adversus eos, qui contra synodum scribere praesumpserunt* (Against Those

Who Dare Write Against the Synod), a defense of the Roman synod of 502 defending Pope Symmachus; *Paranaesis didascalia,* an exhortation to study rhetoric; *Eucharisticum de vita sua,* an autobiographical sketch modeled on Augustine's Confessions; *Benedictiones cerei,* two blessings of the Easter Candle.

3. Twenty-eight *Dictiones* or Orations on various topics.

4. *Carmina* in two books. Book I offers twenty-one longer poems and twelve hymns. Book II has 151 epigrams.

As a writer Ennodius is polished but far from an inspired genius. His writings show the influence of secular thinking and reading in classical literature. His works are rich in thought. Christian and pagan materials are mixed together and there is room for some obscenities. Ennodius coined the phrase, *"Papa a nemine judicatur"* (The pope is judged by no one), and was the first to reserve the name *papa* to the bishop of Rome.

IV. The Writers of Africa

The African Church of the fifth century was devastated by the Vandals who spread Arianism everywhere. Arianism was followed in the middle of the sixth century by the "Three Chapters" controversy. As a result, the writers of Africa in these centuries were almost totally occupied with these heresies. Fulgentius of Ruspe is the only outstanding literary representative of the African Church in this period. Other writers are: Asclepius, Cerealis of Castellum, Dracontius, Eugenius of Carthage, Ferrandus, Facundus of Hermiane, Honoratus, Junilius Africanus, Liberatus the Deacon, Primasius of Hadrumentum, Verecundus of Junca, Victor of Cartenna, Victor of Tunnuna, Victor of Vita, Vigilius of Thapsus, and Voconius of Castellum.

1. FULGENTIUS OF RUSPE (467–533)

Fulgentius of Ruspe was a staunch follower of Augustine and an opponent of the Semi-Pelagians of Gaul. He also waged vigorous battle against Arianism. All in all he was a competent theologian, although he did propose some unusual theological ideas. He denied the Immaculate Conception and excluded unbaptized children from salvation. He traced the inheritance of original sin through the concupiscence of the parents. In his teaching on grace he followed Augustine faithfully.

He was born of a noble family and received a splendid education in Greek over and above the usual studies. He was procurator of his native city Telepte, then retired to become a monk, and in 507 was chosen bishop of Ruspe. He spent the years 508–515 in exile with sixty other bishops. A second exile overtook him during the period 517–523. Both were spent in Sardinia. Ten years later, he died in 533. His disciple, the deacon Ferrandus, wrote a beautiful life of his master.

Fulgentius has left quite a few anti-Arian writings. *Contra Arianos* is an answer to ten questions put by King Thrasamund, and the three books *Ad Thrasamundum* continue this polemic. Other polemical works are: *Contra sermonem fastidiosi Ariani, Contra Fabianum, De Trinitate ad Felicem, De Incarnatione ad Scarilem.* His best non-controversial work was a compendium of dogma that was very popular in the Middle Ages, *De fide ad Petrum.* Another dogmatic work is *De remissione peccatorum ad Euthymium* (On the Remission of Sins), in two books.

Against Semi-Pelagianism Fulgentius wrote three works: *Ad Monimum* in three books, *De veritate praedestinationis et gratiae Dei* (On Predestination and the Grace of God) in three books, and the seven lost books *Contra Faustum Reiensem.* He has left us thirteen letters and seven sermons. Several of the letters are longer and in reality complete dogmatic treatises. Epistle fifteen and epistle seventeen are letters written by all the bishops in exile with him. Of these the latter epistle approves the formula, "One of the Trinity has suffered in the Flesh" (see Proclus of Constantinople). The first seven letters deal with practical moral questions, such as marriage and celibacy.

V. Writers of Spain

We have already noted these "Founders" of the Middle Ages, Boethius, Cassiodorus, and Dionysius Exiguus. With them, or perhaps even ahead of them, should be placed the Spaniard, Isidore of Seville. His contributions to posterity are inestimable. The Spanish Church of this period produced another theologian of no mean stature, Martin of Bracara. Other Spanish writers of the time are: Apringius, Braulio, Hydatius or Idacius, John of Biclaro, Justinian of Valencia, Justus of Urgel, Leander of Seville, and Severus of Malaga.

1. ISIDORE OF SEVILLE (636)

The last of the fathers of the West, Isidore of Seville, has left us little information about himself. He was born about 560, succeeded his brother Leander as archbishop of Seville, presided at the fourth national synod of Toledo in 633, and died three years later, 636. His contemporaries regarded him as the greatest scholar of his time, and twenty years after his death the eighth Council of Toledo declared him to be "the doctor of our age, the most recent ornament of the Catholic Church, last in order of time but not least in doctrinal teaching, and, to be more exact, the most learned scholar of these latter days." How popular Isidore was in the Middle Ages is best shown by the fact that there are about 950 manuscripts of his *Etymologiae* (Etymologies) alone.

But Isidore was neither an original scholar nor a creative thinker. Above all he was the greatest compiler of the patristic age. That was his most valuable service to posterity. His writings have preserved the sum of human knowledge available in his day, and thus he gave to the Middle Ages an epitome of all pagan and Christian learning of antiquity. The most serious defect of his work is its superficiality. Many of his sources were second and third hand. But all this does not dim his achievement. He is truly the bridge between the patristic age and the Middle Ages.

Isidore's writings cover so wide a range that they can scarcely be classified. *Differentiarum libri II* and *Synonymorum libri II* treat of grammar. *De ordine rerum* and *De ordine creaturarum* are treatises on the natural sciences. He wrote a short *Chronicon* of the world extending to the year 615. The *Historia Gothorum* is a chronicle of the Visigoths up to 625. To it are added two short appendixes on the Vandals and the Suevi. He also carried forward Gennadius' continuation of Jerome's *De viris illustribus.* Not the least interesting of his writings are twenty-seven *Titula Isidori.* They are inscriptions that Isidore had on his bookshelves and on the walls of his house. They are valuable for light they throw on the times.

The rest of Isidore's works are mostly religious. There are two exegetical works: *Quaestiones in Vetus Testamentum* and *De ortu et obitu Patrum.* The latter sketches the lives of eighty-six biblical characters. *Sententiarum libri III* is a handbook of dogmatic and moral theology based largely on the *Moralia* of Gregory the Great. There are two polemical works: *Contra Judaeos ad Florentinam sororem* (Against the Jews), and a history of heresy, *De heresibus.* There are two ascetical treatises, *Regula monachorum* and *Commonitiuncula ad sororem.* Important works for canon law and the liturgy are the *Collectio Isidoriana* and *De ecclesiasticis officiis.* The former originated about 500 in Spain and stresses the Spanish councils, though its immediate connection with Isidore is not plain. The latter is most important for the Spanish liturgy. Book I, *De origine officiorum,* treats of the sacraments, especially the Mass, and of liturgical prayers and the ecclesiastical calendar.

Isidore's monumental work is the *Etymologiae* or *Origines.* The contents are best summarized by listing the titles of its twenty books. Here they are outlined.

1. *De grammatica,* On Grammar
2. *De rhetorica et dialectica,* On Rhetoric and Dialectics
3. *De quatuor disciplinis mathematicis,* On the Mathematical Disciplines, Arithmetic, Geometry, Music, and Astronomy
4. *De medicina,* On Medicine
5. *De legibus et temporibus,* On Laws and Chronology with a Chronicle of the World as an Appendix
6. *De libris et officiis ecclesiasticis,* On Ecclesiastical Offices and Liturgy
7. *De Deo, angelis, et fidelium ordinibus* deals with theological matters
8. *De Ecclesia et sectis diversis,* On the Church and the Sects
9. *De linguis, gentibus, regnis, militia, civibus, affinitibus,*

On the World as Divided by Languages, Peoples and
Countries

10. *Vocum certarum alphabetum*, On Certain Etymologies of
Words
11. *De homine et portentis*, On Man and Nature
12. *De animalibus*, On Animals
13. *De mundo et partibus*, On the World and its Parts
14. *De terra et partibus*, On the Earth and its Parts
15. *De aedificiis et agris*, On Buildings and Fields
16. *De lapidibus et metallis*, On Stones and Metals
17. *De rebus rusticis*, On Rural Affairs
18. *De bello et ludis*, On War and Games
19. *De navibus, aedificiis, et vestibus*, On Boats, Buildings, and
Clothes
20. *De penu et instrumentis domesticis et rusticis*, On Victuals,
Home and Farm Tools

The chief sources for this astounding work are the fathers,
pagan writers, and all handbooks of antiquity that Isidore could
lay hands on. All these he used extensively but uncritically. Book
X contains only etymologies and it may be well to cite a few
of these. *Apis*, the Latin word for bee, he derives from *a* (without) and *pedibus* (feet). Therefore the bee is without feet. The
word for friend, *amicus*, he derives from *hamus*, a hook.

VI. Poets

The clamor and uproar of the barbarian invasions were enough
to stifle the song of poetry in these turbulent times but there
are some few voices raised to bring cheer to the hearts of their
Christian contemporaries. Outstanding in an age when it took no
great requirements to stand out are Dracontius, Sidonius, and
Venatius Fortunatus. Other poets of this period are Arator, the
author of *Carmen ad Flavium Felicem*, Rusticus Helpidus, and
Paulinus of Periguex.

1. DRACONTIUS (early fifth century)

Blossius Aemilius Dracontius, a Carthagenian lawyer was a genuine and sensitive poet of the late fifth century. Thrown into prison by King Guntamund (484–496) because he had, it seems, dedicated a poem to the Byzantine emperor, he composed *Satisfactio*, a poem in 158 distichs, confessing his guilt and asking pardon. Three books *De laudibus Dei* (On the Praises of God) in 2,327 hexameters is his most mature work and shows him master of the poetic art. He praises the creator and sustainer of the world. Book III exhorts to mutual charity. His ten *Carmina Romana* (Roman Songs) deal with pagan materials. The *Orestis tragoedia* is most probably also his work.

2. SIDONIUS (c. 490)

Sidonius (Apollinaris Sidonius) was born of noble lineage in Lyons (432) and later became the son-in-law of the emperor. In imitation of Virgil and Claudius Claudianus he composed twenty-four *Carmina*, among them three panegyrics to Roman emperors. These are full of mythological allusions with no trace of Christianity. After his unwilling promotion to bishop of Arverna (Clermont-Ferrand) in 469, he devoted himself to epistolography and has left us nine books of 147 letters. These are verbose and show little profundity of thought, but they are of importance for the cultural history of the time. He has also preserved in them a number of poems, epitaphs, and ecclesiastical inscriptions. He died between 480 and 490. He was a good bishop and tried to be a Christian writer, but the old love of the classics had to be shared by his attempted love of the Scriptures. At any rate there is no theology and little moralizing in his letters.

3. VENATIUS FORTUNATUS (after 600)

Born in Trevision in northeastern Italy (c. 530), Venatius Fortunatus studied rhetoric and law at Ravenna. In 567 he set out on a leisurely pilgrimage to the tomb of Martin of Tours, through whose intercession he had been cured of a malady of the eyes. On the way he met innumerable people, high and low, ecclesiastics and courtiers. He made many stopovers of varied length, delighting in the countryside and the people he met. All these things are reflected in his poetry. He ended his travels at Poitiers. Here he met two pious women, Radegund and her foster-daughter, Agnes. They persuaded him to settle down and be ordained a priest. Thereupon, he assumed the spiritual care of a monastery, founded by Radegund who was the widow of Chlotar I. Toward the end of the century he was chosen bishop of Poitiers. His poetical gifts and affable disposition won him a very wide circle of friends and acquaintances. He was an intimate friend of Gregory of Tours.

Fortunatus was an exceedingly gifted and sensitive poet. He is at his best when describing the little things of everyday life. His sensitive soul reacted to everything that happened and to everything that he came in contact with. He has left more than 300 poems. The best of these are found in his *Carmina miscellanea* (Miscellaneous Songs), a collection in eleven books. There are hymns, panegyrics, elegies, epigrams, epitaphs, and all kinds of occasional poems. The finest of these are hymns composed in honor of the Holy Cross. The occasion for their composition was the presentation of relics of the Holy Cross to Radegund by the emperor Justin II. Two of these are still used in the liturgy, the *Pange lingua* and the *Vexilla regis*. Another poem of eighty-two verses, *De navigio suo* (On His Boat Trip), is an exquisite description of a trip on the Moselle that easily rivals the *Mosella* of Ausonius. The Collection also contains several letters and two prose compositions or treatises, *Expositio Orationis Dominicae* (On the Our Father) and an *Expositio Symboli* (Exposition of the Creed). The latter is dependent on the work of Rufinus, *Commentarius in symbolum Apostolorum* (Commentary on the Apostles' Creed).

- SECTION II -

The East

Introduction

What has been said above about the West during this period of the decline of patristic literature is true to considerable extent of the East. As in the West we find a preponderance of practical writings and works handing down the precious heritage of the past. There are commentaries on the writings of the earlier fathers. There are *Catenae* and *Florilegia*, particularly of the moral, ascetic, and disciplinary writings of an earlier day. We see a rise of poetry in the East. Works of history and chronicles are numerous also. Through all the literature of the East there runs the strain of emphasis on the authority of the fathers. But the Empire was dying in the East. Monophysitism and Nestorianism (later Monothelitism and Iconoclasm) harassed the Eastern Church within. As the barbarians, using the internal strife that plagued the Empire, encroached on the territory of the East, the Empire shrank and the Arab hordes engulfed the outposts of Christianity in the East.

We shall treat the writers of the East in three chapters:
I. Heretical Writers
II. Orthodox Writers
III. Poets

I. Heretical Writers

Severus of Antioch is probably the only heretical writer of this period to be given separate consideration. Other writers are: Cyrus the Monk, Cyrus of Phasis, Dioscorus, John Nikiotes, John

Rufus, Julian of Halicarnassus, Oecumenius, Paul of Constantinople, Pyrrhus of Constantinople, Sergius of Constantinople, Sergius Grammaticus, Stephen Gobarus, Themistius, Theodore of Pharan, Timothy Aerulus, and Zacharias Rhetor.

1. SEVERUS OF ANTIOCH (538)

Severus of Antioch, patriarch of Antioch (512–518), was the keenest and ablest Monophysite theologian of the sixth century. He was also the most ruthless and skillful sectarian politician of his party. Born at Sozopolis in Pisidia of pagan parents, he studied rhetoric in Alexandria and law in Beyrouth. Baptized in 488, he became a monk at Majuma near Gaza and went to Constantinople after his ordination. In 512 the Monophysites made him patriarch of Antioch. In 518 he was banished by the emperor Justin, but Justinian recalled him in 534–535. After a year or so he fled again and died at Xois, south of Alexandria, February 8, 538.

Severus has had to suffer from his own bold and domineering personality. In 518 he entered a controversy with Julian of Halicarnassus on the incorruptibility of the body of Christ. He attacked Chalcedon and the Tomus of Leo the Great, but was in fact not too far from orthodox teaching. His attack on Chalcedon was directed more at the wording than at the substance of the teaching. His great work *Against the Godless Grammarian* shows this. In it he explains his position and supplies some 1,250 quotations from the fathers of the Church. Besides this he has left us *Philalethes*, a polemic against an anonymous work defending Chalcedon, and numerous sections of his writings against Julian Halicarnassus. There are some 125 homilies in the Syriac translation of Jacob of Edessa and about 4,000 letters preserved in an arrangement into twenty-three books. Lastly, the *Oktoechos* contains some of his hymns, the best known being the *Sub tuum praesidium* which is still used by both East and West.

II. Orthodox Writers

The East produced only a few worthwhile theologians during this period, John Damascene, Justinian I Emperor, Leontius of Byzantium, Maximus Confessor, the Pseudo-Areopagite, and Sophronius. Other writers are: Aeneas of Gaza, Alexander of Salamis or Salamina, Antiochus Monk, Ammonius Priest, Anastasius I of Antioch, Anastasius II of Antioch, Anastasius III of Nicea, Anastasius the Apocrisian, Anastasius the Monk, Anastasius Sinaita, Andrew of Caesarea, Barsanuphius, Cosmas Indicopleustes, Dorotheus of Gaza, Ephraem of Antioch, Eulogius of Alexandria, Eustathius the Monk, Eutychius, Gennadius of Constantinople, George Pisides, Germanus of Constantinople, Gregory of Girgenti, Heraclian, Hypatius, Jobius, John Maxentius, John of Carpathus, John of Scythopolis, John the Grammarian, Leontius of Jerusalem, Leontius of Napolis, Macedonius of Constantinople, Nephalius, Olympiodorus, Pamphilus, the author of *Panoplia dogmatica*, Peter of Laodicea, Procopius of Gaza, Roman the Singer, Symmachus, Theodore of Raithu, Thalassius the Abbot, Timothy of Constantinople, and Victor of Antioch.

1. JOHN OF DAMASCUS (c. 675–749)

John Damascene is the last great theologian of the ancient East, in the sense that he was the last to devote himself to the entire range of theology. His writings cover the field of dogma, moral, asceticism, exegesis, and history. He was also an orator and poet, and has left some splendid homilies and contributed some fine hymns to the liturgy of the Greek Church. He was highly esteemed by posterity and his *De fide orthodoxa* became the standard handbook of theology for the Eastern Orthodox churches. However, little is known of his life beyond what has been transmitted to us by legendary accounts of the Middle Ages. Born of a noble Christian family of Damascus which was at the time under the sway of Islam, he rose to a high public office but resigned in 726 to enter the Monastery of St. Sabas, near Jerusalem, with his foster-brother, Cosmas the Younger. Later John was ordained priest. His whole life was then devoted to asceticism and literary activity. After his death (749) an Iconoclast synod of 754 anathematized him, but the seventh general council at Nicea restored his honor for his defense of the veneration of images. He was proclaimed a Doctor of the Church in 1890. The Greeks named him *Chrysorroas*, "He who pours out gold."

John's greatest work is the *Pege gnoseos* (Fount of Wisdom), written in 742 and dedicated to Cosmas. It is in three parts of which the third, *De fide orthodoxa*, is the most important. This is a complete handbook of dogma in a hundred chapters. In the text tradition of the West it was divided into four parts, after the fashion of Peter Lombard's *Book of Sentences*. In this arrangement, Book I treats of God, Book II of creation and providence, Book III of Christology, and Book IV continues Christology and presents the other sections of theology: baptism, Eucharist, the veneration of saints and their images, the canon of the Bible, the problem of evil, and the last things. The presentation and teaching of the *De fide* are prominently influenced by Pseudo-Dionysius (on God), Gregory Nazianzen (on the Trinity), Leontius of Byzantium, Maximus Confessor, Anastasius Sinaita (on Christology), and Nemesius of Emesa (on Creation). Part I of the Fountain is called *Dialectica* and is a philosophical introduction to theology. Part II is a history of heresies that draws heavily on Epiphanius, Theodoret, and others. Only what he writes about Islam and Iconoclasm is original. He has left four smaller treatises, *Institutio ad dogmata* which seems to be a preliminary sketch of his *Dialectica*, *Libellus de recta doctrina* (a Catechism), *De Sancta Trinitate*, and a *Profession of Faith*. The latter two works are not certainly genuine.

The Damascene has left a number of polemical writings. The most important of these laid the scientific basis for the theology of the veneration of images and relics. It is the *Orationes pro sacris imaginibus* (Treatises on Sacred Images), written in three books during the years 726 to 730. They appear to be three developments of the basic subject rather than three separate independent works. There are two treatises against Nestorianism, two against Monophysitism with a letter on the Trisagion written to the Archimandrite Jordanes, one against Monothelitism, and two against Manichaeism. There are also some fragments of a polemic against superstition.

The *Sacra parallela* in three books is John's most valuable moral and ascetical work. It is an extensive collection of texts appropriate to Christian living, taken from Scripture and the writings of the fathers. Only the first two books remain in an abridged form. He has left three short ascetical treatises, *De octo spiritibus nequitiae* (On the Eight Vices), *De virtutibus et vitiis* (On Virtues and Vices), and *De sacris jejuniis* (On Variation in Practice in the Matter of the Fast for Easter).

There is little original in John's commentary on the Pauline Letters. It is mostly a compilation from Chrysostom, Theodoret, and Cyril of Alexandria. He has left nine genuine homilies, among them three on the death and assumption of Mary. In his liturgical hymns John shows genuine poetic gifts. Many of these compositions have been preserved in the *Octoechos*. Spurious works attributed to Damascene need not be mentioned.

John, the last outstanding dogmatician of the Eastern Church, left a monumental legacy to posterity by gathering together and handing down what the fathers and the councils of the East had taught. He is a staunch champion of tradition, a devoted child of Mary, and the peerless theologian of the veneration of images and relics of the saints. Sacred Scripture is for him an important rule of faith and here, though he quotes and approves them, he rejects the Deuterocanonicals from the Old Testament canon and accepts the Apostolic Constitutions into the New Testament canon. No less a rule of faith is the living, unwritten tradition of the Church and the unanimous consensus of patristic opinion.

It is out of tradition that he develops his doctrine and theology of the veneration of saints and their images. God alone receives *latria* and *proskynesis*. He sharply distinguishes the two. *Proskynesis* is veneration given to creatures, to Mary as *Theotokos*, and to the saints as friends of God. The Old Testament prohibition of images he restricts to representation of the invisible God (Greek art of his day used only symbols, no statues, for this) and to according *latria* to images. Christ could be represented in images because He Himself assumed human form. Images of the saints may be given *proskynesis* because such representations re-

mind us of these select ones of God. They take the place of
sermons and reading for the unlettered. But *latria* must unequivocally be restricted to the divinity.

John's Christology is authentic, but his Trinitarian teaching
follows the Easterners in the procession of the Spirit from the
Father through the Son. The angels are incorporeal spirits, readily inclined to evil before the Fall but now fixed on good, not
by nature but by grace. There are nine choirs of three triads
who look after the affairs of peoples and individuals. John treats
only baptism and the Eucharist in the *De fide*. In his eschatology
he teaches that we can help the departed souls, but follows the
widely prevalent opinion that hellfire is not a material fire. John
also taught the assumption of Mary.

2. JUSTINIAN I, EMPEROR (527–565)

Justinian I was a man of extraordinary and varied gifts. He
was statesman, lawgiver, builder, and poet. He also made pretensions to being a theologian, though most of his theological
writings seem to show the pen of Bishop Theodore Askidas. On
more than one occasion Justinian intervened in Church affairs that
were more than purely disciplinary. Among his literary remains
are edicts against Monophysitism, Origenism, Nestorianism, and
the "Three Chapters." We also have thirteen letters to various
popes, some *Novellae*, and an antiphonary hymn, the *Troparium*.
Best known of all his works is the Justinian Code, promulgated
in 534 as the official code of law for the Empire.

3. LEONTIUS OF BYZANTIUM (c. 544)

Leontius is the outstanding theologian of the Greek Church
during the first half of the sixth century and he has, not incorrectly, been called the first Aristotelian or Scholastic. Nothing
is known of his life except that he was a monk and that for a
time he had been seduced by the Nestorians. He is the most
illustrious representative of the school of Constantinople which
held a middle position between Alexandria and Antioch. The
school got its greatest impetus from the patronage of Justinian
which attracted many eminent theologians, among them Leontius.
His writings show him to have been well acquainted with the

Logic of Aristotle as well as with Neoplatonism. Moreover, he was an effective polemicist against Monophysitism, especially against Severus of Antioch and his followers.

Shortly before his death (c. 544), he composed his greatest work, *Libri III adversus Nestorianos et Eutychianos*. This marks the author as a penetrating and keen thinker as well as a man exceedingly well read in the fathers. Book I develops the proposition that, though Nestorius and Eutyches seem to be at opposite poles in their thinking, they base their teaching on the same fundamental suppositions. Book II reproduces an alleged disputation between a representative of orthodoxy and one of Aphthartodocetism. Book III is directed specifically against Nestorianism and cites a series of errors that Leontius attributes to Theodore of Mopsuestia.

Besides this, Leontius has left two smaller works against Severus of Antioch: *Solutio argumentorum Severi et triginta capita adversus Severum*. The little treatise, *Adversus fraudes Apollinistarum*, appears also to be genuine. It exposes a number of forged "patristic" texts. The *De sectis*, that was formerly attributed to Leontius, is most probably the work of Theodore of Raithu.

Leontius brought a penetrating philosophical analysis to his exploration of the mystery of the Incarnation.

4. MAXIMUS CONFESSOR AND THEOLOGIAN
(c. 580–662)

Maximus is the greatest Greek theologian of the seventh century and the orthodox champion against Monothelitism. Born of a noble family in Constantinople, he became secretary to Emperor Heraclius but resigned (c. 614) to enter a monastery in Chrysopolis or Scutari, near Constantinople. In 626 he fled before the Persians and after a stopover together with Sophronius in Alexandria (c. 632), we find him in Carthage. In 645 he routed the ex-patriarch Pyrrhus of Constantinople in public debate in that city. The records of the debate have been preserved. Several African synods condemned Monothelitism and, through the efforts of Maximus, this heresy was finally condemned at the Lateran Council under Pope Martin I, in 649. In 653 Maximus was imprisoned with Anastasius, the monk, and Anastasius, the Apocrisian. They were taken to Constantinople for trial in 655. The records of the trial also are extant. The sentence was separate banishment to different places in Thrace. They were returned to Constantinople in 662 in another attempt to get them to subscribe to the *Ecthesis* of Heraclius (638) and the *Typus* of Constans II (648), both of which had been condemned in Rome at the Lateran Council. When these efforts failed, the three were scourged, had their tongues and right hands cut off, paraded through the streets of the city and sent into perpetual exile. Maximus died a little later that same year.

The writings of Maximus show him to have been widely read in philosophy and patristic literature. He is a keen dogmatician and a profound mystic. Next to John Damascene he is the last Greek theologian of importance. He is the scientific conqueror of Monothelitism.

He has left eleven dogmatic writings and some letters that are in reality also treatises against Monophysitism, twenty-three works against Monothelitism, and three anthropological writings, *De anima*. The most important of his mystical and ascetical writings are: the famed dialogue *Liber asceticus*, the 400 *Capita de caritate*, and altogether 300 *Capita gnostica*. There are two liturgical works; *Mystagogia*, a symbolic interpretation of the liturgy, and the *Computus ecclesiasticus* which treats of problems of heortology. His exegetical writings are chiefly discussions of selected passages of Sacred Scripture. He is mostly preoccupied with a moral and allegorical interpretation of the text. They are: *Quaestiones ad Thalassium*, *Quaestiones et dubia*, an exposition of Psalm 59, and a commentary on the Lord's Prayer. Lastly must be mentioned a commentary on Pseudo-Dionysius, consisting of scholia, most of which John of Scythopolis contributed as collaborator. Maximus also commented on several orations of Gregory Nazianzen.

5. SOPHRONIUS (638)

Sophronius was born in Damascus, taught rhetoric for a time and then entered a monastery in Jerusalem. Next he accompanied his friend, John Moschus, to Egypt and Rome. In 633 he refuted

Cyrus, the Monothelite patriarch of Alexandria, and not much later, Sergius, patriarch of Constantinople, vigorously defending the Council of Chalcedon. Upon his elevation to the patriarchate of Jerusalem (634), he immediately issued a synodal letter that is a masterpiece of exposition of orthodox teaching against Monothelitism. In 637 the Caliph Omar took Jerusalem, and the next year brought the death of Sophronius.

Besides the synodal letter already mentioned, Sophronius wrote another work against Monothelitism that has perished. He published a *Florilegium* of 600 patristic texts on the doctrine of the two operations in Christ. He has also left a hagiographical work, a life of the Alexandrian martyrs, Cyrus and John. There are also eleven sermons of his and twenty-three Anacreontic odes for ecclesiastical feasts.

6. DIONYSIUS THE AREOPAGITE
(end of fifth century or later)

The author of four longer treatises and eleven letters that long circulated under the name of Dionysius the Areopagite whom legend says Paul converted, was one of the most phenomenal forgers of history. He pretends to have observed the eclipse of the sun at Christ's death, when he was in Heliopolis, and maintained that he was present with Peter and John at the interment of the Blessed Mother. With colossal cheek he addressed his writings to the apostles and some of their disciples. We first encounter this mysterious author in the writings of Severus of Antioch. When the Monophysites quoted these works authoritatively at the Council of Constantinople (532), the Catholics under Hypatius of Ephesus repudiated them. However, Leontius of Byzantium, Gregory the Great, and Sophronius accepted them as genuine. When Maximus in his commentary explained away the errors of Pseudo-Dionysius, the future of our forger was assured. Hilduin, abbot of St. Denis, next proceeded to identify our hero with the martyr Dionysius of Paris. Scotus Eriugena translated him (c. 850), thus making the writings available to the Middle Ages. They were universally accepted as genuine until the fifteenth century. It has been established that the author copied shamelessly from Plotinus (270) and Proclus, the Neo-

platonist (485). The author cannot have lived much before the
end of the fifth century. He seems to have been a native of Syria,
because his liturgical explanations are all based on the Syrian rite.

Dionysius dedicated all his treatises to his disciple, Timothy.
They are:

1. *De divinis nominibus* (On the Divine Names) treats in
thirteen chapters of the divine names in Scripture and of the
divine nature and God's attributes.

2. *De mystica theologia* (On Mystical Theology) in five chapters treats of the mystical union of the soul with God, which
is achieved in a state of passivity that leads to an ecstatic vision
of God.

3. *De celesti hierarchia* (On the Celestial Hierarchy) in fifteen
chapters treats of the nature of the celestial realm, of heavenly
spirits, their nature, attributes, and classification into three choirs
of three triads.

4. *De ecclesiastica hierarchia* (On the Ecclesiastical Hierarchy)
expounds in seven chapters the organization of the Church after
the pattern of the celestial hierarchy. Here there are three triads
also: a) the three sacraments: baptism, confirmation, and Eucharist, b) the three ecclesiastical ranks: bishops, priests, and
deacons, c) the three lesser states: monks, laity, and penitents.
Chapter seven has an appendix on the ecclesiastical burial service.

The letters treat of pastoral matters and are in part supple-
mentary to the treatises. They are addressed to such persons as
a monk Caius, the apostle John, and the bishops Titus and
Polycarp.

III. Poets

There are several writers with authentic poetic gifts in this
period. The author of the *Akathistos*, Andrew of Crete, George
Pisides, and Roman the Singer, or Melodos, are important also
theologically. Anastasius and Cosmas the Singer were poets of
lesser stature.

1. AKATHISTOS (seventh century)

Akathistos is the most famous liturgical hymn of the Greek Church. It was composed by an unknown author on the occasion of the deliverance of Constantinople in 626. Its name indicates that it is said standing. The full title is, "Ode in Honor of the Most Blessed Glorious Lady, Mother of God and Ever Virgin Mary." There seems good reason to ascribe the poem to Roman Melodos or Roman the Singer.

2. ANDREW OF CRETE (c. 740)

Andrew of Crete was a defender of the faith against Mono-thelitism and, later, against the Iconoclasts. Born around 660, he was a monk in Jerusalem (c. 678), a deacon in Constantinople (c. 685), archbishop of Gortyna in Crete (c. 692). He died about 740. He has left us twenty-three sermons, a number of liturgical poems put to melody, called *Idomela,* and some hymns called Canons. Among the sermons are three on the Assumption. The hymns called Canons are a new form of ecclesiastical hymnody. Andrew's Great Canon, a penitential hymn of 250 strophes which celebrates the great penitents of the Bible, is still in use in the Eastern liturgy during Lent. Andrew was a great poet and orator. His eight homilies and two Canons on the Blessed Mother are most important in Mariology. Noteworthy is his teaching that Mary died, not as other human beings, but to resemble her Son.

3. GEORGE PISIDES (middle of sixth century)

George Pisides, or the Pisidian, deacon of St. Sophia in Constantinople at the time of Emperor Heraclius (610–641), though a hymnographer of classic beauty and great gifts, devoted most of his efforts to such secular themes as the Persian campaigns and the siege of Constantinople in 626. Among his religious hymns are *Hexaemeron* (1894 verses), *De vanitate vitae,* 262 verses (On the Vanity of Life), *Against the Monophysites,* and some Epigrams. The *Akathistos* was by some ascribed to him.

4. ROMAN THE SINGER (c. 560)

Roman the Singer or Romanos Melodos was the greatest of the early Byzantine poets. Born about 490 in Emesa, he was a priest in Constantinople and died there around 560. He is said to have composed 1,000 hymns and is the greatest hymnographer produced by the East—some say he was the greatest of the Church. Though most of his work has not been preserved, some of his hymns are still used today. Of great beauty are his hymns for Easter and Christmas. Recently more evidence has been presented that the *Akathistos* is the work of Roman with a prooemium added later perhaps in 629 when the city of Constantinople was besieged by Avars, or in 719 when the Arabs were at Constantinople's gates.

BOOK TWO

Other Patristic

Writers and Works

In this book are short notices of writers and of anonymous patristic works that were not discussed in Book One. Those fathers and patristic writings studied in Book One are not included here. Some of them have been mentioned previously, but in this book we have added details which may be of help to the student.

Rather than two separate listings of authors and works we have chosen a single listing of both. The titles of the writings are in italics so that they may be easily distinguished from the names of the authors.

Other Patristic Writers
and Works

Abercius, bishop of Hieropolis (end of second century), composed his epitaph of twenty-one lines in a mystical and symbolic style to safeguard the Discipline of the Secret. The inscription attests to the Eucharist under both species, to the virginity of Mary, to the church at Rome as "the queen with robe and golden shoes," to the acrostic, *Ichthus*, to the Christians as a "people with the splendid seal," to the uniformity of belief he found everywhere from the Euphrates to Rome and the belief in "faithful writings." This Abercius may be the Avircius Marcellus to whom the anonymous Montanist dedicated three books.

Abgar, king of Edessa, figures in an apocryphal correspondence between Jesus and Abgar. See *Acta Edessena, Doctrina Addai,* and the *Acts of Thaddeus.*

Abraham of Ephesus (fifth century), founder of monasteries at Constantinople and Jerusalem, later bishop of Ephesus, left homilies on the Annunciation and the Presentation. They are valuable for the history of these feasts.

Absamya, a nephew of Ephraem the Syrian, is perhaps identified with Cyrillonas.

Acacius of Berea, bishop of Berea in Syria, died after 437, at an age of more than a hundred years. Active in Church affairs and first a friend, then a violent opponent of John Chrysostom, he has left only five letters of a bulky correspondence.

Acacius of Caesarea (366), disciple and successor to Eusebius as bishop of Caesarea (340–366), was the leader of the Homeans in the East. He developed the library founded by Origen.

Though a prolific writer only fragments of his work remain.
Acacius of Constantinople. See Henoticon.
Acacius of Melitene, first a friend, later an opponent of Nestorius,
left a homily preached at Ephesus. Two letters also remain of
his writings.
Acta Archelai. See Hegemonius.
Acta Edessena, written in Syriac during the first half of the third
century, deal with the apocryphal correspondence of Abgar.
See Abgar, *Doctrina Addai, Acts of Thaddeus.*
Acts of Andrew. See under Andrew.
Acts of the Council of Chalcedon (451):

    a. In Greek there are three collections of correspondence about
the Council and the minutes (*Actiones*) of the seventeen
sessions of the Council. Both were published shortly after
the year 451.

    b. In Latin there are several translations and the original ac-
counts:

        1. *Collectio Novariensis de re Eutychis* published under
Pope Leo the Great around 450.

        2. *Collectio Vaticana* published under Pope Hormisdas (514–
523).

        3. A Latin version of collections of correspondence (see
above) published on the occasion of the Three Chapters
controversy, by Rusticus the Deacon.

        4. *Leonis Papae I epistolarum collectiones.* These fifteen col-
lections of 114 letters pertaining to this period go back
to 458. The *Collectio Grimanica* of 104 items dates from
553.

        5. *Codex Encyclicus. Collectiones epistolarum et libellorum
de schismate Acaciano.*

Acts of the Council of Constantinople (553). See John Maxentius.
Acts of the Council of Ephesus (431):

    a. Greek collections:

        1. *Collectio Vaticana* (175 items).

        2. *Collectio Seguiriana* (146 items).

        3. *Collectio Atheniensis* (177 items, fifty-eight of which
are not in the other two collections).

    b. Latin translations:

1. *Collectio Casinensis.* Rusticus the Deacon translated and edited these Acts (564–565) in Constantinople in an effort to prove that the "Three Chapters" had been unjustly condemned. His chief source was the *Tragoedia* of Irenaeus Comes.

2. *Collectio Veronensis* appeared in Rome under Pope Celestine I.

3. *Collectio Palatina* is the work of a Scythian monk (c. 550).

4. *Collectio Sichardiana* (after 553).

5. *Collectio Winteriana* (date unknown).

Acts of John. See under John.

Acts of Justin. See under Justin.

Acts of Matthew. See under Matthew.

Acts of Paul. See under Paul.

Acts of Paul and Thecla. See under Paul.

Acts of Peter. See under Peter.

Acts of Peter and Paul. See under Peter.

Acts of Philip. See under Philip.

Acts of Pilate. See under Pilate.

Acts of Thaddeus. See under Thaddeus.

Acts of the Apostle Andrew. See under Andrew.

Acts of the Apostle Thomas. See under Thomas.

Actus Petri cum Simone. See *Acts of Peter.*

Actus Vercellensis. See *Acts of Peter,* of which it is a Latin version.

Adamantius, the speaker in the dialogue, *De recta fide.* He vanquishes Marcion, Bardesanes, and Valentinus, and champions orthodoxy. Adamantius is also a pseudonym for Origen.

Addai Doctrina. See Abgar, *Acta Edessena,* etc.

Adimantus, a fourth century Manichaean who wrote a book on the alleged contradictions between the Old and New Testaments.

Adrian or Hadrian, priest and monk, wrote an introduction to the Holy Scripture early in the fifth century. He was an Antiochian in exegesis and emphasized the need of Hebrew for finding the literal sense.

Aeneas of Gaza, a contemporary of Procopius, wrote to Theophrastus a dialogue on immortality and the resurrection. He was very popular in the Middle Ages.

Aetheria, or Egeria or Eucheria (393) was a deaconess of southern Gaul who made a pilgrimage to Palestine, Egypt, and Edessa (c. 393). She faithfully narrates all she saw on the three-year trip in her *Peregrinatio ad loca sancta* (Pilgrimage to the Holy Places). The work is of great value in the study of liturgy, especially of Holy Week and Easter Week in Jerusalem. The account also tells about many churches and tombs of martyrs. For a long time the diary was thought to have been written by Silvis, sister of Rufinus of Aquileia.

Aetius of Antioch was an out and out Arian. He became bishop of Antioch under Julian (361–363) and died in 367. Some remains of his literary output, which set about to prove that the Son being "gendered" cannot be "ungendered," i.e., God, have been preserved by Epiphanius.

Agapitus I, Pope (535–536) has left us seven letters. He asserted the primacy of Rome by going to Constantinople, deposing the Monophysite Anthimus, and consecrating Mennas in his place.

Agapitus the Deacon, a deacon in the Hagia Sophia in Constantinople, wrote a directive in seventy-two verses to the Emperor Justinian, on his accession. He may have been Justinian's tutor. The directive explains the obligations of a Christian ruler in seventy-two maxims and came to be used as a textbook in government.

Agathangelos (c. 450) is a pseudonym for the author of the "History of the Reign of Terdat and the Preaching of St. Gregory the Illuminator in Armenia."

Agrippa Castor, wrote against Basilides during the reign of Hadrian (117–138).

Aleatores, Adv., is a sermon against dice players whom it condemns as pagans. Though attributed to Cyprian, the author is a Catholic African bishop (c. 300).

Alexander of Alexandria was a bishop of Alexandria (313–328) who bore the brunt of the fight against Arius. In 318 he called a synod at Alexandria which condemned Arius and his followers. A synod at Antioch in 325 confirmed this condemnation. Later that year he effected, with the help of Athanasius, the condemnation of Arianism at Nicea. Among his seventy extant letters, three are important for the history of Arianism. Only fragments remain of his sermons except for one, *De anima et corpore deque passione Christi* (On the Soul and Body of Christ and His Passion).

Alexander of Jerusalem (c. 250) was Origen's friend and a former disciple of Clement whom he received into his home after his flight from Alexandria. He also conferred the priesthood on Origen and protected him against Demetrius of Alexandria. Born around 160–170, probably in Asia Minor, he was later bishop in Cappadocia or Cilicia. On the occasion of a pilgrimage to Jerusalem he was forcibly detained by the Christians of that city and installed as coadjutor to the aged Bishop Narcissus whom he succeeded (c. 216). Eusebius and Jerome mention many letters of which only fragments remain. Alexander established a Christian library in Jerusalem.

Alexander of Salamina was a monk famed as an orator and exegete during the reign of Justinian.

Alexandrians, Epistle of Paul to the. See under Paul.

Alexius, Life of. In its oldest form this legend of the life of Alexius is a Syriac life (fifth century) of an unnamed saint of Edessa.

Ambrose of Alexandria, bishop of Alexandria (d. 248–253) was a patron of Origen and the author of a few letters.

Ammonas, the disciple of and successor to Anthony as head of the monastic colony at Pispir, has left us seven letters in Greek and fifteen in Syriac. His "Heavenly Journey of the Soul" has an important place in his mysticism.

Ammonius (third century), has left a work, *Accord Between Moses and Jesus*. A synopsis of the Gospels is also attributed to him. There seem to have been two or three writers of that name. See Ammonius of Alexandria.

Ammonius (priest) of Alexandria, lived under Emperor Leo I (457–474). Fragments of his scriptural commentaries are found among the *Catenae*. He is probably the Ammonius who wrote against Timothy Aerulus in 457.

Amphilochius of Side was an opponent of Nestorius. Only a fragment of one letter remains.

Amphilochius of Iconium (403) was a cousin of Gregory Nazianzen and a close friend of the three Cappadocians. Born about 340, he studied under Libanius and practiced law in Constantinople. After a brief retirement from the world he was appointed bishop of Iconium in 373 at the instance of Basil the Great. A champion of orthodoxy, he was present at the councils of Constantinople in 381 and 394. In between he presided at a synod held at Side in 390. He especially attacked the Arians and some of the sects of Manichaean tendencies, as the Apoctites, Encratites, Gemellites, and the Messalians. After 394 when he attended a council at Constantinople he is no longer on the scene. A prolific writer, there have come down to us only 333 *Iambics for Seleucus,* eight sermons on feastdays and a treatise against the Apoctites and the Gemellites. The Cappadocians depict him as a man of action and zealous pastor rather than a theologian.

Ananias is an Armenian writer and translator of the fifth century. Very little is known of him. He was one of the "Holy Translators."

Anaphora Pilati is a forgery of the Middle Ages purporting to be Pilate's report to the emperor.

Anastasius I, Pope (399–402), left three letters: to Simplician, to Venerius, bishop of Milan, and to Bishop John of Jerusalem. Influenced by Jerome in the matter, he backed up the condemnation of Origen by Theophilus of Alexandria in a Paschal letter, but refused to condemn Rufinus as translator of Origen.

Anastasius II, Pope (496–498), left four letters. Of importance is a letter to Emperor Anastasius declaring heretical orders valid and a letter to a Gallic bishop denouncing generationism as heretical, and declaring for creationism.

Anastasius I of Antioch (559–599) spent most of his patriarchate in exile (570–593) because of his opposition to Aphthartodocetism and the Emperor Justinian, who had decreed in favor of that error. His numerous writings, letters, and treatises, one against John Philoponus the Tritheist, have been lost, except for four sermons and five dogmatic treatises on God's nature and immensity, on the Incarnation, the Passion, and Resurrection of Christ.

Anastasius II, patriarch of Antioch (599–609), translated the *Reg-*

ula pastoralis of Gregory the Great into Greek but it is lost. See Gregory the Great, p. 178.

Anastasius the Apocrisian (666) was a companion in exile of Maximus Confessor, an account of whose trial he wrote. He has left us also a letter against Monothelitism replete with quotations from the fathers. His authorship of the *Doctrina Patrum* against Monophysites and Monothelites is not certain. Some attribute it to Anastasius Sinaita. The work is valuable for quotations from otherwise unknown works. See Maximus Confessor, p. 204.

Anastasius III, patriarch of Nicea (c. 700), wrote a commentary on the Psalms.

Anastasius the Monk (d. 662), a companion in persecution of Maximus Confessor, wrote a letter on the two wills of Christ.

Anastasius the Poet wrote a beautiful Threnody. He may be Anastasius Sinaita.

Anastasius Sinaita (c. 630–700), so named because he was head of a monastery on Mt. Sinai, was a vigorous opponent of the Nestorians, Monophysites, Monothelites, and Jews. He has left us a large work, *The Guide against the Monophysites*, an allegorical commentary on the Hexaemeron, some sermons, and a book on 154 theological questions, some of which are a later addition.

Anatolius of Alexandria, bishop of Laodicea (c. 268), wrote a book on Easter, some theological works, and treatises on mathematics.

Andrew, Acts of the Apostle, is perhaps the work of a certain Leukios Charinos (c. 260). Very little remains of this work and it cannot be determined how much other later works depend on it. These later works are valueless and quite fantastic, e.g., "History of Andrew and Matthias in the City of the Man-eaters."

Andrew, Gospel of, a work mentioned in the *Decretum Gelasianum* is probably the "Acts of the Apostle Andrew."

Andrew, History of, may be the work of Leukios Charinos (c. 200). Only fragments have come down to us. Later writings based on this work are hard to evaluate. See "Acts of the Apostle Andrew."

Andrew of Caesarea in Cappadocia wrote a commentary on the

Apocalypse sometime between 563 and 614. He is a protagonist of pneumatic exegesis and an opponent of Oecumenius. He has given us one of the best earlier recensions of the text of the Apocalypse. The commentary on the Apocalypse by Arethas of Caesarea (c. 895) is a free adaption of Andrew's text. We have only fragments of another work, *Therapeutike*.

Andrew of Samosata (c. 430), bishop of Samosata, attacked Cyril of Jerusalem. A few of his letters have been left.

Anianus the Chronist, a monk of Alexandria (412), wrote a chronography of the world.

Anonymous Arian is a commentary on Job by an anonymous Arian of the fourth century attributed to Julius Halicarnassus.

Anonymous Anti-Montanist, whom Eusebius mentions, was a bishop or priest of Eastern Phrygia (c. 192–193). He wrote a treatise in three books.

Anthimus was a Greek hymnographer of the fifth century cited by Theodorus Lector.

Anthony the Hermit (died in 356, age 105), though unlettered, has left us seven letters which show the sound asceticism of the author. Noteworthy among them are a treatise on an introduction to the ascetical life and a letter on sincere repentance to Abbot Theodore. The so-called *Rules of St. Anthony* seem to be genuine also.

Anthony the Hagiographer wrote a life of Simeon Stylites.

Antiochus of Constantinople (c. 408) was a most popular orator in his day but only one of his discourses has been preserved.

Antiochus the Monk, of St. Sabas, wrote his *Pandects* on Sacred Scripture early in the seventh century. This work was much used by later writers, especially John Damascene. It is a moral theology in 130 sections full of quotations from the Scriptures. Sections 1–2 deal with faith and hope. After an introductory discussion of the vices (3–66) the next sections (67–126) discuss the virtues. The last sections (127–130) treat of charity and conclude the work.

Antiochus, monk of the monastery of St. Sabas (c. 620), wrote *Pandects* of the Sacred Scriptures; 130 chapters on the duties of Christians and the duties of the religious life. He ends with a prayer for Jerusalem then under the Persians.

Antiochus of Ptolemais (c. 408) was an opponent of John Chrysostom. No certain works of his authorship remain. He enjoyed great repute as an orator.

Antipater, bishop of Bostra, in the fifth century, wrote against Pamphilius' *Apology* of Origen and against the Apollinarists. Only fragments of his writings are left.

Antonii Placentini itinerarium tells of a pilgrimage to Palestine by the citizens of Piacenza. It was written between 560–570.

Apelles was a disciple of Marcion. He died about 180. His work, *Syllogisms*, was an attack on the Old Testament. His *Revelations* purport to describe the visons of Philomena, a member of the sect. A gospel was also attributed to him.

Aphraates (c. 345), the Persian Sage, is the first of the Syriac Fathers. Monk, ascetic, and probably a bishop, he has left us twenty-three treatises, called Demonstrations, on a wide range of theological subjects, faith, charity, fasting, prayer, penance, exhortations to ascetics, the Resurrection and the Divinity of Christ. He attacks the Jews. Though he covers the whole range of theology, he emphasizes asceticism. He quotes the New Testament from Tatian. He is important for the history of Persian monasticism and the Persian Church in general.

Apion, an anti-Gnostic writer of the turn of the century from the second to the third, composed a work on the Hexaemeron.

Apocalypse of Baruch, see under Baruch.

Apocalypse of John, see under John.

Apocalypse of Peter, see under Peter.

Apocalypse of Stephen, see under Stephen.

Apocalypse of Thomas, see under Thomas.

Apocalypse of Zacharias, see under Zacharias.

Apollinaris of Hieropolis, bishop around 170–175, wrote four apologies, five books against the Greeks, two books on truth, an apology addressed to Marcus Aurelius (161–180), a work on Easter against the Quartodecimans and, with other bishops, an encyclical against the Montanists.

Apollonius is an Asiatic writer (196–197) against Montanism.

Apollonius, Acts of, are an account of the trial of a Roman named Apollonius (183–185) before the prefect Perennis.

Aponius (c. 410) wrote a long allegorical commentary on the Canticle of Canticles that repeatedly emphasizes the primacy of the Church of Rome.

Apostles, Letters of:

1. *Pauline Apocryphal Letters*
   a. *To the Laodiceans* (fourth century).
   b. *To the Alexandrians*, a lost Marcionite work.
   c. *Third Letter to the Corinthians* (second or third century) contains some of the materials of the *Acts of Paul* and treats of prophecy in the early Church, of the Incarnation, the creation, the Virgin Birth, the human nature of Christ, and the Resurrection.
   d. *The Correspondence of Paul and Seneca*, may have originated as school exercises around 300.
2. Barnabas. See Pseudo-Barnabas, p. 18.
3. *Epistola Apostolorum*, a most important and valuable document, purports to be the revelation of Christ to His apostles after the Resurrection. It originated in Asia Minor or Egypt in the middle of the second century. It discusses questions on the Resurrection, Parousia, Last Judgment, signs of the End, the missionary work of the apostles, and the Descent into Hell. It is on the whole orthodox.
4. *Epistola Titi*, on Virginity, is directed against the abuses connected with the *Virgines subintroductae*. It is Priscillianist in outlook.

Apophthegmata Patrum, a collection of sayings and examples taken from the lives of famed monks. The work dates from the end of the fifth century and has undergone many revisions. See *Verba seniorum*, and *Vitae Patrum*.

Apringius, bishop of Badajoz in Spain (c. 540), wrote a commentary on the Apocalypse. Only a few fragments are left.

Aquila translated the Old Testament from Hebrew into Greek (c. 135). Though highly esteemed by the Jews of the time, it was a slavish and inelegant version.

Arabianus was an anti-Gnostic writer mentioned by Eusebius.

Arabic Gospel of the Childhood of Jesus is a late work based on the *Gospel of Thomas* and the *Protoevangelium Jacobi* with additions.

Arabic History of Joseph the Carpenter is a fifth century story of the life of St. Joseph based on the *Gospel of Thomas* and the *Protoevangelium Jacobi.*

Arator, poet, was a protegé of Ennodius and Pope Vigilius (554). A lawyer and comptroller of finances under Athalaric, he composed an *Epos de Actibus Apostolorum* in 2336 hexameters which he read in the church of Peter in Chains. He also wrote some letters in distichs. Sedulius was his model.

Arbela, Chronicle of, dates from the period around 540–569 and has a series of biographies after the pattern of the *Acta Martyrum.* Their historicity is questionable, to say the least.

Aristo of Pella, the earliest Apologist for Christianity against Judaism, wrote a *Dialogue Between Jason and Papiscus on Christ* (c. 140). Jason, a convert from Judaism, converts the Jew Papiscus by a discussion of the Old Testament prophecies. Both the Greek original and the Latin translation have been lost.

Arnobius the Elder of Sicca (c. 327) has left us seven books *Against the Nations,* allegedly composed to prove the genuineness of his conversion. A great and learned rhetorician, his understanding of Christian teaching was not very thorough. In Book one he refutes the old charge that the infidelity of the Christians has brought evil on the Roman Empire. Books two to five expose the immorality and unreasonableness of the pagan myths and beliefs. The last two books denounce pagan worship. The work is valuable for history and archaeology.

Arnobius the Younger (451), though a native of Africa lived as a monk in Rome (c. 432). A Semi-Pelagian, he left an allegorical commentary on the Psalms and exegetical notes on Matthew, Luke, and John. His *Conflictus Arnobii Catholici cum Serapione Aegyptio* is a debate with a Monophysite. The treatise, *Praedestinatus* may be his work also.

Asclepius, bishop of Castellum in Africa in the fifth century, wrote polemics against the Arians but all are lost.

Assumption of Paul. See Paul.

Asterius of Amasea was bishop of Amasea (c. 410), and a great orator. Homilies mentioned in the II Council of Nicea are ascribed to him. Twenty-one of these have been preserved.

The *Catenae* contain other fragments. All are moral in tone and show the pastoral preoccupation of the preacher.

Asterius of Cappadocia (c. 341), also called the Sophist, defended Arianism and attacked Marcellus of Ancyra in a lost work, *Syntagmation*. He was a disciple of Lucian of Antioch and some few of his homilies on the Psalms are useful in the study of Antiochean exegesis.

Athanasian Creed is also called the *Quicumque* after its first word and is still recited in the Office at Prime on Trinity Sunday. A clear exposition of the doctrine of the Trinity and the Incarnation, it has been ascribed to Athanasius only since the seventh century.

Audentius (fourth century) was a bishop mentioned by Gennadius as an opponent of the Priscillianists.

Aurelian of Carthage (429), friend and disciple of Augustine, and bishop of Carthage, wrote a circular letter against the Pelagians in 419.

Aurelianus of Arles, bishop of Arles (546–553), rearranged and enlarged the two rules, *Regula ad monachos* and *Regula ad virgines*.

Ausonius, poet of the fourth century, is still an enigma as to the genuineness of his conversion. Born around 310 in Bordeaux he is best remembered for his relationship with his pupil Paulinus of Nola. He has left us many *Opuscula*, but these show little distinctly Christian spirit. He wrote a description of Treves and the Moselle region. Besides this he has left us *Versus Paschales*, an Easter prayer for Emperor Valentinian I (c. 370) containing the Nicene Creed, *Oratio matutina*, *Oratio versibus rhopalicis*, and twenty-five letters in verse among which are three that try to dissuade Paulinus of Nola from leaving the world.

Auxentius was a Greek hymnographer of the fifth century.

Auxentius of Dorostorium (fourth century), bishop of Dorostorium, is connected with some letters and sermons of Arian tendency. He was a disciple of Wulfilas and has left us an *Epistola de fide, vita et obitu Wulfilae*.

Avellana Collectio is a collection of some 243 letters of popes and emperors dating 367–553, many of them of Hormisdas

(514–523). It was made as a private collection and is named after the Umbrian convent S. Croce di Fonte Avellana.

Avircius Marcellus, an unknown bishop in Asia Minor, dedicated three works against the Montanists to Avircius Marcellus. Some think he is Abercius of Hieropolis.

Babai the Great, abbot of Izla, who lived from 569 to 628, was a fanatical Nestorian who has left us a treatise *On the Union* (of the two natures of Christ), some letters, biographies, hymns, works of asceticism, liturgy, and a commentary on the whole Bible. See Henana of Adiabene.

Bachiarius, a Spanish monk, was compelled to leave Spain because of charges of Priscillianist sympathies. In Rome he wrote a treatise (c. 383) *De fide* against the Priscillianists to justify himself. Later (c. 394–400) he published a work *De lapso* interceding for a fallen deacon. Two letters on ascetical matters may also be from his hands.

Balaeus, or Syrian Balai (c. 460), chor-episcopus or rural bishop of Aleppo (Beroea), was a contemporary of Acacius (432) and left us five panegyric poems on the latter. A few of his hymns found their way into the liturgy of the East but most of his prolific output of poetry has been lost. See Acacius.

Bar Chatar (459) collaborated with Simeon Bar Apollon to write a life of Simeon Stylites (died 459) in Syriac. It is quite full and reliable. Nothing else is known of Bar Chatar.

Bardesanes (Bar-Daisan) of Edessa (c. 222) composed with his son Harmonius 150 hymns and their melodies to teach his doctrines. It is far from clear to what extent he taught Gnostic errors. His students may have distorted his views. There has come down to us in the original Syriac a work *On Fate* or *Book of the Laws of Countries*.

Barkabbas, Prophecy of, was a popular book among the Nicolaites but nothing is known of it.

Barlaam, Life of Barlaam and Joseph, is based on a novel of the seventh century. It is an extravagant romance very popular in the Middle Ages written by a Greek monk of the tenth century. He incorporated into his work (and in doing so, preserved for posterity) the *Apology of Aristides.* This is its only claim to mention here.

Barnabas, *Gospel of*, a work mentioned in the *Decretum Gelasianum* and in a list of canonical books dated eighth or ninth century, has been lost. The so-called Italian Gospel of Barnabas which regards Mohammed as the Messias is the work of a fourteenth century apostate to Islam.

Barnabas, *History of*, belongs to the legendary *Acts* of various Apostles that originated in the fourth or fifth century or even later.

Barsanuphius, monk of Gaza (c. 540) wrote many ascetical letters. Several of those attributed to him may be the work of John of Gaza (c. 530). One hundred of them are addressed to the ascetic Dorotheus, his disciple.

Barsauma (489), bishop of Nisibis, induced Peroz, king of Persia, to make Nestorianism the official form of Christianity in that country. He was the author of many hymns, treatises, letters, and a liturgy. His statutes for the school of Nisibis, revised by his successor Osee or Eliseus, are still extant. He was a Nestorian. See Henana.

Bartholomew, *Apocalypse of*, came to be known only in recent times, but even now nothing is known of it other than that such a work once existed.

Bartholomew, *Gospel of*, dates from the third century and originated in Gnostic circles of Egypt. It is mentioned in the Gelasian Decree. The fragments remaining treat of the questions asked by Bartholomew of Jesus after His Resurrection. The *Descensus ad Inferos* is discussed in great detail.

Bartholomew, *History of*, belongs to the legendary *Acts* that originated in the fourth and fifth century or even later.

Baruch, *Apocalypse of*, is a Jewish work interpolated by Christians.

Basil of Ancyra (364) was a physician who in 336 succeeded the deposed Bishop Marcellus of Ancyra. At the Synod of Ancyra in 358 he and George of Laodicea led the Semi-Arians (Homoiousians). He was banished to Illyria by a synod held at Constantinople (360) which was dominated by Acacius and the Homoieans. He died about 364. He has left us a *Memorial* on the doctrine of the Trinity. Perhaps *De virginitate*, usually attributed to Basil the Great, is also from his pen.

Basil of Cilicia, a monophysite priest of Antioch, wrote a Church

History of the period around 450–540, which is no longer extant.

Basil of Seleucia (c. 468), metropolitan of Seleucia, after some years of vacillation during the Monophysite controversies, remained staunchly orthodox after Chalcedon (451). A number of sermons have come down to us but they are of relatively little worth. His poem, *De vita et miraculis sanctae Theclae Libri II* also is of little value.

Basilides, an Alexandrian Gnostic, wrote his "gospel" and a commentary in twenty-four books, and some Odes. All have been lost.

Basilides was a soldier martyr (c. 202) whose Acts are mentioned by Eusebius.

Benedict, St., born at Nursia in 480, died at Monte Cassino in 547. His rule was adopted by almost all Western monks from the eighth to the thirteenth century.

Beryllus was a bishop of Bosra whom Origen converted. Jerome speaks of a correspondence between the two. Beryllus also produced an anthology or *Philocalia*.

Besa (c. 474), successor to Shenoute whose biographer he was, has left sermons and ascetical treatises, for the most part unedited.

Boniface I, Pope (418–422) left nine letters, of which No. 15 asserts his primacy in the feud at Thessalonica.

Boniface II, Pope (530–532) confirmed the condemnation of Semi-Pelagianism by the second Synod of Orange (529) in a letter to Caesarius of Arles.

Bonosus of Sardica, bishop of Sardica, had denied the perpetual virginity of Mary. Pope Siricius (384–399) condemned him in a letter to Bishop Anysius of Thessalonica.

Braulio of Saragossa (seventh century) was a friend of Isidore of Seville. After Isidore's death he edited and added to the *Etymologies* but he was best known as an orator.

Breviarius de Hierosolyma is a catalogue of the Holy Places in Jerusalem of the fifth or sixth century.

Caius, a Roman priest under Zephyrinus (199–217) rejected the Johannine writings in his efforts to refute the Montanists who abused them.

Callinicus wrote a life of Hypatius (446), abbot of one of Rufinus' monasteries. Callinicus was a monk under Hypatius and wrote around 447–450.

Callistus, Pope (217–222), reputed author of the famed Edict of Callistus or Callixtus, excommunicated Sabellius. The so-called Edict referred to by Tertullian is regarded by most scholars as the decree of an African bishop, not a papal edict. Callistus was scurrilously maligned by Hippolytus.

Candidus was an anti-Gnostic writer of the second century.

Candidus (an Arian) was the author of a treatise *De generatione divina*, refuted by Marius Victorinus.

Canons of Hippolytus. See *Didascalia*, p. 30.

Capreolos (435), a friend and disciple of Augustine, wrote two remarkable letters against Nestorius and his teaching.

Carmen ad Flavium Felicem de resurrectione mortuorum et de judicio Domini (On the Resurrection of the Dead and Judgment); a poem of 406 hexameters was written by an anonymous African (c. 500) and handed down as a work of Cyprian or Tertullian.

Carmen adv. Marcionitas, is a writing of the early fourth century at one time ascribed to Tertullian. However, both place and date of origin are still highly debatable. It is based on Tertullian's *Adv. Marcionem*.

Carpocrates, an Alexandrian Gnostic, contemporary of Valentine and Basilides.

Carpus, Papylus and Agathonice, The Passion of, is an eyewitness account. The first two martyrs were burned at the stake during the reign of Marcus Aurelius, and Agathonice joined them in their martyrdom.

Catalogus Felicianus is the oldest part of the *Liber Pontificalis*, a collection of biographies and letters of the popes. The *Catalogus Felicianus* takes the collection up to Felix III (526–530). It was probably compiled by a Roman cleric under Boniface II (530–532). He used the *Catalogus Liberianus* as the basis of his work.

Catalogus Liberianus is a list of the popes with dates of their reigns up to Pope Liberius (352–366). See *Catalogus Felicianus*.

Celestine I, Pope (422–432), left sixteen letters most of which have to do with Nestorius. Epistle 21 reckons Augustine among the "Magistri optimi" and defends him from Semi-Pelagian attacks.

Celestius, monk and disciple of Pelagius, is known only through citations.

Celsus, a Platonist, wrote a bitter attack on the Christians (c. 178) that can be to some extent reconstructed from Origen's *Contra Celsum*.

Cerealis, an anti-Arian writer, was bishop of Castellum in Mauretania Caesariensis (c. 485).

Cerinthus, a Syrian Gnostic, left no writings. A gospel bears his name.

Chariton, Life of, was written by an anonymous author at the suggestion of Cyril of Scythopolis in the sixth century. Chariton (d. 350) was a founder of Palestinian monasticism.

Chosrowig was one of the "holy translators" (fifth century) in the school founded by Mesrop.

Christus patiens, is a work of the eleventh or twelfth century that was commonly listed among the works of Gregory Nazianzen.

Chromatius of Aquileia (388–407) was a correspondent of St. Ambrose. Parts of eighteen treatises of his have come down to us. They are remarkable for correctness and charm.

Chronicon Horosii is a world chronicle reaching to 334 A.D., based on the chronicle of Hippolytus.

Chronicon Edessena, a Syriac chronicle, covers the period around 133 B.C. to 540 A.D. of the history of Edessa. The author is unknown but of Nestorian sympathies.

Chronicon Paschale is an anonymous work of the early seventh century from Constantinople. The author is preoccupied with the feast of Easter, hence the name given it by Ducange. He covers the years from Adam to 629. Only the last part is of any value.

Chronographer of 354 is perhaps the work of Dionysius Philocalus, secretary to Pope Damasus I. The work contains all manner of lists of civil and ecclesiastical officials and varied information. It contains:

    1. Official Calendar of the city of Rome by Philocalus in 354.

2. Consular annals of Rome to 354.
3. List of the prefects of Rome, 254–354.
4. Paschal tables from 312 to 411.
5. *Depositio episcoporum*, a list of dates of death and burial of popes from Lucius (254) to Julius I (352).
6. *Depositio martyrum* lists the anniversaries of the martyrs venerated at Rome. It is our earliest Martyrology.
7. *Liberian Catalogue*, a list of popes from Peter to Liberius (352–366). The author of the *Liber Pontificalis* used this.
8. A description of Rome by districts, about 334.
9. The *Chronicon Horosii*.
10. A chronicle of Rome up to 324.

Chrysippus was a native of Cappadocia and priest of Jerusalem (after 479). A skilled orator he left us four *Encomia, On St. Theodore, On the Archangel Michael, On the Mother of God,* and *On John the Baptist.*

Claudianus Mamertus, a priest of Vienne and younger brother of Bishop Mamertus (c. 474), wrote *De statu animae,* a work of Neoplatonic and Augustinian tendencies against those who held a certain corporeity of the soul. He develops his thesis in three books, the last of which is directed against Faustus of Riez. His arguments are taken from reason and authority.

Claudius Claudianus, an outstanding pagan poet (404). Though "*a Christi nomine alienus*" (a stranger to the name of Christ), he composed several Christian poems, among them the *Carmen Paschale. Laus Christi* and *Miracula Christi* are not authentic.

Clementine Literature comprises the following items: a second letter to the Corinthians, two letters *Ad virgines,* and the *Clementine Romances.* These latter ar composed of twenty homilies and ten books of *Recognitiones.*

Clementine Romances, also called the Pseudo-Clementines, tell in two forms, the homilies and the *Recognitiones,* the history of Peter, his travels, his encounter with Simon Magus and the conversion of Clement. The twenty homilies purport to be sermons of Peter but they are fanciful in the extreme and betray Judaistic and Gnostic thinking. The *Recognitiones* get their name from the remarkable circumstances that the whole family of Clement of Rome, though dispersed throughout the world, yet meet and come to know or recognize each other.

Clement. *Two Letters to Virgins,* originated in Palestine about the middle of the third century. How they came to be associated with Clement is not known as they are first mentioned by Epiphanius. Both letters are valuable for the history of asceticism. The author, who seems to have been highly respected and prominent, discourses on virginity and excoriates ascetics for abuses in communal life and idleness. His description of the customs and practices of the ascetical life are most valuable. Letter two seems to be a continuation of the first.

Clericorum, De singularitate, a work on the celibacy of the clergy by a bishop of Cyprian's time, is thoroughly permeated with Cyprian's thought.

Climacus, John, a monk on Mount Sinai (c. 649), derived his cognomen from his most important work, *The Ladder to Heaven* (Klimachs). The *Ladder* has thirty rungs, explaining in simple language the vices a monk must fight (1–23) and the virtues he must acquire (24–30). Added to the *Ladder* is *A Book* (or a letter) *to the Shepherd,* written for Abbot John of Raithu. Though immensely popular, hardly any details of John's life are known. Daniel of Raithu wrote his biography but it is unreliable.

Codex Justinianus was promulgated by Justinian I in 534. It includes all earlier laws and decrees up to 534.

Codex Theodosianus was promulgated by Theodosius II in 438. It was accepted by Valentinian III also, and contains the decrees of Constantine the Great and his successors up to 438.

Collectio Avellana. See Avellana.

Collectio Palatina is the work of a Scythian monk in Thrace. It has preserved writings of Marius Mercator, Cyril, Diodore, Theodore, and Theodoret. It is to be dated about 550.

Collectio Sabbatica contra Acephalos et Originistas destinata, contains Canons of Constantinople (536) and Jerusalem (536).

Comes. See Marcellinus Comes.

Commodianus, an ascetic layman, has left us his *Instructiones* in two books of acrostic poems of an apologetic nature. Book one is addressed to pagans and Jews, while book two gives exhortations to Catechumens and the faithful. His long *Carmen*

Apologeticum (1,060 hexameters) shows him to be a crude literary workman and theologically a Sabellian and Chiliast. It is not certain when he lived.

Constantius of Lyon wrote a *Life of Germanus* around 480.

Constitutiones per Hippolytum, or *Epitome,* in five parts, is an almost literal extract from the *Apostolic Constitutions.*

Constitutions of the Apostles. See *Apostolic Constitutions,* p. 31.

Consultationes Zacchaei et Apollonii is an anonymous work of the fifth century. Its three books have Zacchaeus instruct a pagan philosopher Apollonius in the elements of Christianity. It discusses many errors and instructs the reader on Christian living, especially on virginity, the ascetical life, the resurrection, and the end of the world.

Corinthians to Paul, Epistle of the, complains to Paul of Gnostic inroads. It is of no value.

Cornelius, Pope (251–253), wrote seven letters to St. Cyprian and three to Fabius of Antioch. They dealt with the Novatian schism and with the ecclesiastical hierarchy.

Cosmas Indicopleustes (The Indian Traveler) was an Alexandrian merchant who undertook long voyages, visiting the Red Sea, the Gulf of Persia, Ceylon, and the coast of India. Tired of travel, he became a monk and composed his *Christian Topography* (c. 550). It is a strange mixture, in twelve books, of the most unscientific hypotheses on the shape of the earth and its principal phenomena. It has most interesting information about the countries the author visited and the things he saw. He was a Nestorian.

Cosmas the Elder was a learned monk, tutor of John Damascene and Cosmas the Younger, who had been rescued from captivity among the Saracens by the father of John Damascene.

Cosmas the Younger, surnamed the Singer or Melodos, was a foster brother of John Damascene with whom he entered the monastic life in 726. He became bishop of Majuma near Gaza in 743. Though highly regarded as a hymnographer in his day, his work is mediocre. *Scholia* on the poems of Gregory Nazianzen and fourteen canons are attributed to him. However, some of this material is the product of his tutor Cosmas the Elder.

Cresconius, a Donatist, wrote a letter to Augustine in 401 which he answered.

Cresconius (Canonist) composed a *Concordia Canonum* of 300 titles based on the texts of Dionysius Exiguus sometime before the eighth century.

Cyprian of Antioch was a legendary wizard and martyr who was sometimes confused with Cyprian of Carthage.

Cyprian of Toulon was bishop of Toulon and coauthor with Massianus of a life of St. Caesarius, their teacher, shortly before his death in 542 or 549.

Cyprian, the *Proconsular Acts of*, are official documents and date from the early third century.

Cyprian Gallus, a priest of Gaul, first half of the fifth century, composed a metrical recension of the Old Testament which was formerly attributed to Juvencus. He may also be the author of another biblical poem, *Caena Cyprianis*. Though a cultured man and well read in the classics, he was a poor writer.

Cyrillonas, nephew of Ephraem, possessed genuine ability as a poet and has left us six *Carmina*. Two are on the Last Supper and one is a psalm of petition on the occasion of a plague of locusts and a threatened attack by the Huns in 396. He testifies to the sacrificial character of the Eucharist and to the veneration of the saints. See Absamya.

Cyril of Scythopolis (558) is one of the best hagiographers of the sixth century. Born c. 523, he entered the monastery of Euthemium in 544. His last years, 555–558, he spent in the "New Laura" of St. Theognius (522) and St. Abraham (527). Cyril also suggested the life of Chariton to its author. See Chariton.

Cyrus, Monophysite, a monk mentioned by Gennadius, wrote a work against Nestorius. He was a member of the Monophysite party as opposed to the Eutychian party.

Cyrus of Phasis, later of Alexandria (631–641), was a Monothelite. He has left some letters.

Dada of Amida (c. 460), a monk of Amida, and a contemporary of Isaak, wrote some 300 hymns and treatises. None of them are extant.

Dadjesu, patriarch of Seleucia (421–456), has some extant commentaries on the Old Testament ascribed to him.

Dalmatius, archimandrite of Constantinople, wrote an apology and left two letters.

Dalmatius of Cyzicus has attributed to him a source book on Nicea that is of unknown origin.

Damasus I, Pope (366–384), composed sixty metrical inscriptions for the catacombs and monuments he built or restored. They have a certain dignity but they are poor poetry. He also wrote short poems on David and Paul. Ten of his synodal letters remain. They are most important for their vindication of the primacy of Rome. See Jerome, p. 155.

Dasius, Acts of, are important in the study of the history of religions for a description of the Saturnalia as celebrated in the army. Dasius was a soldier (c. 303).

David the Armenian, a fifth century translator of Neoplatonist and Aristotelian works who also wrote some philosophical treatises.

Decretum Gelasianum de libris recipiendis et non recipiendis, is not genuine but the work of a cleric of sixth century Gaul. It contains the following: Decisions of the Synod of Rome (381) on the Holy Spirit and the names of Christ; a list of the books of the Bible; an exposition of the primacy of Rome and the patriarchates; on general councils and the fathers of the Church; a list of apocrypha and some theological writings. See Gelasian Decree, p. 178.

De execrandis gentium Diis is by an unknown author, not, as was long thought, by Tertullian.

De Jona is a poem of 105 hexameters by an anonymous author who composed another work of 167 hexameters, *De Sodoma.* Both poems show considerable ability on the part of the author. *De Jona* tells of the conversion of Nineveh.

Demetrius, bishop of Alexandria, wrote a few letters of little importance. He suspended Origen.

Depositio Episcoporum is a list of popes from Lucius (254) to Julius I (352). It is found in the Roman *Chronographer* of 354.

Depositio Martyrum is a list of martyrs honored at Rome. It is found in the Roman *Chronographer* of 354.

Dêr-Balizeh is a papyrus discovered in a Coptic monastery that gives considerable sections of the Greek liturgy of the Mass of the third century.

De recta in Deum Fide is a dialogue in which Adamantius the orthodox champion defeats the followers of Marcion, Bardesanes, and Valentinus. The work is not well written but was attributed to Origen because of the name Adamantius. The anonymous author was a contemporary of Methodius and an opponent of Origen. He wrote around 300. See Adamantius.

De Sodoma, a poem by the author of *De Jona*. It describes the destruction of Sodom.

De transitu Mariae is an apocryphal account of the death and assumption of Mary attributed to Melito of Sardis. The account served as the basis of many variations of the same theme both in the East and the West.

De vocatione omnium gentium is now generally conceded to be a genuine work of Prosper of Aquitaine. It is the oldest Christian treatise on the problem of the salvation of infidels.

Diadochus, bishop of Photice in Illyria (middle of fifth century), remained aloof from the controversies of his time and left us a sermon on the Assumption and a work important and valuable for the history of mysticism and asceticism: *Capita centum de perfectione spirituali* (A Hundred Maxims on Spiritual Perfection). It was much quoted in the East and its principles are frequently applied today in theology. Diadochus contributed much to the fixing of certain concepts in mystical and ascetical theology.

Dictinius (end of fourth century), bishop of Astorga, a Priscillianist, wrote *Libra* (The Scale) and some other unknown works.

Didascalia Apostolorum Arabica, the *Didascalia Arabica et Aethiopica* is a recension of the first six books of the *Apostolic Constitutions* and consequently of the original *Didascalia Apostolorum*. It is believed that the Ethiopic text is derived from the Greek through Arabic and Coptic translations.

Diodorus of Tarsus (c. 394) brought the theological school of his

native Antioch to its heights during his presidency of that institution. He was well qualified for the position. His most famous
students, John Chrysostom and Theodore of Mopsuestia, developed what was best and what was worst in their master's
teaching. Emperor Valens banished Diodorus but after Valens'
death he became bishop of Tarsus. In his lifetime Diodorus was
a vigorous champion of orthodoxy against heresy and paganism,
but the Synod of Constantinople (499) condemned him as the
originator of Nestorianism. All his many and varied writings
have been lost except a commentary on the Psalms and a treatise
De fato.

Dionysius of Alexandria (c. 264), called the "Great" because
of his scholarship and for his great contribution to the Church
as an ecclesiastic. The most distinguished student and successor of Origen in the school of Alexandria, he was twice
exiled as bishop of that city and died in Antioch about 264.
Only fragmentary remains of his extensive writings are preserved by Eusebius in his *Church History*, book seven of which
was dedicated to Dionysius. He wrote a treatise *On Nature*
against Epicureanism. *A Refutation and Apology* in four books
defended his orthodoxy to Pope Dionysius. A mystical interpretation of the Apocalypse, *On the Promises*, refuted Chiliasm
but denied the Johannine authorship of the Apocalypse. Only
two letters remain of a voluminous correspondence to attest
what a busy and great ecclesiastic Dionysius was. He wrote
letters on the Novatian schism, on the *Lapsi*, and on the controversy over rebaptism. He sent out annual *Festal Letters* of
which the letter to Basilides of Pentapolis became one of the
sources for our Easter law. In it he discusses Lenten regulations
and conditions for the Eucharistic fast.

Dionysius of Corinth, a contemporary of Soter I (166–174), was
one of the most frequently consulted men of his time. Eusebius
was acquainted with eight of his letters and has briefly indicated their contents. The first six are addressed to various
communities; the seventh to Pope Soter, and the eighth to a
Christian lady named Chrysophora.

Dionysius of Tellmahre (845) was long regarded as the author
of a chronicle which was the work of an unknown Monophy-

site monk (c. 775). It reproduces much of the second part of the *Church History* of John of Asia and goes to 754–755. It is important for the history of the Jacobite Church in the sixth century. Dionysius did publish some *Annals* covering the years 583–843.

Dionysius Philocalus, calligrapher to Pope Damasus I, probably wrote the *Roman chronography of 354*. See *Chronographer of 354*.

Dionysius, Pope (259–268), wrote two letters on the divinity of Jesus Christ to Dionysius of Alexandria to correct some of the latter's doctrinal utterances.

Dioscorus of Alexandria (454), successor to Cyril as bishop of Alexandria, was deposed at Chalcedon in 451 and died in 454. He did much to promote the Monophysite party. We know only of letters, a few fragments, and perhaps six anathematisms against the Council of Chalcedon.

Doctrina Addai. See Abgar and *Acta Edessena.*

Doctrine of the Twelve Apostles. See *Didache*, p. 16.

Donatus the Great, bishop of Carthage 313–355, successor of Majorinus the schismatic. A prolific writer, there remain only a letter on baptism refuted by Augustine and *On the Holy Ghost*, which is Subordinationist in tendency. He gave his name to the Donatist schism.

Dormitio B.V.M. (see *Transitus Mariae*) narrates how Mary died in Jerusalem, surrounded by the apostles, and how her body was carried up into heaven. The story contains very ancient elements, but the actual form of the work supposes that the cultus of the Blessed Virgin was already well developed in the early Church. It is the general belief that this work does not date earlier than the fourth or fifth century.

Dorotheus, abbot of a monastery near Gaza and a disciple of Barsanuphius (c. 540) and of John of Gaza (c. 530), has left us twenty-three dialogues on ascetical matters and eight letters to the brethren. See John of Saba.

Duae viae vel Judicium secundum Petrum. See *Didascalia*, p. 30.

Easter Table is an Easter table for the years 312–411 that has been preserved by the Chronographer of 354.

Ecthesis of Heraclius (638). See Maximus Confessor, p. 204.

Ebionite Gospel dates from the early third century.

Edessa, Acts of the Martyrs of, is a legendary account of some martyrs put to death by the Romans.

Edessa, Chronicle of, a Syriac chronicle, covers the period from about 133 B.C. to 540 A.D. of the history of Edessa. The author is unknown but of Nestorian sympathies.

Egeria. See Aetheria.

Egyptian Church Ordinances. See the *Apostolic Tradition of Hippolytus*, p. 29.

Egyptians, Gospel of, was written some time after 150 in Egypt where it was regarded as canonical for a time. It was popular among the Encratites, the Naasenes, and the Sabellians.

Eleutherius, Pope (c. 174–189), wrote against Montanists. He received Iranaeus who, as a representative of the martyrs of Lyon (177–178), pleaded for milder policy toward heretics.

Eliseus the Doctor. See Wardapet.

Elpidius Rusticus. See Helpidius.

Emeritus was a Donatist preacher (412–418).

Endelechius (Severus Sanctus Endelechius), a correspondent of Paulinus and a Gallic rhetorician, wrote a short bucolic poem entitled *De virtute signi crucis Christi* (On the Power of Christ's Cross). Its theme is that the tree of the Cross covers the world and its fruit is the food of mankind.

Enoch, Book of, was interpolated by Christians in the first century. It contains the first reference to the millennium in the section called "Secrets of Enoch."

Ephraem of Antioch (545) was one of the most esteemed men of his time. As patriarch of Antioch (527–545) he was a staunch defender of the faith. Photius tells that he wrote some dogmatic letters, eight discourses, and a treatise defending Chalcedon against Severus.

Epiphanes (Gnostic), son of Carpocrates, died at the age of seventeen and left a treatise *On Justice*.

Epiphanius of Salamis condemned Origen in a synod near Constantinople.

Epiphanius the Monk translated Sozomen, Socrates, and Theodoret's Church histories into Latin. He then used these sources for his *Historia tripartita* in twelve books, which became one of the most important sources for Church history in the Middle Ages.

Epistle of St. Paul to the Alexandrians is a lost forgery by Marcionites mentioned in the Muratorian Fragment.

Epistle to the Laodiceans contains many words and phrases of genuine Pauline Epistles, but it cannot be dated before the fourth century. Harnack mistakenly thought it a Marcionite forgery.

Epistola Apostolorum, or, "Conversations of Jesus with His disciples after the Resurrection," begins as a letter but soon turns into an apocalypse. It was written in Asia Minor or Egypt between 140 and 170. Though the author appears to be orthodox, the work shows some Gnostic traces. The work begins with a profession of faith and an account of Christ's miracles by the eleven apostles. Then follows a discussion between Jesus and His apostles on such questions as the parousia, the Resurrection, the Last Judgment, the signs of the parousia, the fate of the damned, the Incarnation, the Redemption, the *descensus ad inferos* (descent to hell), the commission of the apostles and Paul, warnings against false teachers and concludes with a description of the Ascension. The work, among other errors, teaches Christ's descent to Limbo to baptize the just detained there. The Eucharist is called *Pascha* and the author is a rigorist on the question of penance.

Epitome of Apostolic Constitutions is an adaptation of book eight of the Apostolic Constitutions. It is also referred to as *Constitutiones per Hippolytum*.

Esdras, Fourth Book of, a Christian continuation of the Jewish III Esdras, was for a time regarded canonical and is of importance in eschatology.

Eucherius, bishop of Lyons (d. 450–455), became a monk of Lerins after a successful career in the world while his wife entered a monastery. Later he lived as a solitary until elected bishop in 434. He has left two exegetical works, *Formulae spiritualis intelligentiae* (On the Spiritual Interpretation of the Bible), and *Instructiones ad Salonium libri duae* (On the Literal Interpretation of the Bible). Besides this he wrote two ascetical treatises *De laude eremi* (In Praise of the Desert, to

Hilary of Arles), and *De contemptu mundi* (On Contempt of the World, to Hilarianus). His *Passio Agannensium martyrum* tells of the martyrdom of the Theban Legion. He was one of the outstanding ecclesiastical writers of the fifth century. His two sons, Veranus and Salonius, also were bishops. Eucherius was a staunch defender of Augustine. His writings were very popular in the Middle Ages.

Eudoxius, Anomean bishop of Antioch (358) and later of Constantinople (360–369) has left us two fragments of a work on the Incarnation and some scholia on the Psalms. Later he joined the Homoeans.

Eugenius of Carthage, bishop of Carthage (480–505), was an anti-Arian writer.

Eugenius of Toledo (657), archbishop of Toledo, left some letters and poems.

Eugippius (533) was a disciple of St. Severin (482) and abbot of a convent near Naples where he died sometime after 533. His *Vita sancti Severini* is a valuable source book on the migration of nations and his *Excerpta ex operibus sancti Augustini*, a thesaurus of Augustine's writings, was very popular in the Middle Ages.

Eulogius (607), patriarch of Alexandria (580–607) and a friend of Gregory the Great, was a great champion of the orthodox faith against the Novatians and the Monophysites. Little of his literary work has come down to us and some fragments attributed to him are the work of Sophronius.

Eunomius (394), disciple of Aetius of Antioch and bishop of Cyzicus (c. 394), was an Anomean Arian. Though only small fragments of his writings have survived we have a fair idea of his errors from the works of Basil the Great and Gregory of Nyssa written against him. The Anomeans were also called Eunomians after him. He was their leader after the death of Aetius.

Eusebius of Alexandria was the pseudonymous author of some important sermons (fifth or sixth century).

Eusebius of Emesa (c. 359), a disciple of Eusebius of Caesarea, was a Semi-Arian of Homoean leanings. Most of his prolific and brilliant writings have been lost. We do, however, have seventeen important genuine sermons.

Eusebius of Nicomedia (c. 342) was an influential friend of Arius who, after Nicea, was the real political leader of the Arians and kept them together. He was a prolific letter writer but most of his works have been lost.

Eusebius of Thessalonica left fragments of a long work against an Aphthartodocetist monk.

Eusebius of Vercelli (c. 371), first bishop of that city, was banished to Scythopolis in Palestine for denouncing the condemnation of Athanasius at the Synod of Milan (355). Upon his return from exile he was active against Arianism with Hilary of Poitiers. He died about 371. He left three letters and it may be that *Codex Vercellensis* is his work. His translation of a "Commentary on the Psalms" by Eusebius of Caesarea has been lost.

Eustathius, a monk, wrote a letter against Severus of Antioch, *On the Two Natures*.

Eustathius (337), bishop of Antioch, was a vigorous opponent of Arianism at Nicea (325). The Emperor Constantine banished him to Thrace (330) where he died (c. 337). His only work that has been preserved, though he was a voluminous writer, is a criticism of Origen's allegorizing interpretation of Sacred Scripture, a treatise on the Witch of Endor (*De Engastrimytho*). There are fragments of *Adv. Arianos, Adv. Photinum, De anima*, and of a letter to Alexander of Alexandria. In exegesis he may be regarded as a forerunner of Antioch.

Eustathius of Epiphania wrote a *Chronicle* which stops with the year 502, according to Evagrius. It is, however, the work of Theodore Lector. Evagrius erred.

Eustathius of Sebaste was the teacher of Basil the Great, although later he became his enemy. He was very active in the spreading of monachism. The two *Regulae* of Basil are based on oral material taken from Eustathius. He left no writings and but little is known of him. In 357 he was bishop of Sebaste. In the Arian controversy he vacillated and seems to have died a Semi-Arian.

Eustratius, a priest and historian of Constantinople at the end of the sixth century, wrote a life of the patriarch Eutychius 552–582.

Eutherius, archbishop of Tyana, was an ardent follower of Nestorius. For this he was excommunicated at Ephesus (431) and banished in 434. We have five letters and a *Confutationes quarumdam propositionum*.

Eutropius, a Spanish priest in the first half of the fifth century, probably wrote the Antimanichean treatise *De similitudine carnis peccati* and two ascetical works: *De contemnenda hereditate* and *De vera circumcisione*.

Eutropius of Valencia (c. 608) wrote a little on asceticism and monachism.

Eutyches declared at the Council of Constantinople (448) that he did not regard the humanity of Jesus Christ as consubstantial with ours. Eutyches seems to have written nothing more than a few letters.

Eutychius, patriarch of Constantinople (552–582), is the author of *Sermo de Paschate De Sacrosanctae Eucharistiae*, which is incomplete, and a letter to Pope Vigilius.

Euzoius, a Semi-Arian, usurped the see of Caesarea from Gelasius in 376. Jerome says he wrote on many subjects but nothing further is known.

Evagrius, priest and monk of Lerins, wrote the *Altercatio Simonis Judaei et Theophili Christiani* (c. 430). It is made up of borrowed fragments and is one of the last polemical patristic writings against the Jews.

Evagrius of Antioch (393) succeeded Paulinus as bishop of Antioch in 388. Jerome, whose friend he was, says he wrote treatises, but all that remains is his Latin translation of Athanasius' *Life of St. Anthony*.

Evagrius Scholasticus (c. 600), lawyer in Constantinople and later imperial quaestor and prefect, has left an *Historia ecclesiastica* in six books covering the period 431–594. It is important for the history of Nestorianism and Monophysitism. Though he tries to be objective he is inclined to be a bit gullible especially in regard to miracles. His sources, however, are reliable.

Eve, Gospel of, is known only by title. It was in use by the Nicolaites (Gnostic) and appears to have been an apocalypse.

Evodius (c. 426), bishop of Uzalum or Uzelis and friend of Augustine, has left a few letters and perhaps a *De fide contra Manichaeos*.

Excerpta Latina Barbaris is a chronicle of the world that originated in Alexandria. It goes to the year 387 and is preserved in a Latin version of about the eighth century.

Eznik of Kolb, a disciple of Mesrop, wrote (c. 430) four books against heretics, i.e., the Heathen, the Persians, the Greek Philosophers, and the Marcionites. The date of his death is not known.

Fabian, Pope (236–250), gave written approval to a Numidian synod condemning Bishop Priatus of Lambese.

Facundus of Hermiane (571), an African, defended the "Three Chapters" even after the Council of Constantinople (553) and Pope Vigilius had condemned them. In 550 he published his *Pro defensione Trium Capitulorum* followed by *Contra Moncianum* (550–552) and *Epistola Fidei Catholicae* (568–569). He broke with the pope and was shut up in a monastery in Constantinople (564) where he died (571). Facundus based his position on the point that the emperor's incompetence as a theologian should rule out his intervention in the question of the "Three Chapters." Hence he reasoned that the condemnation of the "Three Chapters" was a depreciation of Chalcedon and an advantage to Monophysitism. This position Facundus defended with clarity and in an irenic spirit at first. Later his violence led to his condemnation.

Fastidius, a British Pelagian bishop (early fifth century), wrote two treatises: *On Christian Life* and *On Riches*, and five letters.

Faustinus (end fourth century) was a violent and bitter anti-Arian Roman presbyter siding with the unmerciful position of Lucifer of Calaris. He wrote:

1. *De fide adversus Arianos*, a very original work on the Trinity (380).
2. *Fides Theodosio Imperatori oblata*, written between 379–381, defending himself from the charge of Sabellianism.

3. He collaborated with Marcellinus on a *Libellus precum* to the emperor (383–384), in favor of the persecuted Luciferians.

Faustus of Milevis (a Manichaean) taught in Carthage 383–386, and published an attack on the Bible. Augustine refuted him at length (c. 400).

Faustus of Byzantium wrote (c. 400), in Greek, a history of Christianity in Armenia covering the time 344–387. It has come down to us in a fifth century translation. Lazarus of Pharp (after 491) continued the work through the years 388–485. It is important for the history of the beginnings of Christianity in Armenia, though it is not entirely free of legendary materials and a certain lack of objectivity.

Felicitas, Passion of, was probably the work of Tertullian. He wrote it in Latin and also translated it into Greek. Felicitas (202–203) was martyred with her mistress Perpetua and three catechumens. The work is important for the belief of Christian antiquity in the afterlife. See *Perpetuae et Felicitatis, Passion of*.

Felix Abbot, abbot in Constantinople, collaborated with the Roman deacon Rusticus in a polemic work now lost, condemning the decision against the "Three Chapters" in 553. Later he wrote *Disputatio contra Acephalos* against the Monophysites. He left us a very valuable Latin edition and translation of the Acts of the Councils of Ephesus and Chalcedon.

Felix, Acts of, tells the martyrdom (303) of this African bishop for his refusal to yield up the Sacred Books.

Felix (Manichaean) was the opponent of Augustine in a disputation held in December, 404.

Felix I, Pope (269–274), left no literary remains. Early in the fifth century Apollinarists attributed a letter to him, which is a forgery.

Felix II (III) Pope (483–492), left us eighteen letters dealing with Church affairs in the East, especially the Acacian schism.

Felix III (IV) Pope (526–530), left us four letters and a decree naming the deacon Boniface as his successor.

Ferrandus, Fulgentius (c. 547), a Carthaginian deacon, disciple of Fulgentius of Ruspe, wrote a beautiful *Vita* of his master and a *Breviatio Canonum* which gives us the Canon Law of his day.

In it he brought together under 232 headings all the available conciliar legislation under the following titles: the bishop (1–84), the priest (85–103), the deacon (104–120), the clergy (121–142), the councils (143–164), procedure (165–198), baptism (199–205), Lent (206–210), and miscellaneous decrees (211–232). He also wrote seven letters of dogmatic and historical importance, especially for the "Three Chapters" controversy. Here he opposed the position of the Emperor Justinian. Ferrandus enjoyed great esteem as a theologian in his day.

Ferreol of Uzes, bishop of Uzes (591), wrote a *Regula ad monachos*.

Filastrius (c. 397), bishop of Brescia, wrote his *Liber de haeresibus* between 385–391. He mentions 156 heresies and provides a valuable source for the study of these heresies. Augustine used it copiously for his *History of Heresies*. Filastrius in turn used Irenaeus and Epiphanius and his work helps to reconstruct the lost *Syntagma* of Hippolytus.

Firmicus Maternus, a Sicilian rhetorician, wrote a serious moral work, *Matheseos libri VIII*, tinged with astrological errors. After his conversion he produced a curious work (346–348) entitled *De errore profanarum religionum* in which he urged the violent eradication of what remained of paganism. His name has also been connected with the *Consultationes Zacchaei et Apollonii*.

Firmillian was bishop of Caesarea in Cappadocia (after 268) and a disciple of Origen. There remains only one letter to Cyprian in which Firmillian sharply attacks Pope Stephen in the matter of heretical baptism.

Firmus of Caesarea in Cappadocia has left us forty-five very interesting letters which do not, however, touch on doctrinal matters.

Flavian, bishop (381–404) of the Meletian orthodox Christians of Antioch in opposition to Evagrius, was the friend of Diodorus of Tarsus and of John Chrysostom. We have a treatise on fraternal charity, some discourses, and two of his letters relative to the Messalians. None are complete however.

Florinus was a Western Valentinian to whom Irenaeus wrote to protest his blasphemous writings.

Forty Martyrs, Acts and Testament of, tells of the death of forty martyrs in Sebaste (c. 320) who had requested common burial.

Fronto of Cirta, the teacher of Marcus Aurelius, attacked Christians in an oration (164–165).

Fulgentius, a Donatist, wrote a treatise on baptism, 412–420.

Fulgentius, Ferrandus. See Ferrandus.

Gaius, Anti-Montanist, Roman priest, wrote a dialogue with the Montanist Proclus during the reign of Pope Zephyrinus, 198–217. He denied that John the Apostle wrote the fourth Gospel and the Apocalypse.

Gaudentius (c. 406), Donatist bishop of Brescia, refuted by Augustine, has left twenty-one sermons of which ten preached in Holy Week are important for the Eucharist. Of interest, also, is a panegyric on his predecessor Philastrius.

Gaudentius of Tingal, a Donatist bishop refuted by Augustine, taught the licitness of suicide.

Gelasius of Caesarea (395) was the second successor of Eusebius as bishop of that see, succeeding Acacius in 367. He continued the *Church History* of Eusebius. Some hold that this continuation served Rufinus as a basis for the last two books (9–10) of his Church history, although traditional opinion regards them as original work of Rufinus. Gelasius may also have written a *Catecheses* modeled on the *Catecheses* of his uncle, Cyril of Jerusalem.

Gelasius of Cyzicus wrote, in Bithynia (c. 475), a church history in three books, covering the ecclesiastical history of the Orient during the reign of Constantine the Great. The work is mostly a compilation from other sources and it is doubtful whether Gelasius contributed anything original to it.

Gelasius of Jerusalem, a nephew of Cyril of Jerusalem, died in 395. His works are lost. Check Gelasius of Caesarea.

Geminus, a priest under Alexander Severus (222–235), wrote a few books, according to Jerome.

Gennadius of Marseilles (505), a Semi-Pelagian priest, continued the *De viris illustribus* of Jerome (480) and wrote works, now lost, against Pelagius, Nestorius, Eutyches, and eight lost books *Adversus haereses,* the concluding part of which may be extant in *Liber ecclesiasticorum dogmatum.* He may also be the real author of a pseudo-Augustinian commentary on the Apocalypse and a profession of faith.

Gennadius I, patriarch of Constantinople (458–471), was the author of a great number of scriptural commentaries, among them commentaries on all Pauline Epistles. Only fragments remain, most of which were saved by finding a place in the *Catenae*. Important are fragments of a commentary on Genesis and Romans. Fragments of a polemic against the twelve anathemas of Cyril (431–432), of at least two books against Parthenion, a partisan account of Nestorius and of an encomium on Leo the Great are all that remain of his dogmatic writings. Orthodox and in line with the Council of Chalcedon, Gennadius enjoyed great esteem as an orator.

George, bishop of the Arabs, a friend of James of Edessa, was called bishop of the Arabs because, residing at Akula, he exercised jurisdiction over the Monophysite Arab tribes. George was a voluminous writer. His episcopacy is to be placed in 687 or 688. To him we owe scholia on the Scriptures and on the homilies of Gregory Nazianzen, several homilies of his own, a commentary on the sacraments, a metrical treatise on the calendar, and his most important work, a translation of Aristotle's *Organon*. To these must be added letters, a chronicle (lost), and the conclusion of the *Hexaemeron* of James of Edessa, which death prevented the latter from finishing.

George of Laodicea (c. 335), Arian bishop, wrote some letters. Only one is extant. Epiphanius mentions a work against the Manichaeans, and Socrates has preserved an outline of his biography of Eusebius of Emesa.

Germanus of Constantinople (733) professed Monothelitism in 712 under imperial pressure as bishop of Cyzicus, but condemned it in 715 as patriarch of Constantinople. He was banished in 730 because of his opposition to the Iconoclasts. His works comprise three dogmatic letters, valuable for the history of Iconoclasm, an epistle *Ad Armenos*, a defense of Chalcedon, *De vitae termino*, a philosophy of life defending divine providence, and *De heresibus et synodis*, an historical work. Of nine homilies, seven are on Mary (three *De dormitione B.V.M.*). He has left many hymns. *Rerum ecclesiasticarum contemplatio*, an explanation of the liturgy, is probably also his work. Together with John Damascene and George of Cyprus, Germanus was excommunicated by the Iconoclast Council of 753 but

restored to honor by the General Council of 787. He was renowned as an orator. He also laid the theological foundation
for the Church's teaching on the veneration of images. Later
theologians did little more than amplify and explain his teaching.

Germinius of Sirmium (366) has left a few letters, treatises, and
sermons of more or less Arian bias.

Gerontius (485) wrote (c. 440–450) a life of St. Melania the
Younger (c. 430). It is partly preserved in Greek and Latin
versions, of which the former appears to be the original. The
work throws much light on the times.

Gilda the Wise (after 569) wrote a *Liber querulus* in three
books that gave a depressing and biased picture of the Church
in the British Isles. The man's historical identity is not altogether clear.

Gobarus. See Stephen Gobarus.

Gorium (c. 450) wrote a life of Mesrop, his master.

Gospel of Andrew. See under Andrew.

Gospel of Barnabas. See under Barnabas.

Gospel of Bartholomew. See under Bartholomew.

Gospel of the Egyptians. See under Egyptians.

Gospel of Eve. See under Eve.

Gospel of Judas Iscariot. See under Judas.

Gospel of Matthias. See under Matthias.

Gospel of Mary. See under Mary.

Gospel of Nicodemus. See under Nicodemus.

Gospel of Peter. See under Peter.

Gospel of Philip. See under Philip.

Gospel of Thaddeus. See under Thaddeus.

Gospel of the Ebionites. See under Ebionites.

Gospel of the Hebrews. See under Hebrews.

Gospel of Thomas. See under Thomas.

Gregory of Elvira (c. 392), bishop of Elvira near Granada, was
a great champion of Nicea and later fought Priscillianism.
After the death of Lucifer of Calaris he headed the Luciferians.
A fertile and original writer his chief works are:
  1. *De fide orthodoxa,* profession of faith.
  2. Twenty *Tractatus Origenis de libris Sacrae Scripturae.*

3. *Tractatus de epithalamio,* five homilies on the Canticle of Canticles in which Gregory is the first Western exegete to interpret the Canticle of Christ and His Church.

4. *De Arca Noe.*

5. *Expositio in Ps. 9.*

Gregory of Girgenti (c. 592), bishop of Girgenti (Agrigenti in Sicily) wrote on Ecclesiastes in ten books, in which he seeks the literal sense. A *Vita Gregorii* by an unknown Leontius is also preserved.

Gregory the Illuminator (c. 332) was the apostle of Armenia, where he, his sons and grandsons, furnished the ecclesiastical leadership for years. Though some letters and homilies have been attributed to him it is most doubtful that he wrote anything at all. The history of Terdat and of the preaching of St. Gregory the Illuminator is an entirely unreliable writing of the fifth century.

Gregory the Syrian, a monk, contemporary of Ephraem, left some letters and a treatise on the ascetic life.

Gregory Thaumaturgus (c. 270), the apostle of Cappadocia, was born of a noble family of Neo-Caesarea in Pontus where he and his brother Athenodorus, while students of Origen, became Christians. Soon thereafter he became bishop of Neo-Caesarea and effectively spread Christianity. His influence was still felt at the time of the three Cappadocians. He has left:

1. A panegyric on Origen delivered when he left his master's school. It throws light on Origen's teaching methods and is witness to the contemporary belief in the guardian angels.

2. A Trinitarian profession of faith, that is very clear.

3. The Canonical Letter, important for the history of penance.

4. A paraphrase of Ecclesiastes. It is no more than that.

5. On the passibility and impassibility of God.

6. A work addressed to Philagrius, on the Trinity.

7. Some homilies and a treatise on the soul are very probably not his.

Hadrian I, Pope, sent a Missal to Charlemagne (c. 790). It is an enlargement of the *Sacramentarium Gregorianum,* and it eventually replaced the *Sacramentarium Gelasianum*.

Hadrian, the Exegete. See Adrian.

Harmonius, the son of Bardesanes, wrote many works in Syriac. All are lost.

Hebrews, Gospel of, was used by Ignatius of Antioch and Clement of Alexandria. It was long thought to be the Aramaic original of Matthew, which it does resemble. The name is derived from its popularity in Palestine.

Hegemonius, a little known Syrian, wrote (c. 350) an anti-Manichaean polemical *Acta Archelai* in which the Catholic bishop Archelaus routs Mani and his disciple Turbo in debate. The remains of this work are most important in the study of Manichaeism.

Helpidius Rusticus is sometimes identified with the deacon Helpidius, who was physician to King Theodoric. He is the author of a poem in 149 hexameters, entitled *De Christi Jesu beneficiis,* and of a collection of twenty-four inscriptions of three verses each, intended to explain the biblical paintings of the Old and New Testaments to which they are affixed. He died c. 502 as bishop of Lyons. See Rusticus.

Helvidius, a poorly educated layman and disciple of the Arian, Auxentius of Milan, denied the perpetual virginity of the Blessed Virgin Mary, maintaining that she had other children after Jesus. He also denied the superiority of celibacy to marriage. His works are lost. Jerome wrote against him (c. 383) *Adversus Helvidium de perpetua virginitate Mariae.*

Henana of Adiabene (c. 596–610), a great and popular teacher in the school of Nisibis who, though accused of error, seems to have been orthodox because Babai attacked him for holding the *Theotokos* and denouncing Theodore of Mopsuestia. He wrote many biblical commentaries in which he followed John Chrysostom rather than Theodore of Mopsuestia. He also published a revision of the statutes of the school of Nisibis.

Henoticon was a profession of faith drawn up by Acacius of Constantinople (471–489). The Emperor Zeno (474–491) had supported the Council of Chalcedon. Basiliscus, the usurper (476–477), briefly dethroned Zeno and issued an encyclical condemning Chalcedon. When Zeno regained his throne,

Acacius proposed the *Henoticon* in the hope of reconciling the adversaries of Chalcedon. Acacius hoped to get recognition for Canon 28 of Chalcedon, which Pope Leo had resolutely rejected. The Acacian schism followed and gave Monophysitism a longer life. Acacius has also left a letter against Peter Fullo, Monophysite bishop of Alexandria, protesting some of the latter's liturgical innovations.

Heraclas was successor to Origen as head of the Alexandrian school. He was followed by Dionysius the Great of Alexandria in 231–232, who also followed him as bishop of Alexandria in 247 or 248.

Heracleon was a disciple of the Gnostic Valentine. Fragments of a commentary on John are left. He wrote between 155 and 180.

Heraclian, bishop of Chalcedon, early sixth century, wrote a treatise against Sotericus, Eutychean bishop of Caesarea in Cappadocia, and a refutation of Manichaeism in twenty books. He is praised by Photius.

Heraclitus was an anti-Gnostic writer and defender of orthodoxy under Septimus Severus. His works are lost.

Hermias is the unknown author of an *Irrisio*, or "Satire on the Profane Philosophers," which is of questionable value. It is primarily a coarse satire and is probably to be dated in the third century.

Hermogenes was a Gnostic painter of Carthage. Tertullian wrote *Adversus Hermogenem* to defend Catholic teaching on creation. Theophilus of Antioch also wrote a work, "Against the Heresies of Hermogenes," but it is lost.

Hesychius of Alexandria revised the Septuagint and the New Testament text about 300. Jerome criticises his work severely.

Hesychius of Miletus (c. 550) wrote a history of the world, of which only fragments remain.

Hexapla. See Origen, p. 77.

Hieracas (c. 300) was head of a numerous community of ascetics of both sexes at Leontopolis, and the first ecclesiastical author to write in Coptic. Epiphanius mentions a work by him on the *Hexaemeron* and many writings on the Psalms that were full of error and exaggerated allegorizing.

Hierocles, governor of Bithynia, rated Apollonius of Tyana above

Christ in a polemical writing. Eusebius attacked him for it.

Hierotheus is an unknown theologian cited by the Pseudo-Areopagite.

Hilarianus Hilarius, proconsul and prefect of Rome (c. 408), has been suggested as the author of *Ambrosiaster*.

Hilarianus, Quintus Julius, wrote a brief chronography in 397 entitled *De cursu temporum*. He was probably an African of Chiliastic tendencies and he endeavored to construct an original philosophy of history. Another work, *De ratione Paschae et mensis*, is also of little value.

Hilary, Pope (461–468), has left eleven letters having to do mostly with matters of ecclesiastical discipline in Gaul and Spain. His extensive correspondence with the East has perished.

Hilary of Arles (449), a monk of the monastery of Lerins founded by Honoratus (421–429), succeeded the latter as abbot and later as metropolitan of Arles. He has left us a panegyric of Honoratus called *Sermo de vita sancti Honorati*. Hilary was most interested in the consolidation of ecclesiastical affairs in Gaul and drew a rebuke from Pope Leo for his attempts to make Arles a kind of primatial see for Gaul. His fine panegyric on Honoratus shows his unusual literary and oratorical gifts. A certain Reverentius has left us a *Vita sancti Hilarii*.

Hilary of Rome, a Roman deacon, was a rabid follower of Lucifer of Calaris. He demanded that all penitent Arians be rebaptized.

Hilduin of St. Denis, abbot of St. Denis (c. 844), is responsible for starting the identification of St. Denis of Paris, the Pseudo-Areopagite and the disciple of St. Paul.

Historia Acephala is a collection of official source material for ecclesiastical history and law that derives from Alexandria. It has been preserved by having been taken into the collection of Theodosius the Deacon.

Historia Lausiaca is a most important history of ancient monachism published by Palladius in 419–420. The name comes from Lausus, the royal chamberlain to whom it was dedicated. It was early translated into several languages. Next it was merged with a work of Timothy of Alexandria, *Historia monachorum*, in Egypt. This last named work was then translated into Latin by Rufinus.

Historia monachorum was written (c. 400) by Timothy of Alexandria and translated into Latin by Rufinus. See *Historia Lausiaca.*

History of Joseph the Carpenter. See Joseph.

Honoratus of Cirta, or Antonius Honoratus, bishop of Cirta in Numidia, was an anti-Arian writer of the end of the fifth century, all of whose writings are lost.

Honoratus of Marseilles (after 492) was the author of many homilies and "Lives," no longer extant. Some identify him as the biographer of Hilary of Arles, whose disciple he had been.

Hormisdas, Pope (514–523), has left some ninety letters and decrees all having to do with the Acacian schism which he settled in 519. His *Libellus professionis fidei,* signed by the emperor and all bishops of East and West says: *In Sede Apostolica citra maculam semper est catholica servata religio* (the Catholic religion has been preserved ever immaculate in the Apostolic See). Then follows the condemnation of Nestorius, Acacius, and other heresiarchs of the East.

Horsiesi, successor to Pachomius (c. 380), left his spiritual testament, *Doctrina de institutione monachorum* in fifty-six chapters.

Hosius of Cordoba (c. 358) did not engage in much literary activity but he was one of the most important churchmen of his time. He was advisor to Constantine the Great and may have presided at Nicea. His influence was also decisive at Sardica (343). In 357 when the aged bishop was almost a centenarian he was forced to sign the second Sirmian Formula. However, he repudiated it immediately. He died in 357 or 358. A number of the canons of the Synod of Sardica are from his pen and we have a letter addressed to Pope Julius I and another to Constantine (354). Two other works, *De laude virginitatis* and *De interpretatione vestium sacerdotalium,* have been lost. He wrote little but staunchly defended Nicea throughout his life.

Hydatius or Idacius (fifth century), a Spanish bishop, wrote a

Chronicon or chronology of the world which continues the
Chronicle of Jerome up to the year 468. For the period from
428 it is an independent work and stands on its own merits.
It is important for Spanish history.

Hymnaeus, Letter to, is a letter purporting to have been written
by six bishops to Paul of Samosata before the synod of 268
to ask him to subscribe to an extensive Creed or rule of faith
found therein. The document, however, remains doubtful.

Hypatius of Ephesus (bishop 531–536) was the leader of Catholic
bishops at the meeting (*Collatio cum Severianis*) in Constantinople in 532. He rejected the authority of Pseudo-Diony-
sian literature (Dionysius the Pseudo-Areopagite) against the
Monophysites who appealed to them. He was the confidant of
Emperor Justinian who sent him to Pope John II. From the
latter he received approval of a formula to be presented to the
Theopaschites. He presided at the Synod of Constantinople
(536) and died some time between 537 and 552.

Ialdabaoth, Books of, are lost writings of the Nikolaites.

Ibas (d. 457), bishop of Edessa, successor of Rabulas, wrote a
Christological letter (c. 433) about Cyril of Jerusalem to Maris,
bishop of Ardaschir in Persia. He was deposed at the Robber
Synod in Ephesus (449) but the Council of Chalcedon (451)
returned him to his see. However, his letter was put among
the "Three Chapters" and condemned with them in 553. His
translations of the works of Theodore of Mopsuestia and of
Aristotle have perished together with his hymns. After his
death many teachers transferred from Edessa to Nisibis and the
former school closed around 489.

Idacius of Emerita was an opponent of Priscillianism. See
Hydatius.

Ildefonsus of Toledo (667), a nephew of Fulgentius and disciple
of Isidore, continued the *De viris illustribus* of Gennadius
after Isidore. He added fourteen ecclesiastics, eight of whom
were writers. He wrote much but there are left only his "Defense of the Perpetual Virginity of Mary," *De cognitione
baptismi*, a treatise on baptism, and an ascetical work, *De
itinere deserti quo pergitur post baptismum* (A Journey into
the Desert). The desert of this work is the spiritual life of

faith and works into which baptism introduces the Christian.

Innocent I, Pope (402–417), contributed more than any other pope before Leo the Great to the prestige and authority of the Roman Pontiff. He constantly insisted that all local customs and practices must give way to the decisions of Rome, which has its authority from Peter. We have about thirty-eight letters of which some are of great doctrinal importance especially the following:

> Epistle 2. On the validity of baptism by heretics and on celibacy.
>
> Epistles 6 and 25. On public penance and reconciliation.
>
> Epistles 6 and 7. On the canon of Scripture and on the *apocrypha*.
>
> Epistles 25,3,8. On confirmation by the bishop only and anointing of all the faithful in extreme unction.
>
> Epistles 29,31 deal with Pelagianism.
>
> Epistles 29,1 states of the Holy See: *a quo ipse episcopatus et tota auctoritas nominis huius emersit* ("from whom [Peter] have come this episcopate [of Rome] and all authority belonging to this name").

Instantius was a follower of Priscillian. There are eleven anonymous treatises that were ascribed to Priscillian. These have also been attributed to Instantius. The three most important are *Liber Apologeticum, Liber ad Damasum episcopum,* and *De fide et de apocryphis.* They are, however, of disappointing value for the history and teaching of Priscillian. There are also seven homilies and a liturgical prayer.

Irenaeus, Comes (c. 450), archbishop of Tyre who was friendly to the Nestorians, collected conciliar acts which found their place in later collections. See *Collectio Atheniensis* under Acts of the Council of Ephesus.

Isaac of Amida was a Monophysite priest who visited Rome about 404. See Isaac of Antioch.

Isaac of Antioch wrote several treatises against the Nestorians and Monophysites and a threnody on the destruction of Antioch by an earthquake in 459. None of these writings have survived. There is no little confusion among the various men named Isaac. Jacob of Edessa (708) mentions three teachers named

Isaac but no Isaac of Antioch. He mentions Isaac of Amida and two Isaacs of Edessa, one a Catholic, the other a Monophysite. More than 200 writings associated with the name Isaac are extant but have not yet been edited.

Isaac of Edessa is a confusing name as there was an orthodox Isaac of Edessa (c. 522) and a Monophysite Isaac of Edessa. The latter wrote (c. 468–488) a poem (still extant) of 2,137 verses on a parrot that could pronounce the *Trisagion* with the addition, "who was crucified for us."

Isaac of Nineveh was a great Nestorian ascetic and mystic of the late seventh century. After five months he resigned as bishop of Nineveh (661) and became first a hermit and then a monk near Susa. He was a prolific and popular writer but because of the confusion about the various men named Isaac it is difficult to ascribe any of our literary remains to him. See Isaac of Antioch.

Isaac the Great Armenian (439) has the Armenian name Sahak. See Sahak the Great; also Mesrop, p. 131.

Isaias, Ascension of, is of Jewish origin but with Christian interpolation in the first part. This contains the account of the martyrdom of the Prophet. Part two (6–11) is of Christian origin (second century) and contains purported prophecies about Christ and His Church.

Isidorus (Gnostic), son of Basilides, left three works: *On the Second Soul*, i.e., the soul of man dominated by passion, *Ethica*, and *Exposition of the Prophet Parchor*.

Itinerarium Burdigalense is a dry but concise account of a pilgrimage to the Holy Land by a pilgrim from Bordeaux who arrived in Constantinople in May, 333. After visiting Palestine he returned home via Rome and Milan. The full title is *Itinerarium Burdigala Hierusalem usque.*

James Baradeus (578) wrote very little but it was through his efforts that Monophysitism was not eradicated by the vigorous measures of the emperors. The Monophysite Church is called Jacobite after him. Consecrated bishop of Edessa (c. 543), he had authority over all Monophysites. He died in 578. He is also called Jacob of Tella or James Baradai.

James of Edessa (708) is a Monophysite writer important in many fields. Elected bishop of Edessa (c. 684), he left his see (688) to teach in various monasteries until he returned in 708. Shortly after that he died, June 5, 708. He wrote a Syriac grammar and treatises on orthography and punctuation. *Enchiridion* is a treatise on technical terms used in philosophy. He composed a liturgy of his own and revised that of St. James. His *Book of Treasures* is a collection of official prayers. He also compiled an *Ordo* and a Calendar. He revised the Old Testament of the Peshitta and wrote commentaries on numerous books of the Bible. Add to all this his canons on discipline, his homilies, his wide correspondence, and the encyclopedic quality of his literary activity becomes evident.

James of Sarug (521), bishop of Batna near Edessa, spent his whole life in literary work undisturbed by the controversies of his time. Though his Monophysite admirers called him "Harp of the Orthodox Church" he was not tinged by Monophysitism but remained Catholic. His many beautiful homilies won for him the appellation "Flute of the Holy Ghost." In prose he left many letters, sermons, funeral orations, biographies for edification, and translated the "Six Centuries" of Evagrius Ponticus. His poetry comprises "metrical homilies" (e.g., one of 3,300 verses on the Passion of our Lord) and religious hymns, many of which found their way into the liturgy. There are several liturgies or *anaphora* as well as baptismal and confirmation rituals that are attributed to him.

James the Deacon wrote the life of Pelagia, the harlot, which was translated from Greek into Latin by a certain Eustochius. Nothing further is known of either man.

Jeu, two Books of, are Gnostic writings of around 170–200. Little more is known of them. See Pistis Sophia.

Jobius, an anti-Monophysite monk of the first half of the sixth century, has left a treatise against Severus and a commentary on the Incarnation. Photius mentions his works. He is not to be confused with an earlier Jobius who was a bishop and disciple of Apollinaris of Laodicea.

Johannes Monachus (c. 530), a Greek hymnographer and monk of a convent near Gaza is the author of some of the letters in a collection of the letters of Barsanuphius.

John, Acts of the Apostle (150–180) is the oldest of the apocryphal acts of the apostles. Though we have no complete text, there is a considerable portion of the Greek original and some parts of a Latin version. John's missionary career in Asia Minor, his miracles, sermons, and death are told. The author shows Docetic and Gnostic tendencies and a penchant for the miraculous. It is noteworthy as the oldest witness to Mass for the dead and presents a very old Eucharistic prayer. The hymn attributed to Christ is heretical in coloring.

John, Apocalypses of, two of them, were in circulation besides the canonical one. One treats of Antichrist and the end of the world. The other discusses fasting, the liturgy, Sunday worship, and other points.

John, Apocryphon of, is a Gnostic work refuted by Irenaeus.

John I, Pope (523–526), probably John the Deacon, who wrote *Epistola ad Senarium*, important for the liturgy of baptism, and a treatise *De fide catholica* which was attributed to Boethius.

John II, Pope (533–535), left five letters.

John III, Pope (561–574), when a Roman subdeacon, translated *Verba seniorum* into Latin. See *Apophthegmata Patrum* and *Vitae Patrum*. Perhaps he also compiled an *Expositum in Heptateuchum*.

John Bar Cursus (538), the Monophysite bishop of Tella, is the author of a commentary on the *Trisagion* which was to serve as a profession of faith for the monks and clerics of his diocese. He was the organizer of Syrian Monophysitism.

John Climacus. See under Climacus.

John Diakrinomenos wrote a Church history (c. 500) covering in ten books the period from 429 to Emperor Anastasius I (491–518).

John Malalas (577) is probably John Scholasticus (Malalas means rhetorician or scholastic) who became patriarch of Constantinople in 565 and died in 577. He wrote a chronography in seventeen books of Monophysite coloring, to which he later added an orthodox Book XVIII. The text, as preserved, goes to 563 but originally it went to 574. Written in common style it was a very popular and influential work. He also gathered a collection of synodal canons in fifty titles. This collection was probably begun earlier in Antioch around 378 and enlarged until it reached the size of John's publication.

John Mandakuni (c. 498) was appointed patriarch of Constantinople when an old man. A member of the nobility, he had received a good education. He is said to have left sermons, liturgical prayers, and a penitential canon but this is difficult to prove. He was among the "holy translators," as the group was called, who translated prominent Greek and Syrian writings under the direction of Sahak the Great and Mesrop.

John Maxentius, leader and spokesman of the Scythian monks who defended the Theopaschite formula, *Unus ex Trinitate carne passus est* (One of the Trinity suffered in the flesh) in Rome and Constantinople (519–520), is the author of *Libellus fidei*, a dialogue *Contra Nestorianos*, and several shorter *Libelli* including the acrimonious *Ad Epistolam Hormisdae responsio*. Canons 1–8 of the Synod of Orange (529) are from his writings. He also edited the Canons of Constantinople (553). He wrote in Latin.

John Monk, of Gaza (c. 530) left several hundred letters of an ascetical and pastoral nature. See Barsanuphius.

John Moschus (619) a monk of Jerusalem, Egypt, Sinai, and Antioch was born in the middle of the sixth century and died in 619. In 614, when the Persians took Jerusalem, he journeyed to Rome with his friend Sophronius. His chief work, *The Spiritual Meadow*, is a collection of more than 300 anecdotes and miracle stories, chiefly about contemporary ascetics. With Sophronius he wrote a biography of John the Almoner, patriarch of Alexandria.

John Nikiotes (c. 700) wrote, from the Monophysite point of view, a chronicle beginning with the origin of the world. It is important for what it relates of the seventh century of our era.

John Philoponus, i.e., "man of work" (565), was an Alexandrian grammarian who bent his efforts to reconciling Aristotelianism and Christian teaching. Besides a number of grammatical works and commentaries on Aristotle, he has left several theological works: *De aeternitate mundi* against the Neoplatonist Proclus; *De opificio mundi*, a commentary on the creation account in

Genesis, and *De Paschate*. His chief theological work, "The Arbiter," is tritheistic.

John Rufus composed, in the early fifth century, his *Plerophoriae* which, though purporting to be history, are stories of visions, prophecies, and miraculous happenings crudely directed against the Council of Chalcedon. He also wrote the life of Peter the Iberian.

John Scholasticus. See John Malalas.

John of Antioch (sixth century), friend of Theodoret and official leader of the party against Cyril of Jerusalem, left a few letters. He is not to be confused with a John of Antioch, a chronicler of the end of the fifth and beginning of the sixth century who has left us a few fragments.

John of Asia (586), also called John of Ephesus, was an ardent Monophysite and bishop of Constantinople under Justinian. In 572 he was imprisoned by Justinian II and after his release he wandered about visiting ascetics in the East. He wrote a Church history in three parts of six books each, from Julius Caesar to 585. Only Part III covering 571–585 has come down to us. He also wrote a history of the saints of the East, an account of the lives of fifty-eight men, reflecting the practices of Monasticism.

John of Biclaro (c. 621) was abbot of Biclaro and later bishop of Gerona. He continued, in the same dry and incoherent style, the *Chronicle of Victor of Tunnuna*, for the period 567–590.

John of Carpathus (end of seventh century), bishop of the island of Carpathus, an island between Crete and Rhodes, was an ascetical writer of around 680. Photius mentions a *Book of Consolation* to the monks of India, containing 100 sayings. Other collections of monastic sayings are attributed to him.

John of Ephesus. See John of Asia.

John of Euboea (c. 750) left a sermon on the Holy Innocents and a long homily, *On the Conception of Mary*.

John of Jerusalem, successor to Cyril in the see of Jerusalem (386–417), was a man of eloquence and virtue but did much to fan the Origenist controversy. He, supported by Rufinus, attacked Jerome and Ephiphanius. He has left us a profession of faith, and some fragments from a memoir on Origenism. His letters and other works are lost. Some manuscripts ascribe the *Mystagogical Catecheses* of Cyril of Jerusalem to John but without reason.

John of Nikiu, See John Nikiotes. Nikiu is a city on an island in the Nile.

John of Rome. See John I, Pope.

John of Saba was a Nestorian mystic of the eighth century. The *Doctrina 24* attributed to Dorotheus of Gaza is the work of John. He is also called John of Saba the Elder.

John of Scythopolis (sixth century) is the author (515–520) of a long apology for the Council of Chalcedon and later of a work against Severus cited by the Sixth General Council (680). He and John the Grammarian were outstanding opponents of Severus.

John of Thessalonica (early seventh century), bishop of that city, left some sermons on St. Demetrius, patron of Thessalonica, a homily on the Dormition and a homily on the Gospel accounts of the Resurrection.

John the Almoner (617) wrote a life of St. Tycho. John Moschus in turn wrote a life of John the Almoner.

John the Faster (595) caused Gregory the Great much trouble. As patriarch of Constantinople (582–595) he assumed the title of Universal Patriarch. A work, *Rescriptum de sacramento baptismatis,* is lost. The other works occasionally ascribed to him are spurious. He was held in high repute as an ascetic in the East. In the West he is remembered for his struggle with Gregory the Great over the ecumenical title.

John the Grammarian, cited sometimes as bishop of Caesarea in Palestine, wrote a criticism of the *Philaletes* of Severus (c. 510) and an apology (515–520) for the Council of Chalcedon, which Severus answered in his treatise *Contra Grammaticum.* See John of Scythopolis.

John the Prophet, a disciple of Barsanuphius, left a few letters of spiritual direction.

John the Rhetorician, an otherwise unknown chronicler of Antioch, wrote a chronicle that reached to 526. It is lost.

Jordanes wrote a Universal History, part two of which is a history of Rome, *De summa temporum vel de origine acti-*

busque Romanorum, 551. He made considerable use of the *Chronicle* of Marcellinus Comes. He also abridged Cassiodorus' *De origine actibusque Getarum.*

Joseph, St. See History of Joseph the Carpenter.

Joseph the Carpenter, History of, seems to have been written to furnish liturgical readings for the feast of St. Joseph. It originated around the fourth century and purports to tell of an account by Jesus Himself of the life and death of Joseph.

Josua Stylites (sixth century) probably wrote the chronicle attributed to Dionysius Tellmahre.

Jovinian, a monk, denied the superiority of the celibate state to marriage. He also taught that faith alone saves and that good works are useless. He was condemned by the Synod of Rome (390) and died before 406. See Pope Siricius; also Jerome, p. 157.

Judas Iscariot, Gospel of, is mentioned by Irenaeus as in use among the Cainites.

Julian of Eclanum (454) was driven from his bishopric, Eclanum, near Beneventum in 418; lived for a time with Theodore of Mopsuestia and Nestorius in Constantinople, dying about 454. He was the systematic theologian of Pelagianism and an exegete of Antiochian tendency. As a disciple of Pelagius he wrote *Libri IV ad Turbantium* and *Libri VIII ad Florum.* These, though lost, can be in great part reconstructed from three works of Augustine written against them. Commentaries on Osee, on Joel, and on the Psalms are today regarded as his work. The last work shows definitely the influence of Theodore of Mopsuestia.

Julian of Halicarnassus (527), a bitter opponent of Severus of Antioch, was the leader of the *Aphthartodocetae* or *Incorrupticolae* who held that Christ's body was incorruptible even during His earthly life. We have 154 fragments of four treatises he wrote against Severus and three letters.

Julian of Saba was a hermit who is celebrated in the *Carmina Nisibina* of Ephraem.

Julian of Toledo (690) wrote much on a variety of topics. His chief extant work is *Pronosticon futuri saeculi* (A Look into the Next World), an ascetical dialogue on the Last Things.

Julianus Pomerius (c. 500), a native of Africa and teacher of
Caesarius of Arles, composed eight books on the soul and
several works of spirituality, according to Gennadius. Extant
is *De vita contemplativa* (On the Contemplative Life) an
excellent book of spiritual reading for clerics treating of the
active life and the practice of Christian virtues.

Julius Africanus (240–250) was born in Jerusalem, lived in Em-
maus-Nikopolis after extensive travels and attended the lectures
of Heraclas in Alexandria where he became a friend of Origen.
He was on friendly terms with the nobility of Edessa in the
East and Emperor Alexander Severus in the West, for whom
he established a public library in the Pantheon. His *Chronicle*,
in five books, is a history of the world from Adam to 217.
According to Julius the world will exist 6,000 years; Christ was
born in 5500 and the year 6000 will inaugurate the millennium.
This work served as a model for many years but only a few
fragments remain today. Another work entitled *Embroidered
Girdles*, concerning the greatest variety of things, such as
farming, warfare, magic, etc., in twenty-four books was dedicated to Emperor Alexander Severus. It is also lost for the
most part. What remains shows Julius to have been a believer
in magic and witchcraft. Two letters of Julius are interesting.
One, to Origen, questions the canonicity of the Susanna narrative in Daniel and the other, addressed to an unknown Aristides, tries to solve the discrepancies between the genealogies in
the Gospels according to Matthew and Luke.

Julius Cassianus, a Valentinian dissenter, an Encratite, wrote in
Alexandria or Antioch around 170. No writings remain, but
Clement of Alexandria mentions commentaries and *On Con-
tinence*, a condemnation of marriage.

Julius I, Pope (337–352), has left us two letters preserved by
Athanasius. The first (341) is a vigorous defense of Athanasius
and Nicea. It severely criticises the Eusebian and Arian bishops
of the East for "not having reported on the Church in Alexandria" in order that they might have received a decision from
Rome. The second is a letter of commendation for Athanasius
returning home in 346.

Junilius Africanus (c. 542), the *quaestor sacri palatii* to the Court of Emperor Justinian, translated and edited, at the suggestion of Primasius of Hadrumentum, the *Instituta regularia divinae legis* of Paul of Nisibis. This is an introduction to the study of Scripture that faithfully reproduces the ideas of Theodore of Mopsuestia.

Justin and His Companions, Acts of, are official court records and of indubitable authenticity. After an introduction there follow the interrogation of the court and the sentence.

Justinian (after 546), bishop of Valentia, wrote a *Liber responsionum ad quendam Rusticum de interrogatis quaestionibus* which may be preserved in part in the *De cognitione baptismi* of Ildephonse of Toledo.

Justus of Urgel (after 546), brother of Justinian of Valentia, left a brief explanation of the Canticle of Canticles.

Juvencus, a Spanish priest and poet, composed around 330 a Gospel harmony in 3,211 hexameters, *Evangeliorum libri IV*. The verses are a fairly accurate paraphrase of the text. He follows Matthew for the most part. Only about a fifth of the work is devoted to the other Gospels. His full name was Gaius Vettius Aquilinus Juvencus. Other works have been lost.

Korium was a bishop in Georgia who between 445–451 wrote a life of Mesrop, his teacher.

Laodiceans, Epistle of Paul to. See Epistle to the Laodiceans.

Laudes Domini, a poem of 148 hexameters celebrating a miracle that happened between 316–323. A woman long buried raised her hand in greeting when her mate was buried beside her. To the narrative is added the *Laudes Christi,* as Creator and Redeemer. The poem closes with a blessing on Constantine and his household. The author obviously used Virgil as his model. It is the oldest Christian poem of Gaul.

Latronianus was a poet of the fourth century. He was a Priscillianist.

Laude Martyrii De, is a poorly written treatise (third century) long attributed to Cyprian.

Laurentius, bishop of Novara (307–317), was surnamed *Orator Mellifluus.* He has left us two homilies, *De paenitentia* and *De eleemosyna.* Another homily, *De muliere Chananaea,* is probably the work of John Chrysostom but translated into Latin by Laurentius.

Lazarus of Pharp (after 491), called the Rhetorician, wrote a good history of Armenia from 388–485 based on Agathangelos and Faustus of Byzantium whose works he continued. His style is adulterated and shows Greek influence.

Leander of Seville (600–601) was born before 549 in Cartagena of noble ancestry. His father, Severianus, and his brothers, Isidore and Fulgentius, both bishops, all played important parts in the history of the Church in Spain, especially in bringing the Arian Visigoths to the Catholic Church. He presided at the Council of Toledo (589) at which Reccared was received into the fold. His letters and anti-Arian treatises have perished. There remain his sermon *In laudem Ecclesiae* at the Council of Toledo and a rule for Nuns, *De institutione virginum* in twenty-one chapters for his sister Florentina.

Leonine Sacramentary. See Sacramentarium Leonianum.

Leontius, abbot of St. Sabas in Rome, wrote a life of Gregory of Girgenti or Agrigentum.

Leontius of Jerusalem has left two works: *Adversus Nestorianos* and *Contra Monophysitas* which formerly were attributed to Leontius of Byzantium. Leontius of Jerusalem was present at the Council of Constantinople (536) and at an earlier meeting with the Severians (c. 532).

Leontius of Neapolis in Cyprus (c. 650) wrote biographies of John the Almoner and the monk Simeon of Sali (565). His *Vita Spyridonis* of Trimithus is lost.

Leporius, a priest expelled from Gaul, was induced by Augustine to write a retractation of his Nestorian and Pelagian heresies in his *Liber emendationis*.

Letter of the Alexandrians is mentioned as a Marcionite writing by the Muratorian Fragment, but it has perished.

Leucius Charinos was perhaps the author of some pseudo-Johannine writings. Whether a real name or pseudonym, the name Leucius Charinos appears first in Photius.

Liber diurnus Romanorum Pontificum was long thought to have been the papal official formulary, but is today recognized as a work book for chancelleries. Some elements go back to Gregory the Great and, therefore, throw light on the procedure of Canon Law of that time.

Libri Generationis are a double Latin edition of the "Chronicle of Hyppolytus" of Rome.

Liber Judicii is perhaps Jerome's name for the *Didascalia* and Rufinus' name for the *Duae viae vel judicium secundum Petrum*.

Liber pontificalis is a collection of papal biographical sketches from Peter to Hadrian II (872) and Stephen V (891). Its oldest part is the *Catalogus Felicianus* which seems to have been based on the *Catalogus Liberianus*.

Liber propositi finis was a work used by the Marcionites. It was meant to take the place of the Acts of the Apostles, just as the Marcionites had a special collection of psalms meant to supplant the Psalms of the Old Testament.

Liberatus, a deacon of Carthage (560–566), wrote *Breviarum causae Nestorianorum et Eutychianorum*, one of the best brief sources for Nestorianism, Monophysitism, and the other heresies up to 553. His work is based on good sources. He was an opponent of the "Three Chapters."

Liberianus Catalogus is a list of the popes up to Liberius (352–366) and is the last part of the work of the Roman Chronographer of 354.

Liberius, Pope (352–366), was a controversial figure in the Arianist controversy. He has left us thirteen letters, three of them to Eusebius of Vercellae and four controverted letters written in exile which seem to compromise the pope, although they are unquestionably genuine. See *Catalogus Liberianus*.

Licianus of Cartagena wrote a letter to Pope Gregory the Great in which he calls Hilary, Ambrose, Augustine, and Gregory Nazianzen *doctores defensoresque ecclesiae* (Doctors and Defenders of the Church).

Linus, Pope, was, according to Irenaeus, the successor to St. Peter but a *Martyrium beati Petri Apostoli a Lino conscriptum* is a sixth century forgery dependent on the *Actus Vercellensis*.

Lives of the Desert Fathers. See Vitae Patrum.

Logia of Jesus, are two fragments of the Logia of Jesus unearthed at Oxyrhynchos. Papias (c. 130) also wrote his five books of commentary on the Logia.

Lucian of Antioch (312) was the founder of the Antiochian school (c. 260). He was a priest of Samosata and is not to be confused with a pagan Lucian of Samosata. Lucian has the questionable honor of having been the teacher of Arius and was himself a subordinationist, but died a martyr in 312. He is distinguished for his textual work on the Septuagint and the New Testament. His influence on the text of the New Testament has today not yet been entirely clarified. His text was so widely accepted that it was called Koine, i.e., the common text or the text in common usage.

Lucian of Samosata, a pagan rhetorician (c. 170), wrote *De morte peregrini*. The work mocks Christians for their brotherly love and contempt for death.

Lucian the Presbyter wrote (c. 415) in Greek a work describing the finding of the relics of St. Stephen. See Apocalypse of St. Stephen.

Lucidus was a priest of Gaul condemned in the Synods of Arles and Lyons (473–474) because of his teaching of predestinationism. See Faustus of Riez, p. 183.

Lucifer of Calaris or Cagliaris in Sardinia (370–371), together with Eusebius of Vercelli, refused to condemn Athanasius at the Synod of Milan (335) and was banished. Thereafter, he lived in Syria, Palestine, and the Thebaid. In Antioch he consecrated Paulinus bishop and thereby disrupted whatever beginnings of harmony between the Niceans and the Homoiousians had been made at the Synod of Alexandria (362). In this way he started the Antiochian schism. Though he died outside the Church he is venerated as a saint in Sardinia. Five treatises of his directed to Constantine, though inferior works in content and style, are important for the history of Latin and for a study of the pre-Hieronymian text of the Bible. The works are: *De non conveniendo cum haereticis* (On not Consorting with Heretics), *De regibus apostaticis* (On the Wicked Kings of the Old Testament), *De sancto Athanasio*, *De non parcendo in Deum delinquentibus* (That the Enemies of God are not to be Spared), *Moriendum esse pro Dei Filio* (That One Should

Die for the Son of God). A man of violent temperament, he alienated many friends, and his schism hardly outlasted the century.

Lucius I, Pope (253–254), wrote a letter to Cyprian on the *Lapsi*.

Lupus, bishop of Troyes (427–479), came from Lerins. His immense correspondence has perished almost entirely.

Macarius of Antioch, submitted a profession of faith to the Council of Constantinople but was condemned by that council in 680. The name Macarius has caused no little confusion since it was used as a title of address much as we use the title, "Venerable."

Macarius of Magnesia, bishop of Magnesia in Caria, or Lydia, assisted at the synod held at the "The Oak" in 403. He is believed to be the author of an apology in five books, in the form of objections and answers, entitled *Monogenes,* or *Unigenitus,* (*Reply to the Heathen*), written probably around 410. The objections are taken mostly from a work against the Christians by the Neoplatonist Porphyry.

Macarius the Egyptian, also called the Elder or the Great (c. 390), lived sixty years in the desert of Scete. Neither Palladius' *Historia Lausiaca,* nor Rufinus' *Historia Monachorum* has anything to say of his literary activity. There are ascribed to him some sentences or *apophthegmata*, some letters, fifty spiritual homilies, and two small prayers. All must be questioned. The anonymity of the author may well be concealed behind the general term, Macarios, i.e., Blessed. He is not to be confused with Macarius the Alexandrian, who wrote nothing.

Macarius the Younger, also called the Alexandrian (died c. 394 a centenarian), was an anchorite in the desert of Scete and the Nitrian desert. No authentic writings have come down to us.

Macarian Writings are some varied writings whose origin and history are not clear. There was a catechism of the Messalians and an *Asketikon* condemned at Ephesus in 431. Symeon, one of the founders of the Messalians, may have had something to do with them.

Macedonius of Constantinople, patriarch of that city (496–511), was the author of a *Florilegium Patristicum* against Monophysitism. He is not to be confused with Macedonius (362), the Semi-Arian usurper of the see of Constantinople who gave his name to the Macedonians.

Macrobius (Donatist) was the author of a book to virgins and confessors which some think is the *De singularitate clericorum* attributed to Cyprian. The *Passion of Sts. Maximinus and Isaac*, written in 366, is attributed to him.

Malchon Presbyter of Antioch had a disputation with Paul of Samosata. It is lost.

Mambre Verzanogh (fourth century) has left us three homilies on New Testament subjects.

Mamertus. See Claudianus Mamertus.

Mar Aba (552) was a disciple of Ephraem and bishop of Seleucea 536–552. He was among the famous teachers of the school of Nisibis. He was a convert from Mazdaism but fell into Nestorianism. A commentary on the Gospels and other exegetical works are ascribed to him.

Mandakuni. See John Mandakuni.

Marcellinus, together with Faustinus, presented a *Libellus precum* (383–384) to the "Emperors Valentinian II, Theodosius II, and Arcadius" successfully petitioning protection for the Luciferians from attacks by Catholics.

Marcellinus Comes, an Illyrian, wrote a chronicle of the Eastern Empire for the years 379–534.

Marcellus of Ancyra (c. 374) was an ardent supporter of Athanasius at Nicea and later. Zealous in defense of orthodoxy, he was not the best of theologians. His polemic against the Arian Asterius (335) was challenged as Sabellianism. He was deposed in 336 and condemned as a heretic in 381 at Constantinople. We have 129 fragments of his polemic preserved by Eusebius, who wrote against it and quoted it. He also stirred up much antagonism against Marcellus though the latter was entirely orthodox.

Marcellus, Acts of, tell of a centurion who refused to take part in the army's festivities on the emperor's birthday.

Marcianus was a Greek hymnographer of the fifth century.

Marcion, the heretic, rejected the Gospels of Matthew, Mark, and John. He also expunged, so he claimed, Jewish influence from Luke. He rejected the Pastoral Epistles and Hebrews and arbitrarily edited the other Paulines. Thus he reduced the New Testament to the Gospel of Luke, ten Epistles of Paul, and his own book, *Antitheses*.

Mark of Gaza (c. 420), a deacon, wrote a life of St. Porphyry (395–419). It has come down to us in a sixth century revision.

Mark the Gnostic taught in Asia Minor about 180.

Mark the Hermit, disciple of John Chrysostom and contemporary of Nilus, was abbot of a monastery in Galatia, but became a solitary in his old age. Photius was acquainted with nine ascetical and dogmatic treatises by him, which we still possess. He is said also to be the author of two series of maxims for monks treating of Christian perfection, treatises on baptism, on penance, and on the frequent thought of God.

Marius of Avenches (594) wrote a badly organized history or chronicle of the world covering the time 455–481. He continues where Prosper left off.

Marius of Lauzanne (end of sixth century), bishop of Lauzanne, wrote a sequel to the chronicle of Prosper of Aquitaine, adding notices from 455–481.

Marius Victor (died between 425–450), rhetorician of Marseilles, is the author of *Aletheia*, a poem in hexameter, in three books. It is a paraphrase and commentary on the materials of Genesis from creation to Sodom.

Marius Victorinus (c. 362), African by birth, was a celebrated rhetorician in Rome under Constantine (337–361) who came to the Church by way of Neoplatonism. When he asked to be baptized in 355 Augustine wrote: "Rome marvelled and the Church rejoiced" (Conf. 8,2,4). Julian the Apostate forced him to quit teaching. Before becoming a Christian, he wrote many studies and commentaries on the rhetorical and philosophical writings of Cicero, Aristotle, Porphyry, Plotinus, and some original writings of his own. As a Christian he ventured into the theological field and his writings on Trinitarian subjects are based more on Neoplatonist metaphysics than on Scripture and tradition. These works are: *De generatione divini Verbi; Adversus Arium; De Homoousio recipiendo*, and three hymns on the Trinity. He has left commentaries on Galatians, Ephesians, and Philemon, all specimens of literal exegesis.

Marouta (fifth century), a Persian bishop, wrote a history of the Council of Nicea and the *Acta* of the Persian martyrs under Sapor II (310–380).

Martin of Bracara or Braga (580), born in Pannonia about 515, was a monk in Palestine, in Spain, then abbot and bishop of Dumio. Finally as metropolitan of Bracara (c. 572) he was most active in converting the Arian Suabians. He was a keen theologian, an accomplished translator, but above all a practical pastor and good shepherd. He died in 580. He has left moral and ascetical writings: *Formula vitae honestae* (Map of an Honest Life), *De ira*, and three works that originally made one, *Pro repellenda jactantia* (On Overcoming Depression), *De superbia* (On Pride), *Exhortatio humilitatis* (On Humility). Another work, *De correctione rusticorum* (On Instructing the Unlettered) is important for the light it throws on the superstitious beliefs of the common people of the time. He has left also some writings important for canon law and liturgy. The *Capitula Martini* is a collection of canons of the Eastern, African, and Spanish Synods. *Epistola de trina mersione* (On the Triple Immersion), *De baptismo*, and *De Pascha* are not certainly authentic. Besides these he has left a collection of Greek *Apophthegmata Aegyptiorum Patrum sententiae* (Sayings of the Egyptian Fathers). He had a monk, Paschasius of Dumio, translate another such collection.

Martin of Dumio. See Martin of Bracara.

Martyrium S. Clementis is a legendary work of the fourth century on Clement of Rome.

Martyrologium Carthageniense dates from about the middle of the fourth century.

Martyrologium Hieronymianum is misnamed. Its original form dates from the middle of the fifth century. It contains a Greek Martyrology (middle of fourth century), a Roman Calendar that stops at 422, though most of its materials are older, and an African Calendar (fourth century). Its present form dates from about 600.

Martyrologium Syriacum was collected by an Arian and published in Greek. It is the largest collection to that date.

Martyrs of Lyons suffered martyrdom in Lyons 177–178. The churches of Lyons and Vienne wrote a letter to the churches of

Phrygia and Asia to tell of the courage, love, and brotherliness of the martyrs and the care of the Church for its heroic martyrs.

Maruthas, bishop of Maipherkat, collected (410) the *Acts* of the Persian Martyrs and wrote a history of the Council of Nicea and some homilies.

Mary, Gospel of, is a Gnostic work purporting to give revelations made to the Blessed Mother.

Massianus collaborated with Cyprian, bishop of Toulon, to produce an interesting life of Caesarius of Arles, their master.

Matthew, Acts of, is legendary and of late origin (about fifth century).

Matthias, Gospel of, is an heretical work that may be the Matthias traditions and Gnostic teachings mentioned by Clement of Alexandria. It may date from the first half of the second century.

Maxentius. See John Maxentius.

Maximillian, Acts of, tell of a young Christian of Numidia who refused to become a soldier (c. 295).

Maximinus, Arian Gothic bishop, attacked Ambrose in his *Dissertatio Maximini contra Ambrosium.* He had a disputation with Augustine at Hippo in 427 or 428 and has left forty sermons and three polemic writings.

Maximus was a champion of orthodoxy against Gnosticism at the end of the reign of Commodus and the beginning of the reign of Septimus Severus.

Maximus (Arian), a Gothic bishop of Arian bias whom Augustine refuted, has his name connected with some letters, sermons, and treatises.

Maximus of Turin (born c. 380) attended a Roman synod in 456. Beyond this nothing is known of him. He was as great a preacher as his contemporary Peter Chrysologus. His sermons, several hundred in number, are short and to the point. They are valuable for the cultural history of the times. Twenty-two lenten homilies are important for the history of the liturgy. He was also an outstanding anti-Pelagian.

Memnon of Ephesus championed St. Cyril against Nestorius. We have a letter of his to the clergy of Constantinople (431).

Mesihazek, author of the *Chronicle of Arbela,* a list of biographies after the manner of the *Acta Martyrum*, wrote between 540–569 but is not too trustworthy.

Mesrop is also called Mashtots.

Methodius of Olympus (c. 311), named after his native Olympus and probably bishop of Philippi in Macedonia, was a vigorous opponent of Origen though himself an allegorizing exegete. He died in Chalcis, a martyr, around 311. Of his numerous writings in dialogue form, *The Banquet* or *On Virginity* has come down to us. Fragments of other treatises are also known. They are: *On the Resurrection, On the Freedom of the Will, On Contentment,* and pieces of exegetical works. A polemic against Porphyry has been lost. He had read in the classics widely and was an elegant writer. His aversion to Tertullian is said to have cost him a place in Eusebius' *Church History* and hence little is known of his life.

Miles, bishop of Susa, a martyr under Sapor II (309–379), left some writings, now unknown.

Miltiades was an apologist and anti-Gnostic writer of the late second century. His works are lost. There were two books against the Greeks, two against the Jews and an apology for Christian philosophy.

Modestus was an anti-Gnostic apologetic writer under Marcus Aurelius and Commodus.

Modestus of Jerusalem (634) has left a sermon on the Dormition, locating the tomb of Mary in Jerusalem, and fragments of other writings.

Monarchian Prologues are prologues to the Gospels which originated in Priscillianist circles at the end of the fourth century or beginning of the fifth. Formerly they were dated in the third century and were given far greater importance and authority than they deserve.

Monoimus was an Alexandrian Gnostic who left *A Letter to Theophrastus.*

Moschus John. See John Moschus.

Moses of Chorene (487) seems to have been a disciple of Mesrop (fifth century), but the works attributed to him, such as the *History of Armenia* and a *Geography of Armenia*, etc., must now be dated early in the ninth century.

Muratorian Fragment, The, is the oldest list of canonical books; it came into being during the controversy over the inspired books of the New Testament. This fragment is so named after the discoverer, the archaeologist Muratori. It may have been composed by Hippolytus in his early years toward the middle of the second century. The list gives details about the various New Testament books. It begins with a broken sentence on Mark and omits Hebrews, James, and I and II Peter. It also lists some non-canonical books as heretical and others as recommended reading, though not inspired.

Musanus was an anti-Gnostic apologist under Marcus Aurelius and Commodus (161–192).

Narsai (c. 503) was a foremost champion of Nestorianism. In 437 he became head of the school of Edessa and when driven out in 457 he founded the school of Nisibis at the invitation of Bishop Barsauma. He died around 503, aged 103. His enemies called him the Leper but the Nestorians extravagantly referred to him as the "admirable Doctor," "the tongue of the East," "the poet of the Christian religion," and the "harp of the Holy Ghost." He was a gifted poet but there remain only some of his metrical homilies and liturgical hymns.

Nemesius, bishop of Emesa in Phoenecia early in the fifth century, has left us a work on the nature of man that was very popular in the Middle Ages.

Nephalius (c. 508), a Palestinian monk and defender of Chalcedon early in the sixth century, published a discourse against Severus of Antioch and an *Apology* for the Council of Chalcedon.

Nepos was bishop of Arsinoe in Egypt. Dionysius of Alexandria attacked his views on the millennium and his work *Against the Allegorists.*

Nicephorus Confessor (829), patriarch of Constantinople, deposed (815) because of his attacks on the Iconoclasts, has left some letters, a history, and several polemical works.

Nicodemus, Gospel of, originated early in the fifth century but is based on older materials and attempts to use Pilate as testimony against the Jews. It is interesting to note that the Coptic Church venerates Pilate as a saint and martyr. The first two parts are the *Acta Pilati,* while part three purports to be the testimony of two witnesses to the *Descensus ad Inferos Christi* (The Descent of Christ into Hell), who had returned from the dead.

Nikiotes. See John Nikiotes.

Nilus of Ancyra (c. 430), formerly erroneously called Nilus of Sinai, was a staunch supporter of Chrysostom and head of a monastery in Ancyra. Well trained in theology and of great literary gifts, he has left numerous ascetico-moral treatises meant chiefly for monks. He has also left a number of short letters which are chiefly selections and extracts from ascetical writings of earlier fathers.

Noetus of Smyrna, a patripassianist (*pater passus est*), was a proponent of monarchianistic teaching on the Logos and the originator of Modalism. Tertullian attacked his teaching when Epigon and Cleomen, disciples of Noetus, spread it in Rome.

Nonnus of Panoplis wrote his *Epos Dionysiaca* celebrating the travels of the god Dionysos to India and (after 431) a paraphrase of John's Gospel in hexameters. From the tenor of the *epos* one would conclude that he was not a Christian at the time of its writing.

Noria is the title of a Gnostic book used by the Nicolaites.

Novatianum, Ad, is a work on the problem of the *Lapsi* to Cyprian. The author is a bishop who agrees with Cyprian.

Octateuch is a work on the Apostolic Constitutions. It seems of Syriac origin.

Octoechos is a book of liturgical hymns, some still in use. Severus of Antioch and John Damascene wrote many of them. The Marian hymn, *Sub tuum praesidium*, by Severus is one of them.

Odes of Solomon (second century) are hymns of mystic beauty and piety. Written in Greek, further details about the odes will probably never be settled. Ode seven is on the Incarnation. Ode twelve is a hymn to the Logos. Ode seventeen tells the *Descensus ad Inferos Christi*, and Ode nineteen witnesses to the virginity of Mary, *inter et post partum*. Ode twenty-eight tells of the Passion and Ode forty-two deals with the Resurrection. Ode two has been lost.

Oecumenius, a philosopher and rhetorician, was a follower of Severus of Antioch. In the first half of the sixth century he composed a commentary on the Apocalypse in twelve books. Fragments of his scholia on Chrysostom's *Homilies on St. Paul* have come down to us in a commentary on the *Acts* which was formerly ascribed to Oecumenius. He is not to be confused with Oecumenius, bishop of Trica in Thessaly, who lived in the tenth century.

Olympiodorus, an exegete and deacon of Alexandria, wrote (first half of the sixth century) on Ecclesiastes, Jeremias, Lamentations, and Baruch. There remain only some scholia or fragments of his work on Job, Proverbs, and Luke. A polemic against Severus of Antioch also is lost.

Olympius was an anti-Priscillianist bishop mentioned by Gennadius.

Optatus of Mileve, bishop of that city in Numidia, wrote in 365 his *Contra Parmenianum Donatistam* in six books. In 385 he published the second revised edition of this work and added Book VII. The work is irenic in tone but incisive in its analysis of the problems of the Donatist schism. Book I sketches the history of the Schism. Book II teaches that there is only one true church united in the *una cathedra Petri, apostolorum caput* in Rome (one chair of Peter, head of the apostles in Rome). Book III explains that Catholics did not originate the measures against the Donatists taken by the state. Book IV attacks the false interpretation by the Donatists of Isaias 66:3 and Psalm 140:5. Book V is directed against rebaptism. Book VI describes the fury and the fanaticism of the Donatists in destroying altars, etc., and Book VII outlines a lenient policy in dealing with *traditores*.

Optatianus Porfyrius, a native of Africa, was the first Christian to write good religious poetry in Rome.

Opus Imperfectum in Matthaeum is an anonymous Latin commentary of considerable worth but imperfectly preserved. It has been variously attributed to Chrysostom (until the sixteenth century), Ulifas, or the Gnostic bishop Maximinus. The work originated around 550 in Arian circles of northern Italy.

Orator Massiliensis may be the Victorinus Rhetor Massiliensis mentioned by Gennadius. He died after 425. Marius Victor is also called "Orator Massiliensis."

Ordinances of the Apostles is a disciplinary work of the beginning of the fourth century, very valuable for the history of ecclesiastical law. Its full title was *Ordinances Transmitted by Clement and Ecclesiastical Canons of the Holy Apostles.* Only the last part is valuable. It is sometimes also called *Apostolic Church Order.* It contains moral precepts based on the *Didache* in the first part, while the rest contains canonical legislation on bishops, priests, deacons, lectors, and widows.

Orientius (c. 430), bishop of Auch (Augusta Ausciorum), wrote a *Commonitorium* in two books of verse, in unaffected and plain style. Other poems under his name are of doubtful authenticity.

Osius. See Hosius of Cordoba.

Pachomius (346) was the founder of the cenobitical life. In 320 he founded a monastery in Tabennisi in the Thebaid and later added eight male and two female monasteries to the group under his rule. He left us a rule in Coptic. This has been preserved in a Latin translation by Jerome, who added fragments from other exhortations of Pachomius. Pachomius also has left us eleven letters, two of them in cipher.

Pacian (c. 392), bishop of Barcelona, was the father of the prefect to whom Jerome dedicated his *De viris illustribus.* His three letters against the Novatian Sympronianus and a short treatise, *Paranaesis sive exhortatorius libellus ad poenitentiam* are valuable for the history of penance. His sermon *De baptismo* discusses original sin. He coined the phrase *Christianus mihi nomen est, Catholicus cognomen* (Christian is my name; Catholic is my surname). Attempts have been made to establish his authorship of other writings but without success.

Palestinian Martyrs is a work of Eusebius on the martyrs of 303–311.

Palladius (431) was a disciple of Evagrius Ponticus. He was a monk in Egypt and Palestine (388–399) and bishop of Helenopolis in Bithynia after that; he died before 431. In 419–420 he published his famous *Historia Lausiaca.* See Timothy of Alexandria and *Historia monachorum in Egypto.* In 408 he wrote, during his stay at Syene, his Dialogue *De vita sancti Joannis* on his friend Chrysostom. It is patterned on Plato's *Phaedo* and important as an historical source.

Pamphilus (309), the learned priest and disciple of Pierius, was one of the greatest masters of the school and library at Caesarea. He was imprisoned in 307 by Maximinus Daja, and there wrote in five books his *Apologia* for Origen, his teacher and predecessor. Eusebius, his slave and disciple, added a sixth book. Only the first book has been preserved in Rufinus' translation. His efforts in textual criticism of the biblical text are most important. Eusebus wrote his biography in three books, but it is lost. Pamphilius died in 309 or 310 as a martyr.

Pamphilus of Jerusalem was a friend of Cosmas Indicopleustes and was thought to have been the author of an anonymous writing called by A. Mai the *Panoplia Dogmatica*. However, the author of that work is dependent on Leontius of Byzantium and Justinian's work, *Confessio rectae fidei*. He must have written sometime between 560–630.

Panodorus, an Alexandrian monk, wrote between 395–408 a *Chronicle of the World,* which is known only through later Byzantine chroniclers.

Panoplia Dogmatica. See Pamphilus of Jerusalem.

Pantaenus (206), "The Sicilian Bee," was the teacher of Clement of Alexandria. He was the first president of the catechetical school in Alexandria. It is doubtful whether Pantaenus published any works.

Parmenianus was the successor to Donatus the Great, as Donatist bishop in the see of Carthage (c. 355–391). He wrote (c. 362) five treatises against the church of the *Traditores*, which were refuted by Optatus and (c. 378) a Letter to Tychonius which was refuted by Augustine.

Pascha Computus, De, is a revision of Hippolytus' Easter calendar attributed to Cyprian. It dates from about 243.

Paschasius of Dumio translated the *Verba seniorum* into Latin.

Pastor, bishop of Galicia, was an anti-Priscillianist of the early fifth century.

Paul, Acts of, already known to Tertullian, must date before 190. Originally the work contained the three works known to us as:

  1. *Acta Pauli et Theclae.* This is patently fiction but it has influenced Christian literature and art. It has the oldest description of Paul's appearance.

2. The correspondence of St. Paul with the Corinthians which purports to be letters written by the Corinthian Church to Paul.

3. *Martyrium* or *Passio Pauli*, a legendary story of Paul's labors in Rome and his death there. This account has also influenced Christian art and literature.

Paul, Apocalypse of, is a forgery of the fourth century. It elaborates on II Cor. 12:2 and tells how Paul visited heaven, hell, and the garden of Eden.

Paul, Assumption of, is a lost Gnostic work written in the second or third century. See Paul, Apocalypse of.

Paul and Seneca is a fictitious correspondence of Paul and Seneca.

Paul and Thecla, Acts of. See Acts of Paul.

Paul to the Alexandrians, Epistle of, is a lost forgery by the Marcionites mentioned by the Muratorian Fragment.

Paul to the Laodiceans, Epistle of, contains many words and phrases of genuine Pauline epistles but cannot be dated before the fourth century; Harnack, who thought it a Marcionite forgery, to the contrary.

Paul of Constantinople was a little known letter writer (641–645).

Paul of Elusa, abbot of Elusa, wrote (c. 526) a life of St. Theognius.

Paul of Emesa, bishop of Emesa, was a follower of Theodoret against Cyril. In 433 he acted as mediator between Cyril and John. He left a letter and some homilies.

Paul of Nisibis, a Persian of Nisibis, wrote *Instituta regularia legis*, an introduction to the Bible which is faithful to the opinions of Theodore of Mopsuestia. He wrote it in Greek and (c. 542) Junilius Africanus translated it and edited it in Latin.

Paul of Samosata was tried by three councils and finally deposed as bishop of Antioch for Monarchian errors and others that foreshadow Nestorianism. His discourses with Sabinus are not genuine. He left fragments of a dispute with Malchon.

Paul of Tella, bishop of Tella in Syria, translated (616–617) the Septuagint according to the *Hexapla* of Origen, called the "Syriac Hexapla." It was very popular but has not come down to us.

Paul the Deacon was an English monk and hagiographer.

Paulinus of Beziers wrote a satire on contemporary manners, around 400–419.

Paulinus of Milan, a deacon, was the secretary of Ambrose but he moved to Africa about 422 and there at the instance of Augustine wrote a life of Ambrose.

Paulinus of Pella (c. 459) seems to have been the grandson of Ausonius. He was born around 376 and came to Gaul at the age of three. In 459 at the age of eighty-three he composed *Eucharisticos Deo sub ephemeridis meae textu,* an autobiography in 616 hexameters of beautiful sentiments but poor poetry.

Paulinus of Perigeux wrote (c. 470) a long *De vita sancti Martini* in 3,622 hexameters which is mainly a redaction of the work of Sulpicius Severus on Martin. He has also left smaller poems on Martin, one in twenty-five, another in eighty hexameters.

Paulonas was a disciple of Ephraem. He wrote some hymns and treatises against heretics.

Pectorius, Epitaph of, belongs epigraphically to the fourth or fifth century but its code language, like that of the Abercius inscription, belongs to the second or third century. It may be using the phraseology of even older poems. It attests the Eucharist, baptism, and prayers for the dead.

Pelagius, heretic, wrote a letter to Demetriades (c. 412 or 413), *Libellus fidei* to Pope Innocent in 417, and treatises *On Freewill* and *On Nature.*

Pelagius I, Pope (555–561), was a Roman deacon and papal apocrisiary in Constantinople. He was against the condemnation of the "Three Chapters" and defended his position in, *In defensione Trium Capitulorum.* He agreed to the condemnation of 553 and later as pope most of his some one hundred letters were written to reconcile opponents of the condemnation.

Pelagius II, Pope (570–590), has left us seven letters.

Peregrinatio ad loca sancta. See Aetheria.

Perpetua and Felicitas, Passion of, may be the work of Tertullian (c. 202–203) who almost at once translated it into Greek. He used an account by Perpetua of her visions and experiences. It is a moving story of the last day of Perpetua and her slave Felicitas, both young mothers, and three catechumens. The account is an important testimony to the belief in the afterlife of the early Church.

Persian Martyrs, Acts of, are a Syriac account of the martyrs under Sapor II, 339–379.

Peter, Acts of, comprises three works dating around 180–190, two of which are found collected in the *Actus Vercellensis,* so named after Vercelli. Their place of origin is Syria.

    1. *Actus Petri cum Simone.* This tells of Peter's triumph over Simon Magus, Paul's trip to Spain, and Peter's death. It is Docetic; it has Peter preach against marriage and teaches the use of water instead of wine in the Eucharist.

    2. *The Martyrdom of Peter,* which tells the story of *Quo vadis.* This also shows some Gnostic influences.

    3. The third work, the *Martyrium beati Petri Apostoli a Lino conscriptum* was written in Latin and dates from the sixth century.

Peter and Paul, Acts of, dates from the third century, shows no heretical tinge and tells of the friendship and labors as well as the martyrdom of the two apostles. Some Latin and Greek fragments are preserved.

Peter, Apocalypse of, dates from the second century and describes a vision of heaven and hell.

Peter, Gospel of (before 150), tells the passion and resurrection of our Lord with accounts of many miracles. The guilt of the Jews in the death of Jesus is emphasized and Herod gives the order of crucifixion. Roughly the work uses the material of the fourth canonical Gospel.

Peter of Alexandria (311) became bishop of Alexandria in 300, was obliged to flee in the Diocletian persecution in 303 and died a martyr in 311. During his exile, Meletius of Lycopolis usurped primacy powers in Egypt (the right to ordain, etc.) and attacked Peter's mild policy toward the *Lapsi.* This started the Miletian schism which was to harass the Church for centuries. The Acts recounting Peter's martyrdom are of later date. His works have come down to us in fragments only. There were treatises and letters. There are fourteen penitential canons probably taken from a Paschal letter on penance (306). Other writings are, *On the Pasch, On the Divinity of Christ, On the Resurrection,* and *On the Soul,* the last three against Origenist errors. There was also a letter to the Alexandrians on Meletius. Peter was a leader of the opponents of Origenism.

Peter of Laodicea (seventh century) had some Commentaries ascribed to him but, de facto, we know nothing about him.

Peter the Iberian was a Monophysite bishop (453–488) of Majuma near Gaza. An anonymous Greek life of Peter appeared in Syriac around 500. See Zachary the Rhetorician.

Petilianus, the Donatist, was the author of several letters refuted by Augustine, and of a book on the unity of baptism.

Philastrius, bishop of Brescia, wrote around 383–391 a *Liber de haeresibus* in which he tells about 150 heresies in a heavy, monotonous manner.

Phileas, bishop of Thmuis, was martyred in 306. He has left fragments of two letters.

Philip, Acts of, is of late date (fourth century) and of small value. It confuses Philip the deacon and Philip the apostle.

Philip, Gospel of, is a Gnostic work in part.

Philip of Gortyna in Greece was an anti-Gnostic champion of orthodoxy.

Philip of Side in Pamphilia wrote in thirty-six books an uncritical and badly composed Christian history (c. 430).

Philo, bishop of Carpasia (c. 400), left fragments of a commentary on the Canticle of Canticles.

Philokalus. See Dionysius Philocalus and the *Roman Chronographer of 354.*

Philoponus. See John Philoponus.

Philostorgius was an Eunomian who wrote (c. 425–433) a church history in twelve books of the period from Arius to 425. The work is entirely lost except for fragments in Photius and other later documents. It is more a plea for Arianism than an impartial history but it is of value for information about contemporary thought.

Philoxenus of Mabug or Mabbogh (523), Monophysite metropolitan of Mabug or Mabbogh since 485, was banished to Thrace in 518 or 519 and died there in Gangra in 523. He is one of the greatest Syriac literary men. A Syriac translation of the Bible authorized by him bears his name (*Philoxenian*). He has left some eighty writings of which there have been edited thirteen orations on Christian life (*De correctione morum*), five treatises on the Trinity and the Incarnation, and several letters.

Phoebadius of Agen (392) in southern France was a vigorous opponent of Arianism. He attacked the second formula of Sirmium in *Liber contra Arianos* written in 357 or 358, most of which he borrowed from Tertullian and Hilary. Jerome mentions a few small lost works. He died after 392.

Photinus of Sirmium, Arian bishop of Sirmium in Pannonia, belonged to the Anomeans, i.e., pure Arians, though he was a disciple of Paul of Samosata. Nothing is left of his writings.

Photius (c. 891) published a library (*Myriobiblion or Bibliotheca*) containing 279 notices of authors and works, many of which would be otherwise unknown today. He left an extensive correspondence, many homilies and sermons as well as doctrinal works. He is important in patrology for his *Bibliotheca* but he is best known in Church history for the Photian Schism.

Physiologus was a Christian handbook of nature symbolism. A Greek edition of the above work is attributed to Epiphanius of Salamis but it is a forgery.

Pierius (c. 309), president of the school of Alexandria 281–300, was a renowned orator. Photius mentions twelve *Logoi* or Sermons, among them one on the *Theotokos*. He died after 309 in Rome.

Pilati, Acta forms the first part of the Gospel of Nicodemus (1–11). Epiphanius and Tertullian seem to have been acquainted with the materials of this work. It tells of the trial of Jesus and purports to be based on a report to Tiberias by Pilate. The *Anaphora Pilati* and the *Paradosis Pilati* are Middle Age forgeries.

Pinytus of Gnossus, bishop of that see, wrote a letter in answer to a letter from Dionysius of Corinth.

Pionius, The Martyrdom of, recounts the death of Pionius under Decius.

Pistis Sophia is a Gnostic work of the second half of the third century. It purports to give the conversation of the risen Savior with His disciples and followers, among them John and Mary Magdalen. These accounts relate to the fall and redemption of the Pistis Sophia, a creature of the world of Aeons. See Odes of Solomon.

Polemon, a disciple of Apollinaris of Laodicea.

Polycarp, Martyrdom of, is the oldest account of the death of the martyr, though it really is a letter. It was sent out by the Church at Smyrna, shortly after Polycarp's death. It belongs to the second group of *Acta Martyrum.*

Polychronius (430), bishop of Apamea in Syria, was the brother of Theodore of Mopsuestia and an exegete of the Antiochian school. He wrote commentaries on many of the Old Testament books but only a few fragments have come down to us in the *Catenae.* He died around 430.

Polycratus of Edessa, bishop of that see, wrote a letter to Pope Victor (c. 190) in which he vindicates for the churches of Asia their right to follow their own tradition in the celebration of Easter.

Pomerius. See Julianus Pomerius.

Pontianus, bishop of an unknown see, wrote to Justinian against his condemnation of the "Three Chapters."

Pontianus, Pope (230–235), communicated the decision of the Roman Synod of 231 or 232 against Origen.

Pontius, deacon, is said to have written a *Vita* of St. Cyprian. It is very uncritical and in the nature of a panegyric or a *Martyrium.*

Possidius of Calama, a disciple and friend of Augustine, wrote a *Vita* of his Master shortly after Augustine's death. To it he added a detailed list of Augustine's writings.

Potamian, Acts of, tells the martyrdom of the virgin Potamiana and the soldier Basilides in Alexandria, 202–203.

Potamius (c. 360), Arian bishop of Lisbon (355–357), has left us two letters and two sermons written before he embraced heresy. His name is linked with Hosius in the composition of the second Sirmian Formula (357), but that cannot be established.

Praedestinatus is a work in three books written under Sixtus III (432–440). It is attributed to Arnobius the Younger and is closely related in style and thought to his commentary on the Psalms. Book I is based on Augustine's *De haeresibus* and gives ninety heresies of which "the last and greatest" is that of the Predestinationists. Book II reproduces Augustine's teaching on grace and predestination and was long attributed to him. Book III attacks the thoughts of Book II and shows up the Semi-Pelagian position of the author.

Praxeas was a patripassianist. Tertullian wrote his *Adversus Praxean* against him. Praxeas, however, blocked the attempts of Montanus to be accepted into the Roman Church.

Preaching of Paul is mentioned in the *Liber de rebaptismate*.

Preaching of Peter comprises a series of spurious missionary discourses of the Apostle, together with a connecting narrative.

Presbyters. See p. 21; see also Papias, p. 18.

Primasius (552), bishop of Hadrumentum, approved the condemnation of the "Three Chapters" and died soon after in 552. He wrote a commentary on the Apocalypse that is of value because of its many quotations from the lost commentary of Tychonius. A history of heresies by Primasius is lost.

Priscillian (385), the founder in 375 of the sect named after him, was a rich, gifted layman of strong character. In 385 he was put to death in Treves on the charge of magic by the usurper Maximus. Eleven treatises, the most important of which are *Liber apologeticus*, *Liber ad Damasum episcopum* and *De fide et de apocryphis*, have been attributed to him or to Instantius.

Proba was the wife of C. Celsinus Adelphius, prefect of Rome. In 360 she tried to put the Bible into a *Centro Virgilianus* of 694 hexameters. The result was a very odd, obscure, incomplete, even ridiculous work.

Proclus (Montanist) was a defender of Montanism in Rome under Pope Zephyrinus (198–217). The priest Caius argued against him. He probably wrote something but nothing is left.

Proclus of Constantinople and Proclus of Cyzicus are the same.

Proclus, Neoplatonist (485) was copiously used and even copied verbatim by the pseudo-Areopagite.

Procopius of Gaza (c. 538) was one of the earliest composers of *Catenae*. He has left one on the Octateuch and on parts of Kings, Chronicles, Isaias, and Canticles. There are 163 letters of great biographical though of little theological interest. Only a panegyric on Emperor Anastasius is left of his orations.

Prologues to the Gospels and Epistles: 1. The Anti-Marcionite Prologues date around 160–180. 2. The Prologues to the Pauline Epistles seem to be the work of Marcion and some of his followers. 3. The Monarchian Prologues to the Gospels seem to have originated in Priscillianist circles around 400.

Prophetiae ex omnibus libris collectae is a collection of biblical prophecies that is important for the study of the Old Latin African Text. The collection originated in the first quarter of the fourth century.

Proto-Evangelium Jacobi is quite old and may have already been used by Justin. It was one of the most popular of the apocryphal gospels. The author calls himself James and professes to tell the story of Mary from her birth to the slaughter of the Innocents and the martyrdom of Zachary in the temple. The entire subject matter is the product of fantastic imagination. It mentions Joachim and Anna as the parents of Mary. It gives emphatic witness to the perpetual virginity, especially *in partu,* of Mary, and is the first ancient document to advance the theory that the "Brethren of the Lord" were sons of Joseph by an earlier marriage. It has been suggested that there are three older works in the *Proto-Evangelium:* 1. the story of Mary, 2. an *Apocryphum Josephi,* and 3. an *Apocryphum Zachariae.*

Ptolemy was a disciple of Valentinus. He has left us a letter to Flora, the complete text of which was preserved by Epiphanius. Flora was a Christian lady who hesitated to undertake the study of Gnosis imposed by the Gnostics. To convince her, Ptolemy undertakes to prove that at least part of the Old Law was the work, not of the supreme God, but of the Demiurge.

Ptolemy and Lucius, Acts of, is mentioned by Justin.

Pyrrhus was a Monothelite writer, 638–641.

Quadratus is the oldest Christian apologist (c. 124) but we know nothing of him except what Eusebius tells. The latter quotes him as saying that some whom Jesus healed are still living. All other speculation about him is erroneous. Recently the Epistle to Diognetus has been ascribed to him.

Quodvultdeus a disciple and friend of Augustine was bishop of Carthage until driven into exile by Geiseric in 439. He died 453 in Campania whither he had fled. Twelve pseudo-Augustinian sermons of the years 437–439 are probably his. Perhaps some six or seven other sermons and also the work *De promissionibus et praedictionibus* ascribed to Prosper of Aquitaine are his.

Rabulas (436) was converted to Christianity (c. 400), made bishop of Edessa (c. 412), and became a follower of Cyril of Alexandria after the Council of Ephesus (431). A great champion of orthodoxy against the Nestorians in the school of Edessa, he died 436. The Peshitta, the Syriac New Testament, came into being at his instance. He left three treatises on *Rules of Life for Clergy and Monks*. He wrote in Syriac and Greek. Little is left of his forty-six Greek letters. There is a sermon of his against Nestorius, a translation of Cyril's *De recta fide*, and there are some hymns of doubtful authenticity.

Rebaptismate, De, is a work by a contemporary of Cyprian that tries to solve, ineptly, the question of heretical baptism by distinguishing between baptism in water and the conferring of the Holy Spirit by the imposition of hands by the bishop.

Remigius, bishop of Rheims, 459–533, left us four letters, a testament of doubtful authenticity, and a metrical composition.

Reticius, bishop of Autun, is the only Gallic writer of the third century known to us. He became a bishop before 313 and died in 334, having taken part in the Council of Rome and the Synod of Arles (in August, 314) that crushed Donatism. He has left us a commentary on the Canticles and a treatise *Adversus Novatianum.*

Reverentius, probably a contemporary of Caesarius of Arles, wrote a *Vita s. Hilarii Arelatensis.*

Rhodon, an Asiatic and disciple of Tatian, wrote against Marcion, against Apelles, and perhaps also against Tatian himself.

Roman Chronographer of 354 A.D. See Dionysius Philocalus.

Rufinus Syrus wrote (c. 412) *Liber de fide* propounding the root principles of Pelagianism.

Rufus, John. See John Rufus.

Ruricius of Limoges left eighty-two letters and died sometime after 507. Faustus of Riez corresponded with him.

Rusticus Deacon collected (564–565), in Constantinople, available conciliar Acts to try to prove the wrong of the condemnation of the "Three Chapters" in 553 by Constantinople. He was a Roman deacon and nephew of Pope Vigilius (537–555).

Rusticus Helpidius (c. 502) wrote *Carmen de Christi Jesu beneficiis* in 149 hexameters and twenty-four Tristichs on biblical materials in beautiful poetry. See Helpidius Rusticus.

Sabinus of Heraclea (c. 378), semi-Arian bishop of Heraclea in Thrace, wrote a lost history of the fourth century councils from Nicea to those under Valens 364–378. Socrates and Sozomen mention his writings and charge them with many misstatements.

Sacramentarium Leonianum is our earliest Roman Missal. Based on materials of the fourth and fifth century, it is to be dated about 550. It is not the work of Leo.

Sahak the Great, patriarch of Armenia (390–439), and Mesrop are the fathers of Armenian Christian literature. They promoted the translation into Armenian of the Bible and of the outstanding works of the Greek and Syriac fathers. They also prepared an Armenian liturgy. In this way they saved Armenian Christianity when Armenia lay under Persian domination. Sahak has left some letters and hymns. See Isaac the Great and Mesrop.

Sahdona, Nestorian bishop of Mahoji of Arewas, abjured heresy and was forced to flee to Edessa where he became bishop (c. 630). He has left us a biography and funeral oration on his master Rabban James. He also has left treatises on the goodness of God and on different virtues.

Salonius, a son of Eucherius and bishop of Geneva or Vienne, wrote a commentary on Ecclesiastes and *Expositiones mysticae in Parabolas Solomonis*.

Scillitan Martyrs were six Christian martyrs in Carthage under the pro-Consul Saturnius in 180. They were the earliest African martyrs and the *Acta* give a very simple but moving account of their heroic faith. They are named after their birth-place, Scilium in Numidia. The Acts are the oldest Latin, African document.

Secundinus wrote a letter to Augustine which evoked his *Contra Secundinum Manichaeum* in 405. Secundinus left other writings about which we know little or nothing.

Secundus the Gnostic was an Eastern disciple of Valentine, the Egyptian Gnostic.

Sedatus of Beziers (c. 589) left a few homilies.

Serapion of Antioch, bishop of that see (c. 191–212), has left the following: *To Domnus* who had apostatized and became a Jew, *To Pontus*, and *To Caricus*. Most important is his letter to the Christians of Phossus on the Gospel attributed to Peter in which he forbade reading that apocryphal work.

Serapion of Thmuis in Lower Egypt (after 362), abbot and since 339 bishop of Thmuis, has left us two letters and a treatise, *Against the Manichaeans*. His most important work is his Prayerbook (*Euchologium*) a collection of thirty liturgical prayers. Details of his life are to be found in Athanasius' *Life of Anthony*. He was a great friend and supporter of Athanasius in the Arian struggle.

Sergius Grammaticus, a follower of Eutyches, held (c. 515–519) a discussion by correspondence with Severus of Antioch, the record of which is still extant. In the end, Sergius confessed himself beaten.

Sergius of Constantinople, patriarch (610–638) and leader of the Monothelites, has been suggested as the author of the *Akathistos*.

Seta was a Greek hymnographer of the fifth century. We know only his name.

Severian, bishop of Gabala in Syria (after 408), was a popular court preacher and vigorous defender of Nicene teaching against heretics and Jews, though he was an enemy of Chrysostom. As a preacher he displays unusual knowledge of Sacred Scripture. We have fourteen Greek homilies, eight Armenian and one Ethiopic. His sermon on the finding of the Cross, *Sermo in dedicatione pretiosae et vivicae Crucis*, is doubtful but fragments of his commentary on the Pauline letters have been preserved in the *Catenae*.

Severus of Malaga opponent of Vincent, Arian bishop of Saragossa, was the author of a treatise on virginity, entitled *Annulus* (The Ring). Nothing is left of his work.

Sextus was an anti-Gnostic apologist of the second century. Nothing is known of him but Eusebius mentions a work of his on the Resurrection.

Sextus, Sayings of, are pagan axioms of life, interpolated by a Christian (c. 200).

Shenoute of Atripe (466) was head of a monastery from 385 on. Next to Pachomius, he is the most important organizer of Egyptian monasticism and the greatest writer of Coptic Christianity. In 431 he accompanied Cyril of Alexandria to the Council of Ephesus. He left many letters, sermons, and several "Apocalypses" or "Visions" in Coptic. The name is found in various spellings: Shenoute, Schenoute, Schenoudi, Schenute, Schenudi, Chenoute, and Sinuthius. He was an irascible and extreme disciplinarian, having once killed a monk for theft and disobedience.

Sibylline Oracles are a mixture of varied pagan, Jewish, and Christian materials, of a religious, political, and historical nature. Books VI, VII, and VIII are Christian, and the other books seem to have Christian interpolations, as Celsus charged. In the Middle Ages they were highly esteemed. Book VI has a hymn to Christ; Books VII and VIII are eschatological.

Simeon Bar-Apollon collaborated with Bar-Chatar on a life of Simeon Stylites (459) that is much more reliable than the Greek life by one of his disciples named Anthony.

Simeon Bar-Sabbai, patriarch of Seleucia, a martyr under Sapor II (309–379), left some writings.

Simeon Stylites the Younger (596) is said to have left thirty treatises on ascetical matters. Two of his letters are cited by the Seventh Ecumenical Council.

Simplicianus corresponded with Ambrose and succeeded him in the see of Milan in 397. Unfortunately, his letters have disappeared.

Simplicius, Pope (468–483), has left us twenty letters that have to do with the Monophysite troubles in the East. Letter 3;5 insists on the permanent validity of papal decisions in matters of faith. He tried in every way to heal the widening rift between East and West.

Siricius, Pope (384–399), has left seven letters of which the most important is the decretal to Bishop Himerius of Terragona (385) in which the pope answers fifteen disciplinary questions. In most collections of canonical legislation this is the oldest item. In 390 he directed an encyclical against Jovinian and his teaching that marriage and virginity are of equal value. A letter to Bishop Anysius of Thessalonica condemns Bishop Bonosus of Sardica for denying the perpetual virginity of Mary.

Sixtus II, Pope (257–258), probably wrote a treatise on heretical baptism. Rufinus tells that Sixtus translated into Latin the so-called *Sayings of Sextus*, but Jerome already refuted this.

Sixtus III, Pope (432–440), has given us the best continuation of the Church history of Eusebius. In seven books he covers the years 305–439. He uses many varied sources such as imperial and episcopal letters, acts and decisions of councils. He generally identifies his source and strives for objectivity although he failed to repress a certain sympathy for the Novatians.

Sophia Jesu Christi is a Gnostic work attributed by some to Valentinus.

Sophronius (Translator) wrote a book on Bethlehem, another on the destruction of the Serapheum at Alexandria, and translated into Greek several Latin works of Jerome. Of these translations perhaps only the *Life of Malchus* has been preserved.

Soter, Pope (c. 166–174), wrote a letter to Corinth (see Dionysius of Corinth). According to Tertullian he seems also to have written a letter against the Montanists.

Sozomen, a lawyer of Constantinople, wrote (439–550) a Church history in nine books covering the years 324–425. He often copied from Socrates but though superior to him in style he is far inferior in objectivity. He introduced much new material but a great deal of it is legendary.

Stephen, Apocalypse of. Nothing is known of this work. The so-called Gelasian Decretals mention it.

Stephen Bar Sudaili was an apostate Monophysite monk, born at Edessa in the second half of the fifth century, who was attacked by Philoxenus, and James of Sarug. *A Book of Hierotheos* that later enjoyed some popularity is ascribed to him.

Stephen Gobarus, a tritheist, wrote under Justin III (565–578) in Syria or Egypt. According to Photius he treated, in fifty-two chapters and an appendix, the greatest variety of theological questions after the *sic et non* method of Abelard.

Stephen I, Pope (254–257), left some letters on the question of baptism by heretics, among them some addressed to the churches of Syria and Arabia and to the bishops of Asia Minor. A letter to Cyprian is important for the Church's teaching on the validity of tradition. It contains the famous statement: *Nihil innovetur nisi quod traditum est.*

Sulpicius Severus (c. 420) was born in Aquitaine of noble lineage and became a lawyer. When his wife died, he was induced by Martin of Tours to become a monk. He wrote a chronicle or world history from Adam to 400 that has value especially for the history of the author's times. He has left also a life of St. Martin, three letters, and two dialogues that have as subject matter St. Martin. They are interestingly written in simple, homely language and relate much fanciful material. But the chronicle shows genuine critical use of sources and is well written history.

Syagrius was an anti-Priscillianist bishop of the fifth century, who wrote a treatise, *De fide*, against them.

Sylvester, Pope (314–335), left no writings though some have been falsely ascribed to him.

Symeon of Messala, one of the founders of the Messalian heresy according to Theodoret, may have left some writings.

Symmachus, a Samaritan, became a Jew and then went over to the Ebionites. He produced (193–211) a Greek version of the

Old Testament that is more concerned with elegance of language than accuracy. Only pieces of it remain. Some other works chiefly among the Clementines have been attributed to him.

Symmachus, Pope (498–514), left nine letters and some synodal letters occasioned by the Laurentian and Acacian schisms and by the jurisdictional dispute between Arles and Vienne (502). The Emperor Theodoric convoked the Palmary Synod to sit in judgment on Pope Symmachus but the synod decreed, *Summa sedes a nemine judicatur* (The Holy See is judged by none).

Symmachus the Exegete (end of fifth century), an exegete of allegorical and moralistic tendency, left an exposition of Proverbs and a commentary on Canticle of Canticles.

Sympronianus sent four treatises defending Novatianism to Pacian of Barcelona, who refuted them (end of fourth century). Sympronianus leaned heavily on Tertullian's *De pudicitia*.

Synaxarium ecclesiae Constantinopolitanae is the best known of the martyrologies of the Greek Church. *Synaxarion* and *Menaeon* are counterparts of the Western martyrologies.

Te Deum is ascribed since the eighth century variously to Ambrose, Hilary, Augustine, and others. It has also been ascribed to Nicetas of Remesiana.

Testament of Our Lord is in two books, the first eschatological, the second disciplinary. It is based on the Church Ordinances of Hippolytus.

Testament of the Twelve Patriarchs purports to give the last words of the twelve sons of Jacob. Though of Jewish origin, it contains Christian elements.

Thaddaeus, Acts of, is a collection of legends made in the first half of the third century dealing chiefly with the story of Abgar and our Lord.

Thaddaeus, Gospel of, is mentioned in a decree of Pope Gelasius. It is lost.

Thalassius (c. 650) was abbot of a monastery in Libya (c. 650) and a friend of Maximus Confessor. He is the author of 400 *Sententiae,* or maxims on charity, continence, virtues, and the pursuit of happiness. They are divided into four *Centuriae* or hundreds.

Themison was a Montanist who wrote a letter called *Catholic*.

Themistius was a follower of Severus of Antioch. He helped found the sect of Agnoetae and wrote a treatise in defense of his error and a treatise against Philoponus.

Theodore Abbot (368) was coadjutor abbot to Horsiesi. He left a work on Easter and some fragments of a conversation with two Alexandrian deacons.

Theodore Askidas, Origenist bishop of Caesarea, was very influential at the court of Emperor Justinian (527–565). It is probable that he wrote some of the treatises attributed to Justinian.

Theodore Lector (after 527) took the Church histories of Socrates, Sozomen, and Theodoret and worked them over to produce his *Historia tripartita* (c. 530) in four books. Next he wrote in four books his own history which continued the other work to 527. Most of this has unfortunately been lost.

Theodore of Ancyra (c. 446) was a great champion of orthodoxy against Nestorianism. His works have been lost except for a commentary on the Nicene Creed and some homilies that are of high caliber in form and doctrinal content. Three of these refute Nestorianism and two are on the Mother of God. All are valuable for Mariology.

Theodore of Heraclea was Homoean bishop of that city (335–355). Jerome praises his writings and his exegesis but we have only citations from his works.

Theodore of Paphos, bishop of Paphos in Cyprus, wrote in 655 a life of St. Spiridion of Trimithus, popular saint of that island.

Theodore of Pharan, bishop of Pharan, was condemned at the Lateran Council in 649 because of statements in his *De operationibus Christi*.

Theodore of Raithu, a monk and priest in Raithu on the southeast coast of Sinai Peninsula, wrote between 537–553 a treatise which he entitled "Preparation." It is often incorrectly called "On the Incarnation" because the first part, eight chapters, is so entitled and deals with errors on the Incarnation. The second part, *De terminis philosophicis*, has to do with the clarification of philosophical terms involved in a discussion of the mystery. Another work, *De sectis*, attributed to Leontius of Byzantium is probably from the pen of Theodore.

Theodorus Cenobite is Theodore the Abbot.

Theodorus of Petra, bishop of Petra, wrote in 547 the life of St. Theodosius.

Theodosius the Archdeacon was probably a native of northern Africa. About 520–530 he wrote *De situ Terrae Sanctae*. He is otherwise unknown.

Theodosius the Deacon made a collection of source material for a Church history and preserved for us the *Historia Acephala*.

Theodotion translated the Old Testament.

Theodotus (Gnostic) was a writer of the Eastern Valentinian branch of Gnostics.

Theodotus of Ancyra wrote six books (now lost) against Nestorius, some homilies and an exposition of the Nicene Creed against Nestorius.

Theognis of Nicea (c. 342), bishop, is credited with a letter by Socrates and Sozomen, now known to be from Eusebius of Nicomedia.

Theognostus (280) was the successor of Dionysius in the catechetical school of Alexandria (264–280). He wrote seven books of *Hypotyposes* (Essays) which present a systematic treatment of all Christian dogma, strongly influenced by Origenistic theories. It might be called the earliest handbook of dogma.

Theophilus of Alexandria (385–412) was a bitter and violent opponent of Chrysostom. There are left a few letters, homilies, and a proposed Easter table covering 380–479 which he sent to Emperor Theodosius around 388. He also vehemently attacked Origen's teachings and the "Tall Brothers." Theophilus was an incessant troublemaker. He has left us Paschal letters for the years 401, 402, 404 and a virulent attack on Chrysostom.

Theotimus, a representative of Western Valentinianism, wrote on the figures of the Old Testament.

Thomas, Acts of the Apostle, was written in Syriac in the third century. The complete text has been preserved in Greek, Latin,

Armenian, and Ethiopic versions. Gnostic and even Manichaean in outlook it tells the story of Thomas' labors in India.

Thomas, Apocalypse of, seems to be a short work of Manichaean background.

Thomas of Edessa (early sixth century) was the Greek teacher of Mar Aba in Edessa. He is said to have written treatises on the Nativity and Epiphany, on psalmody, on astrology as well as sermons and works against heretics.

Thomas, Gospel of, originated in Gnostic circles (Naasenes) and has been lost.

Thomas of Heraclea (after 616), former bishop of Mabug, revised the Philoxenian Version of the New Testament (c. 616). This revision is important for textual criticism though it is not always easy to identify his work in the manuscripts.

Timocles was a Greek hymnographer of the fifth century mentioned by Theodore Lector.

Timothy Aelurus (c. 477) was the Monophysite successor to Dioscorus of Alexandria. He wrote two polemical works against the Council of Chalcedon and the *Tome of St. Leo*, some letters, and a *Book of Accounts* sketching the controversies of his times.

Timothy Apollinarist was a disciple of Apollinaris and wrote a letter to Prosdocius.

Timothy of Alexandria was archdeacon in Alexandria and, about 412, probably wrote a *History Of The Monks*.

Timothy of Antioch has attributed to him five sermons on the Transfiguration, although they seem to be the work of an author who lived in the sixth or eighth century.

Timothy of Constantinople, priest of the Hagia Sophia, wrote (c. 600) a work enumerating and describing heresies and schisms up to the sixth century. He describes how such are to be reconciled to the Church.

Timothy of Jerusalem has been associated with the sermons attributed to Timothy of Antioch.

Titus of Bostra (c. 378), bishop, wrote against the Manichaeans in four books shortly after 363. The first two books refute Manichaeism philosophically and Books III and IV defend

the Old and New Testaments by explaining misinterpreted passages. He shows himself a skilled polemicist. The work is valuable for its quotations from Manichaean works. The *Catenae*
have preserved fragments of his homilies on Luke. We also
have fragments of a sermon on the Epiphany.

Transitus Mariae. See *Dormitio B.V.M.*

Triphyllius was bishop of Ledra in Cyprus during the reign of
Constantius. His writings are lost but Jerome tells of his eloquence.

Trithemius Trypho (third century), bishop of Alexandria, wrote
some exegetical opuscula according to Jerome.

Turribius, bishop of Astorga, a vigorous anti-Priscillianist, wrote
often to Pope Leo (440–445) warning him of the dangers to the
Catholics of Spain from heresy.

Tychonius was a Donatist who broke with them on the question
of the Church holding that there are both good and bad in the
Church. Though the Donatists excommunicated him he did not
return to the Catholic fold. Augustine praised his eloquence and
sharp mind. His two works on the Donatist schism have perished. His *Liber regularum* or *De septem regulis* (c. 380) is the
first Latin compendium of biblical hermeneutics. It was highly
valued by Augustine and Cassiodore. His commentary on the
Apocalypse too was very popular. Primasius used it extensively.
It rejects all chiliastic and historical interpretation and limits the
meaning entirely to a spiritual one.

Ulfilas (383) or Wulfilas, the famous Arian bishop of the Goths
known to every student of English and German literature, has
left a profession of faith that is not too clear about the Second
Person and denies the divinity of the Holy Ghost. He translated
the Bible into Gothic but only fragments of the version remain.
Codex Argenteus is associated with him.

Unknown Gospel, consists of a few fragments of an apocryphal
Gospel dependent upon the canonical fourth Gospel.

Valentinus (Apollinarist) wrote a work against Timothy and
Polemon.

Valentine (Gnostic) was an Egyptian who spent the years 135–
160 in Rome where he gathered disciples. His last years were

spent in retirement on Cyprus. He was a gifted man and wrote letters, homilies, and psalms. His chief disciples were Secundus and Heracleon in the West and Theodotus and Marcus in the East. A lost Gospel bears his name.

Valerian (middle of the fifth century), bishop of Cemele, a city near Nice, wrote twenty homilies and an ascetical work, *Epistola ad monachos.*

Verba Seniorum is a collection of sayings of monks underlying the *Apophthegmata Patrum* and forming Books V to VII of the *Vitae Patrum.*

Verecundus (552 in Chalcedon), bishop of Junca in Byzacena, poet and exegete, wrote *Excerpta de gestis Chalcedonensis Concilii, Commentariorum super Cantica ecclesiastica libri IX* (On Nine Old Testament Canticles) and *De satisfactione poenitentiae,* a penitential poem in 212 hexameters.

Victor, Claudius Marius, the rhetorician, who taught in Marseilles and died sometime between 425–450, wrote a long hexameter poem entitled *Alethia.* In three books he both paraphrases and comments on the materials of Genesis from the beginning to the destruction of Sodom and Gomorrha.

Victorinus, C. Marius, a brilliant African rhetorician (c. 300), went to Rome to teach in 340. Here he was converted by a deeper study of the Christian teaching which he was engaged in refuting. Nothing is known of him after 362. He wrote some treatises against Arianism: *De generatione Verbi Divini* (358), four books *Adversus Arium* (359) and *De Homoousio recipiendo* (360). He also left a few hymns and commentaries. The latter showed little theological ability according to Jerome.

Victorinus of Pettau (304), bishop of that city in Upper Pannonia, present day Yugoslavia, though a Greek by birth, was martyred in the Diocletian persecution in 304. He wrote some biblical commentaries in poor Latin of which only the one on the Apocalypse has come down to us. Jerome used it but it is shot through with chiliasm. Another small work, *De fabrica mundi* on the week of Creation, is tainted with the same error. Victorinus may also be the translator and editor of a small Greek work, *Adversus omnes haereses* that has been handed down as an appendix to Tertullian's *De praescriptione.* In his exegesis

Victorinus is dependent on Papias, Irenaeus, Hippolytus, and especially Origen. According to Jerome, he is the earliest Latin exegete, though a poor one.

Victor of Antioch (fifth century) is said to be the author of a commentary on Mark. Actually this is not a commentary but there is question of a *Catena* of the sixth century, the chief source of which, besides the homilies on Matthew by Chrysostom, are Origen (*In Matt.*), Cyril of Alexandria (*In Luc.*), and Titus of Bostra (*In Luc.*). Victor may be the compiler. Other *Catenae* mention the name Victor repeatedly.

Victor of Capua (554) is a Latin exegete whose chief work is a Gospel harmony, which is a rearrangement of Tatian's *Diatessaron*.

Victor of Cartenna was an anti-Arian writer and bishop in Africa (fifth century). His works are lost.

Victor of Tunnuna (after 566), an African bishop, wrote a world chronicle from the creation to the year 566, but only the second part covering the years 444–566 has come down to us.

Victor of Vita, bishop of Vita in Byzacena in Africa, wrote (c. 488) his *Historia persecutionis Africanae provinciae temporibus Geiserici et Hunerici regum Vandalorum*. In it he tells the horrors of the Vandal persecution under Geiserich (428–477) and Huneric (477–484). He gives much authentic information but is not too critical. Other works that have been attributed to him are not from his pen.

Victor I, Pope (c. 189–198), wrote encyclical letters that are important for the history of the Easter controversy and the primacy of the bishop of Rome. Another letter condemned the Monarchian Theodotus, the tanner of Constantinople. Whether Victor already wrote in Latin is questionable.

Vienne and Lyon to the Churches of Asia and Phrygia, Letter of, is a moving report of the persecution in Lyon 177–178.

Vigilantius, native of Aquitania, a priest, attacked the monastic life, the veneration of the saints and their relics and certain liturgical practices. Jerome refuted him in 404 and 406.

Vigilius, Pope (537–555), issued twenty-six letters and decrees having to do with the "Three Chapters" controversy. See Rusticus the Deacon (his nephew).

Vigilius of Thapsus was one of the Catholic bishops summoned by Huneric to a disputation between Arians and Catholics in Carthage, Feb. 1, 484. He has left us *Dialogus contra Arianos, Sabellianos et Photinianos* and five books *Contra Eutychetem.* Two other works against the Arians have been lost and other works attributed to him are spurious.

Vigilius of Trent was a correspondent of Ambrose. He died a martyr 405.

Vita, Simeon Stylites, a Greek biography of Simeon Stylites (459), was written by his disciple Anthony who utilized chiefly the material of Theodoret. A Syriac biography, more extensive and accurately detailed has come down to us from the pen of two other disciples, Simeon Bar Apollon and Bar Chatar.

Vitae Patrum is a Latin collection of legends of the saints comprising ten books and dating from the sixth century. Books five to seven of the *Vitae Patrum* are composed of the *Verba Seniorum.* See *Verba Seniorum, Apophthegmata Patrum.*

Vitalis, an Apollinarianist, wrote a profession of faith addressed to Pope Damasus. It was current under the name of Pope Julius.

Vitellius, Donatist, wrote (337–350) on polemical, dogmatic, apologetical, and disciplinary subjects but all his works are lost.

Voconius of Castellum was an anti-Arian writer of Africa (fifth century), all of whose works are lost.

Wardapet, Eliseus Wardapet (c. 480) was a disciple of Mesrop. Attributed to him is a cycle of homilies on the life of Christ, *Words of Exhortation to Anchorites,* a commentary on Josue and Judges, and an exposition of the Lord's Prayer. These may be genuine. An historical work on the war of 449–451 is not his but the work of a writer in the seventh century.

Zachaeus of Caesarea, bishop of Caesarea, is said to have written against Valentinian at the end of the second century.

Zacharias, Apocalypse of, is mentioned in the catalogues but the work is lost.

Zacharias Rhetor or Zacharias of Mitylene (553), of which city he died as bishop shortly before 553, was a Greek Monophysite historian who used his art and science in the interest of Monophysitism. He wrote a valuable history covering the years 450–

491, and an anti-Manichaean treatise, a dialogue, *Amonius*, proving the creatibility of the world against pagan cosmology, and several biographies (Severus of Antioch, Peter the Iberian, and Isaias the Ascetic).

Zeno of Verona (372), bishop of that city (362–371 or 372), was most active against dying paganism and the growing evils in his diocese, and in the battle against Arianism. He has left us sixteen long and seventy-seven shorter sermons in which are valuable and beautiful thoughts on the Trinity, Mariology and especially on the baptismal and Paschal liturgies. He was a trained rhetorician and an accomplished preacher who was much influenced by Apuleius of Madaura, Tertullian, Cyprian, and Lactantius.

Zenobius, deacon of Edessa and disciple of Ephraem, wrote some epistles and some treatises against Marcion and Pamphilus. He is the author also of a life of Ephraem, his master.

Zephyrinus, Pope (c. 198–217), is said in a questionable statement of Optatus to have defended the Faith in treatises, but nothing is left of any writings he may have published. A statement attributed to him in the Sabellian controversy is also much debated, but he cannot be accused of Modalism.

Zosimas (early sixth century), abbot of a monastery in the vicinity of Caesarea in Palestine, gave to his monks a series of conferences, which one of them, perhaps, put down in writing.

Zosimus, Pope (417–418), has left some sixteen letters. The important *Epistola tractoria*, which contained papal approval of the dogmatic canons of the Council of Carthage (418) on original sin and grace, has survived in fragments only. *Epistola* XII has the interesting statement that the authority of Rome is so great that a decision of Rome can never be rescinded. The statement was elicited by the Pelagian controversy.

APPENDIX

Less Known Heresies
of the Early Church

(This short appendix lists and briefly describes most of the less known heresies of the early Church. Most of them are of little importance but their very obscurity would seem to make a short notice of them here a great saver of time for the student and reader.)

Abelites, a sect in North Africa in the fourth century, were also called Abelians, Abeloites, and Abelonians. They became extinct in the reign of Theodosius the Younger (408–450). They contracted spiritual unions, condemned the use of marriage and adopted children to continue the sect. Their name was taken from their belief that Abel, though he had a wife, did not seek progeny.

Acacians were followers of Acacius, disciple and successor of Eusebius, bishop of Caesarea in Palestine (340–366), who favored Arianism in a milder form. They were also called Omei from the Greek word *homoios* (like). They rejected Anomoeanism, the *homoousios* of Nicea and the *homoiousios* of the semi-Arians.

Accaophori. See Hydroparastatae.

Acephali is a general term applied to any group refusing to recognize a leader or head. There were Monophysite Acephali and Nestorian Acephali. The term was also applied to priests who refused to recognize the authority of their ordinary bishop and to a suffragan bishop who refused to accept the authority of his metropolitan.

Acoemetae, literally "the sleepless ones," was an establishment of monks who divided the day into three "watches" or shifts of eight hours each to insure continuous and uninterrupted worship in their monastery. Later they were called "Studites" after Studius, a rich Roman who built them a monastery.

Actistetes denied that the Son of God really became man. The name is derived from the Greek word *aktistos*, i.e., "uncreated."

Acuanites were the followers of Acuan, a prominent Manichaean in Mesopotamia in the time of Epiphanius.

Adamites were a Gnostic sect in second century Africa. They renounced marriage and worshiped naked like Adam in Paradise.

Adecerditae were a curious group that held that Christ by the *descensus ad inferos* was able to rescue some souls from Hell.

Adelophagi, an obscure sect of perhaps the end of the fourth century whose name would indicate that they would not eat with a member of another sect, seem to have denied the divinity of the Holy Ghost.

Adelphians were Euchites, followers of Adelphius of Mesopotamia whom Flavian of Antioch excommunicated and caused to be banished.

Adoptionism is the Christological error that regards Christ not as the natural Son of the Father but as adopted only. See Subordinationism.

Aerians were a short-lived sect of followers of an Arian monk, Aerius, who among other queer ideas condemned fasting and prayers for the dead, and denied a difference between priest and bishop.

Aetians were followers of Aetius of Antioch who denied Nicea and held the Son to be like the Father. See Homoiousians. Aetius was banished twice, in 350 and in 360.

Agapeti and Agapetoi, the Greek words for "beloved women" and "beloved men" are less used than *Virgines subintroductae* or *Syneisactai*. They were male and female ascetics living together.

Agionites were a sect condemned by a Council of Gangra between 360 and 380, but nothing is known of them.

Agnoitae, "the ignorant ones," were an obscure fourth century sect who professed to be ignorant of God's omniscience. Another similar sixth century sect of the same name claimed to have no knowledge of Christ's divinity.

Agonistici, literally "contenders," were Donatist zealots who went about Africa trying to win converts. They also were called *Circuiti* and *Circumcellions.*

Alogi is the name given to second century groups who rejected the Johannine writings and ascribed them to Cerinthus because the Montanist appealed to these books. Epiphanius and Augustine used the term.

Anomians is another name for Antinomians.

Anomoeans and Anomoeanism, derive from the Greek word *anomoios,* i.e., dissimilar. The Anomoeans were a sect founded in the last half of the fourth century by Actius and Eunomius. They were strict Arians and held that the Son is dissimilar from the Father because He is generated.

Antidicomarians or Antidicomarianites were a sect in fourth century Arabia that denied Mary's virginity. They were refuted by Epiphanius.

Antinomians is a designation for any group that erroneously interpreted the New Testament doctrine of the freedom of the Christian from the Law.

Antitactics is a designation given by Clement of Alexandria to those who held that while God the Father made all things good, an adversary or rebel creature originated evil.

Antitrinitarians is a self-explanatory term.

Apellianists or Apellites were the followers of the second century Gnostic Apelles.

Aphthartodocetae got their name from the Greek word *aphtharsia,* i.e., incorruptibility. See Docetae or Docetism.

Apoctites. See Apotactics.

Apocatastasis, a Greek word meaning "restoration," is used to designate the error taught by Origen and based on a misinterpretation of some passages of the New Testament that in the end all men, including those in hell, would be restored to God.

Apocryphans is a term used to designate those sects, e.g., the various Gnostic sects, that appealed to the Apocrypha in support of their doctrine.

Apollinarianism is the error of Apollinaris, condemned in 377 and in 382, that Christ's human nature consisted only of flesh and

a sensitive soul and that the Logos took the place of and functioned as the *Nous* in the person of Christ.

Apostolici is another name for Apotactics. It is used by Epiphanius
and Augustine.

Apotactics were an obscure sect that seems to have advocated the
renunciation of private property.

Aquaei were a sect mentioned by Augustine and may be the *Hy-
drotheitae*.

Aquarians is a generic designation for all those varied sects of the
early church that condemned the use of wine in any way, as
the Ebionites, Marcionites, Encratites, and pretended to celebrate the Eucharist with water instead of wine.

Archontics were a second century Gnostic sect that took its name
from the Archons that rule the universe in the Gnostic system.
They denied the resurrection, baptism, Eucharist, and marriage—for they regarded woman as evil. They had their own
sacred books.

Arianism taught that the Logos is not eternal, but generated in
time and not the same substance as God. Christ is only an
adopted Son of God, therefore.

Artemonites were followers of Artemon who early in the third
century denied the divinity of the Second and Third Persons of
the Trinity, though Christ did receive, they conceded, a certain
measure of divinity later.

Artotyrtae were a Montanist sect that used cheese and bread in
their Eucharist, bread representing the fruit of the earth while
cheese represented the fruit of the flock.

Ascitae were a second century group of Montanists who took their
names from the Greek word for wineskin (*askos*). They perhaps got from Matthew 9: 17 the idea for their practice to dance
around an inflated wineskin at certain festivals. See Ascodrugitae.

Asclepiodotians were followers of Asclepiodotus, a disciple of
Theodotus of Byzantium. They held Jesus to be a mere man.

Ascodrugitae were a sect of Marcosian Gnostics who denied all
the sacraments and preached only of spiritual knowledge in
typical Gnostic fashion.

Ascophites appeared as a sect about the end of the second century.
They denied the Eucharist and the Old Testament Scriptures.

Assuritans were a sect mentioned by Augustine. It sprang up under Pope Liberius (c. 358) and was condemned in 394.

Audiani were the followers of a certain Audaeus of Mesopotamia in the fourth century. Nothing is known of him except that he was an extremist.

Barbeliotes were a Gnostic sect in Iberia, named after Barbelos who was claimed to have been the son of the Father, and a woman named Ialdabaoth. They are mentioned by Irenaeus, Epiphanius, and Augustine but information about them is scant and confusing.

Barsanians were Acephali of the fifth century and have been identified with the Semidalites. They are named after a certain Barsanius.

Barsanuphites were Acephali of the fifth century named after Barsanuphius.

Basilidians were followers of the Gnostic Basilides, one of the earliest (c. 139) Alexandrian Gnostics.

Basmotheans are mentioned in the Apostolic Constitutions. They seem to have denied providence, the immortality of the soul, and the creation of the universe. Some think the name is a corruption of "Masbotheans."

Borbelites is another name for Barbeliotes.

Borborians is a derogatory name for the Barbeliotes. The Greek word *borboros* means filth.

Cainites were a second century sect that placed Cain and other sinners of the Old Testament above the innocent Abel; Abel represented lower powers while Cain, etc., were from higher regions.

Carpocratians were followers of the Platonist and Gnostic Carpocrates of Alexandria in the second century. His son Epiphanes who died at seventeen was apotheosized.

Cathari were Novatian's followers.

Cerdonians were named after a Syrian Cerdo who taught in Rome (c. 138). Fanatical ascetics, they condemned marriage and the use of wine and flesh meats. They held the birth and sufferings of Jesus to have been unreal.

Cerinthians were followers of Cerinthus toward the end of the first century.

Chiliasm is the error that there will be a rule of a thousand (*chilios*) years by the Messias and the Just on this earth.

Circumcellions. See Donatism and Agonistici.

Collyridians are mentioned by Epiphanius. The name comes from the Greek word for cakes because the women of the sect offered cakes to Mary and then ate them.

Corpiani is probably a corruption of Scorpiani, a name sometimes given to the Gnostics.

Damianites were the followers of Damianus or Damian, Monophysite patriarch of Alexandria (570), who was also accused of being a tetratheist.

Demiurge in Gnosticism is the creator of the visible universe. He was created in turn out of physical substance by Hachamoth.

Dimoeritae were a sect of Apollinarians that existed only a few years.

Docetism was current in varying forms in the early Church. The Docetae all taught in some way the unreality of Christ's humanity.

Donatism was a schism that threatened the whole African Church. Donatus the Great, the founder of the schism, was a great organizer and leader (see Circumcellions), while Parmenianus, Ticonius, Petilianus and others were brilliant propaganda writers for the sect. The Donatists held that the Church can have only saints as members and that sinners cannot give the sacraments.

Ebionites were a Jewish-Christian sect in Palestine in the apostolic age. *Ebion* means poor in Hebrew. At the end of the first century the Ebionites came into contact with the Essenes and the Esseno-Ebionism found in the Clementines resulted. In short Ebionism is a garbled mixture of Christian, Jewish, and Essene elements and practices.

Elkesaites were a branch of Ebionites toward the end of the second century, whose sacred book of revelations was called *Elkesai*.

Encratites were Judaizing heretics who abstained from wine, meat, and the use of marriage for Manichaean motives. *Enkrateia* in Greek means continence, self-mastery. Small groups of this tendency were apotactici (abstinents), hydroparastatae (aquarians), and saccophori (they wore sacks).

Enthusiastae was another name for Euchites.

Entychites were perhaps the Eutychetae or Euchites.

Essenes, a Jewish sect that lived a common celibate life and observed a strict rule and order of life that included daily labor, fasting, lustrations, common meals, and prayers.

Ethnophronians was a name given to Christians who mingled pagan superstitions with Christian practices.

Euchites were an heretical sect in Syria toward the end of the fourth century. Man, they taught, is born with a demon that can be expelled only by concentrated prayer that induces an ecstatic state, in which the Trinity can be seen with bodily eyes. Thus man is cleansed.

Eudoxians were followers of Eudoxius of Antioch who was an extreme Arian and condemned by several Semi-Arian councils.

Eunomians were strict Arians named after Bishop Eunomius. They were also called Anomoeans because they taught that the Father and Son were unlike. Another name, Exucontians, was given them for saying that the Son was made out of nothing (Greek, *ex ouk onton*).

Eunomio-Eutychians were Eunomian followers of Eutychius of Constantinople. These terms reflect some of the bitter political battles connected with the theological discussions of the day. See Eunomio-Theophronians.

Eunomio-Theophronians were Eunomian followers of Theophronius of Cappadocia.

Euphemites was another name for the Euchites according to Augustine.

Eutychianism is the Christological heresy that finds only one nature in Christ. It is also called Monophysitism. The error is named after Eutyches, archimandrite of Constantinople.

Eutychetae are a sect mentioned by Theodoret. Whether they were the same as the Entychites mentioned by Clement of Alexandria is uncertain.

Excalceati were an ancient sect about whom nothing is known except that they went barefoot in imitation of Isaias.

Exotians is derived from the Greek phrase, *exo tes poleos*, i.e., outside the city, and designates the Arians who were driven out of the city by Theodosius Augustus.

Exucontians. See Eunomians.

Helvidians were followers of Helvidius who toward the end of the fourth century denied the perpetual virginity of Mary and depreciated the value of celibacy and virginity in general.

Hieracites were an obscure sect, followers of Hierax of Leontium in Egypt (early in the fourth century) who denied the resurrection, the existence of paradise and of marriage, and abstained from meat and wine. Another bizarre idea of his was that Melchisedech was the Third Person of the Trinity.

Homoeans, a political group between the Anomeans and the Semi-Arians, held no distinctive special doctrine.

Homoousian designates the correct Catholic doctrine. It means consubstantial.

Hydroparastatae were a sect that used water instead of wine in the Eucharist. They were also called Accaophori.

Hypistarians were a fourth century sect who claimed to worship only the Most High (*upsistos*). They kept the Sabbath but rejected sacrifice and circumcision. They are referred to by the two Cappadocian Gregorys.

Iconoclasts, from *eikon* and *Klao*, i.e., "I break images," were the eighth century heretics who attacked the veneration of images.

Kataphrygian designates any error along the lines of Montanism. It was in Phrygia that many errors in enthusiasm originated and several of the Fathers speak of it as a "queer" land.

Latrocinium is another name for the "Robber Synod" which acquitted Eutyches at Ephesus in 449. Pope Leo coined the name.

Luciferians were followers of Lucifer of Calaris who was a vigorous supporter of Athanasius and therefore exiled by Constantius from 355–361. When the exiled bishops were returned to their sees in 361, he went to Antioch and refused to hold any communion with bishops who had fallen into Arianism even though returned to orthodoxy. Theodoret brands him a heretic but he seems merely to have been leader of a political party rather than a schismatic or heretic.

Macedonians got their name from Macedonius, bishop of Constantinople (360), who, however, seems not to have held their error which was a denial of the divinity of the Third Person of the Trinity, whom they held to be a creature of the Son. They were condemned at Constantinople in 381. Marathanius, bishop of Nicomedia, was one of their leaders and they are more properly named after him.

Mandaeans were an Oriental sect whose religious beliefs were a mixture of Babylonian, Persian, Jewish, and Gnostic ideas. They had no influential contacts with Christianity in any way.

Manichaeism, named after Manes or Manet, a Persian philosopher, taught an essential dualism in all things, good and evil, spirit and matter, light and darkness.

Marathonians. See Macedonians.

Marcellians were followers of a certain woman, Marcella, a disciple of Carpocrates, who came to Rome (c. 155) where her image was worshiped by her followers.

Marcianists were Euchites, so called after one of their leaders in the sixth century named Marcian.

Marcionism was the movement inaugurated by Marcion after his expulsion from the Church. He established his own hierarchy and ecclesiastical organization.

Marcosians were a Gnostic sect of the middle second century named after Marcus who belonged to the school of Valentinus.

Maronites seem originally to have been an heretical sect made up of remnants of Monothelites and Monophysites. John Damascene refers to them as such. Their later development does not concern us here.

Maximianists were a schismatic group within the Donatists, named after their leader.

Menandrians were followers of the Samaritan Menander who, according to Irenaeus and Eusebius, was the successor to Simon Magus. He seems to have taught a primitive form of Gnosticism.

Merinthians is found as another name for Cerinthians.

Messalians was the original Syriac name for Euchites.

Millenarianism. See Chiliasm.

Modalism teaches that the three Persons of the Trinity are not divine realities but simply different aspects of the one God. However, Modalism is a complex heresy. See Patripassianism, Sabellianism.

Monarchianism. See Modalism.

Monophysites are the followers of Eutyches who held the Christological error that there is only one nature in Christ.

Monothelitism is the last of the great Christological heresies. It taught that there is in Christ only one will, thus mutilating Christ's human nature as Apollinarianism and Monophysitism had done earlier.

Montanism was a heresy of fanatic asceticism originated in Phrygia (c. 170) by a certain Montanus. Essentially it was a way of life rather than a teaching or doctrine. Ecstacy and other strange phenomena were part of the movement. Two women, Priscilla and Maximilla, were prominent in the movement.

Naasseni is another name for Ophites, derived from the Hebrew word for serpent.

Nestorians were followers of Nestorius who taught that there was only a moral union of the two natures in Christ and that Mary was not *Theotokos* (God's mother) but *Christotokos* (bearer of Christ).

Nicolaites were a sect of Syrian Gnostics.

Ophites was a name given to a number of Gnostic sects in which the serpent as a symbol of enlightenment plays a part. Such sects were Cainites, Perates, Sethians, Naassenes, Barbelo-Gnostics, Severians, Nicolaitans, Archontics, Justinians, and others.

Patripassianism. See Modalism and Monarchianism.

Pelagianism was the error propagated by the Breton monk, Morgan or Pelagius, who came to Rome around 400. It was a simple naturalistic system that exalted man's natural moral strength to the disparagement of the supernatural.

Pepuzans were Montanists so named after their headquarters at Pepuza in Phrygia.

Peratici was another name for the Essenes after their settlement in Perea.

Periodentae were an order of itinerant Nestorian preachers whom Cosmas Indicopleustes reports active in India.

Phantasiasts. See Docetae.

Photinians were followers of Photinus, bishop of Sirmium in Pannonia. His error was condemned at Constantinople in 381. His error was a variation of Modalism.

Pneumatomachists is a generic term covering all sects that deny the divinity of the Holy Ghost.

Primianists were another schismatic party among the Donatists and were named after Primian, Donatist bishop of Carthage. Their opponents were the Maximianists.

Priscillianists were the followers of Priscillian. The council of Braga (563) condemned them for Sabellianism, Arianism, Docetism, and pantheism and for disparaging marriage and corrupting the text of the Bible.

Psathyrians were Arians, followers of Theoctistus Psathyropola (the cake seller) of Constantinople.

Quintillianists seem to have been named after a certain Quintilla. They seem to have been Priscillianists.

Sabbatians were condemned at Constantinople (381). They were followers of a convert Jew, Sabbatius, who spread the errors of Novatian.

Sabellianism. See Modalism. Sabellius was an Eastern priest who came to Rome toward the beginning of the third century.

Semi-Arians were Arians who tried to water down the decisions of Nicea. The chief Semi-Arians were the Anomeans, the Homoeans, and the Homoiousians.

Semi-Pelagianism was a mitigated form of Pelagianism.

Severians were an Encratite group.

Studites. See Acoemetae.

Subordinationism was the heresy of the second and third century that placed the Logos between God and creation, thus paving the way for Arianism.

Symmachians was a name sometimes applied to the Ebionites after Symmachus, author of a Greek version of the Old Testament.

Tertullianists were followers of Tertullian after he joined the Montanists.

Tetratheist is a designation hurled at some who seemed, by distinguishing between God Himself and the three divine Persons, to teach the existence of four persons in God.

Theodotians held bizarre Christological errors and distorted Trinitarian views. According to them Jesus, a man born of the Virgin, became God after His Resurrection. Other details of their teaching are not too clear. They originated early in the third century and are named after Theodotus.

Theopaschism (God suffers) is an error springing from Monophysitism, which taught that in Christ, His human nature had been absorbed by the divine, and, therefore, there was only the latter to suffer and die.

Tritheism denied the possibility of three persons in one nature. Hence, each divine Person must have His own nature and there are in reality three Gods.

Valentinians were followers of the Egyptian Gnostic, Valentinus, who died in Rome around 160. By the end of the second century he seems to have had a considerable following.

Valesians were a Gnostic sect who seem to have practiced self-mutilation.

Zacchaeans is the name given to Gnostics by Epiphanius.